THE MEDIA REVOLUTION
OF EARLY CHRISTIANITY

The Media Revolution
of Early Christianity

An Essay on
Eusebius's *Ecclesiastical History*

DORON MENDELS

WILLIAM B. EERDMANS PUBLISHING COMPANY
GRAND RAPIDS, MICHIGAN / CAMBRIDGE, U.K.

© 1999 Wm. B. Eerdmans Publishing Co.
255 Jefferson Ave. S.E., Grand Rapids, Michigan 49503 /
P.O. Box 163, Cambridge CB3 9PU U.K.

Printed in the United States of America

04 03 02 01 00 99   7 6 5 4 3 2 1

Library of Congress Cataloging-in-Publication Data

ISBN 0-8028-4610-6

Selections from *Eusebius: The Ecclesiastical History,* translated by J. E. L.
Oulton, J. H. Lawlor, and Kirsopp Lake (2 vols.; Loeb Classical Library 153 and
265; Cambridge, Mass.: Harvard University Press, 1926-32), are reprinted by
permission of Harvard University Press and the Loeb Classical Library.

Selections from Denis McQuail, *Media Performance: Mass Communication and
the Public Interest* (London: Sage Publications, 1992), and Denis McQuail,
Mass Communication Theory: An Introduction (London: Sage Publications,
1994), are reprinted by permission of Sage Publications Ltd.

For Orit and Dan
With great appreciation and love

Contents

Preface

In 1993 I started to study Eusebius's *Ecclesiastical History* in line with my general interest in ancient historiography. In 1996, during a semester at the Center of Theological Inquiry, Princeton N.J., I shaped my ideas and wrote a first draft of this long essay. My purpose was limited and so was my focus. The focus remained the genre of the *Ecclesiastical History*. My initial purpose was to deal only with the issue of genre, but during the process of research I realized that genre cannot be dissociated from content. The result, I hope, is a contribution to the interpretation of Eusebius's understanding of the rise of Christianity.

In this study I apply modern studies of media performance to Eusebius's historiography in the conviction that this research can be used to clarify the kind of history writing that Eusebius employed as a medium for the promotion of the Christian mission. As readers will see, I am not attempting any broad sociological theories about the rise of Christianity, but am rather taking them through the text of the *Ecclesiastical History,* using media performance methods as tools.

When we think of media, we immediately think of news, but other genres and orders of discourse fall under the purview of media research. It is common to associate news with the notion of immediacy, but immediacy can be subjective. What has been known for a long time may be news to us: we become aware of the death of a friend long after the person died; historians get their hands on archival material that has been unavailable for fifty years or more. The same situation could obtain in antiquity: news of the battle of Marathon came in very fast and apparently spread swiftly all over Greece; news of the battle at Afek arrived immediately and so shocked the High Priest Eli that he fell from his seat and broke his neck; but the interval between an occurrence and its becoming common knowledge was sometimes very long. Hence, when I speak of Eusebius as a mediator of information in his *Ecclesiastical History,* I mean that he recounts events (even two centuries after their occurrence) that could still be considered late-breaking news to his readers. The concept of news was well known to him, as the very vocabulary he uses attests (among others, he uses the term *diangellō, Hist. Eccl.* 6.41.9).

I have been working at history long enough to know that analogies between modern and ancient phenomena are dangerous and sometimes even misleading. However, with caution modern examples and analogies may still be used to sharpen our understanding of life in antiquity; illustrations from modern media events can only improve our ability to appreciate ancient modes of discourse.

Since this book is addressed not only to scholars but also to a wider audience, I have all but dispensed with quoting Greek and have cited only the most necessary bibliography. Nor have I endeavored to tackle the problem of Eusebius's sources. I have adopted the English translation of Eusebius's *Ecclesiastical History* by Kirsopp Lake, J. E. L. Oulton, and H. J. Lawlor in the Loeb Classical Library, with some modifications here and there. The somewhat archaic English translation nicely contrasts with my own "modern" narrative.

I take this opportunity to thank Debby Gera, Joseph Geiger, Angelo Di Berardino, and Etan Kohlberg, who were so kind as to read the entire manuscript and make many useful suggestions. Martin Elton and Menahem Blondheim, who deal with different fields of communication studies, read drafts and discussed various points with me during the final stages of my study. Mira Reich was extremely helpful in editing the manuscript. Special thanks are due to Dan Harlow, my editor at Eerdmans, whose excellent editorial comments helped to give the manuscript its final shape. At the Center of Theological Inquiry I had a very fruitful semester thanks to its members and staff. The book is dedicated to my children Orit and Dan, who showed great interest in what I was doing. My wife Michal was as supportive as ever.

The Hebrew University of Jerusalem
Spring 1998

CHAPTER 1

Media Studies and Historiography

I n his *Ecclesiastical History,* Eusebius of Caesarea describes the propaga-
tion of early Christianity by means of a media revolution.[1] Of course
Eusebius did not speak specifically of a media revolution, since the modern concepts of "media" and "revolution" were unknown to him. But what
emerges from his description constitutes what we would consider a media
revolution. Whether this picture reflects reality is a matter for future research and is not the purpose of my present study.[2] Eusebius is an especially interesting case, since, as I will argue, he himself employed a new
genre of history writing. He is neither a Thucydides, a Josephus, a
Polybius, nor an Appian.

Eusebius's *Ecclesiastical History* offers a wonderful opportunity for
the historian to ask new questions concerning historiography. Since historiography is and always has been considered a medium, we may reasonably
attempt to apply some of the scholarly methods used in the field of media
studies to ancient historiography. I will not draw upon communication
studies that deal with literary aspects (semiotics and various fields of literary criticism) or with sociology, but will restrict myself to research done
on modern media performance as such. Viewing Eusebius against this

---

1. This is why my bibliography focuses on Eusebius, rather than on the history
of the rise of Christianity. For a sociological approach, see Michael Mann, *The Sources
of Social Power: A History of Power from the Beginning to* A.D. *1760,* vol. 1 (Cambridge:
Cambridge University Press, 1986).

2. This is a long-term project launched by me at the Hebrew University.

THE MEDIA REVOLUTION OF EARLY CHRISTIANITY

background shows that he produced a type of historiography different from anything before his time. He did not write a rationalistic history like Thucydides or "creative" history like Hecataeus of Abdera. He did not compose biographies like Suetonius and Plutarch.[3] He was not interested in ethnography, as Herodotus and Diodorus Siculus were, nor was he a pragmatist historian like Polybius. He did not even endeavor to compose a universalistic history in line with Timaeus, Polybius, or Diodorus Siculus.[4] So what kind of history did he actually write?

The *Ecclesiastical History* as "Media History"

I would suggest that Eusebius wrote a "media history," a special genre on a new topic. I shall define medium in antiquity as *any means, agency, or instrument that stands between information and the public.* Historical writing is considered a medium because its authors are conscious of representing a historical reality and thus "produce *works* of communication."[5] Our problem as those who study ancient history is our inability to measure the impact that such communicative messages had on their audiences. At present we cannot examine the recipients' reactions to communication efforts. However, by applying the results of media studies we can at least analyze our texts somewhat differently than has been done so far and begin to understand the audiences that the communicators — that is, the ancient historians — had in mind. In certain instances we can speculate about the reaction of audiences in antiquity. For instance, the degree of redundancy in a work of ancient history may suggest the nature of the community to which the text is addressed. In general, a historian who builds redundancy into his message

3. His section on Origen in Book 6 has some aspects in common with biographical writing, but this does not mean that the *Ecclesiastical History* is a biography. On ancient biography, see M. J. Edwards and Simon Swain, eds., *Portraits: Biographical Representation in the Greek and Latin Literature of the Roman Empire* (Oxford: Clarendon, 1997); Patricia Cox Miller, *Biography in Late Antiquity: A Quest for the Holy Man* (Berkeley: University of California Press, 1983).

4. Cf. F. W. Walbank, *Polybius* (Berkeley: University of California Press, 1972); Kenneth S. Sacks, *Diodorus Siculus and the First Century* (Princeton: Princeton University Press, 1990); and Charles W. Fornara, *The Nature of History in Ancient Greece and Rome* (Berkeley: University of California Press, 1983).

5. John Fiske, *Introduction to Communication Studies,* 2d ed. (London: Routledge, 1990), 18.

is "audience centred."[6] Another example would be an author who uses "hysterical" language. We shall see that Eusebius used it in the case of heresies because he was aware that this kind of language was effective as a media device.

Unlike Thucydides, Polybius, and Josephus, Eusebius did not write a comprehensive history of his topic, the rise of Christianity. Rather, he wrote in the manner of our modern media. In his *Ecclesiastical History* we see him working more like a modern journalist or editor, shaping what people should know and deciding what they should forget (a matter he himself bluntly acknowledges in *Hist. Eccl.* 8.2.2-3). Unlike other ancient historians, in many instances Eusebius gives his context a higher degree of redundancy in order to make it more accessible to his audience. It is not that this sort of media awareness cannot be found in historians before him.[7] But, from both the content and the historiographical devices to be found in the *Ecclesiastical History*, we can learn something about the intensity of his use of new methods. We can also say that Eusebius used some ancient historiographical methods in an extreme manner. Thus his history represents a genre that is different from the writings of his predecessors.

That Eusebius wrote missionary literature as well strengthened his awareness that historiography was a useful media tool. (His work should be viewed not only against the background of the Christian mission, but also against that of the revolution in the accessibility of books in the second and third centuries.[8]) His *Ecclesiastical History* as well as his *Demonstratio Evangelica* and *Praeparatio Evangelica* are saturated with the concept that, in order for Christianity to fulfill its universal role in world history, it had to spread rapidly and aggressively. Eusebius knew that many people would read his books and that they would thereby become yet another channel to propagate Christianity. In Chapter 6 we will discuss mis-

6. Ibid., 13, following Claude Shannon and Warren Weaver, *The Mathematical Theory of Communication* (Urbana: University of Illinois Press, 1963).

7. Eusebius's work shares historiographical features with such sources as the "historical" books of the Hebrew Bible, 1 Maccabees, 2 Maccabees, the Gospels, Xenophon's *Anabasis,* Aristotle's *Athenaion Politeia* 1-41, and Plutarch's *Lives.* My purpose here, though, is limited to clarifying the much disputed genre of the *Ecclesiastical History* with the help of media studies. I do not intend to detail all the elements that may be found in Eusebius's predecessors, but to try and explain his chaotic narrative and to rehabilitate his name as a historian. Eusebius's comprehensive approach to history and historiography is what matters, not whether he took one element or another from his forerunners.

8. See Chapter 6 below.

sion in the *Ecclesiastical History*. Here it will suffice to say that the basic principle guiding missionaries in their efforts at communication was the achievement of publicity through the use of media channels of various kinds. The accumulation of channels is a crucial factor when assessing the "media effects" on audiences.[9] From the outset, the Church acted through its media channels, and this became an expression of the strength of its organization vis-à-vis the Roman Empire.

Here we must make a distinction between "static" and "dynamic" media. The emperor's statues all over the Empire were static media symbols that were just "there" and taken for granted. Coinage can also be seen as a medium that transmits a message, but coins too are static and passively received: people living with portraits of the emperor and other symbols associated with the Empire were aware that he existed somewhere, sometimes fantasized about him, but did not have to listen to orators or watch a shifting presentation in order to communicate with him. The same applies to various symbolic scenes on mosaics and reliefs in public buildings. In other words, in this kind of communication no ongoing active role was required on the part of either communicator or recipient. The other kind of media activity is the "dynamic" one. Here we include all media activity of noise (verbal or other) and movement (gestures, mimicry, acting). This activity involves a continuing communicative interaction between communicator and recipient. In pagan societies, dynamic media were public affairs (so too, of course, were static media) — sacrifices performed with hymns and liturgies in cult centers, gladiator shows, sports competitions, theater, wandering philosophers, and also much of the religious activity in the temples.[10]

Eusebius grew up amidst all of this and against this backdrop wrote his *Ecclesiastical History*. In this work he surveys the rise of Christianity with hindsight, and his account reflects his strong belief that the publicity and exposure enjoyed by Christianity were the key to its success.[11] From the *Ecclesi-*

---

9. For media effects in modern media studies, see J. M. McLeod et al., "On Understanding and Misunderstanding Media Effects," in *Mass Media and Society*, ed. James Curran and Michael Gurevitch (London: Arnold, 1991), 235-66.

10. See Ramsay MacMullen, *Paganism in the Roman Empire* (New Haven and London: Yale University Press, 1981); Robin Lane Fox, *Pagans and Christians* (New York: Knopf, 1986); and S. R. F. Price, *Rituals and Power: The Roman Imperial Cult in Asia Minor* (Cambridge: Cambridge University Press, 1984).

11. Eusebius would have resented the observation of Ramsay MacMullen, *Christianizing the Roman Empire (A.D. 100-400)* (New Haven and London: Yale Univer-

astical History it emerges that the publicity implemented by the Church through its media channels became part of a communicative action that had the effect of a well-organized, uniform, assertive, and universal activity. Was this "publicity campaign" of three centuries read into the history of Christianity by Eusebius, or was it really "what happened," to use von Ranke's phrasing? Probably a combination of both. In this study, though, I intend to limit myself to Eusebius's picture in the *Ecclesiastical History,* which presents Christianity as posing a serious competition — or rather threat — to the traditional media channels of the Roman Empire. This picture fits in with an observation made in modern communication studies by James Curran: "the introduction of new techniques of mass communication has tended to undermine the prestige and influence of established mediating organizations and groups. By providing new channels of communication, bypassing established mediating agencies, new media have also posed a serious threat to the stable, hierarchical control of social knowledge."[12] Eusebius, when he wrote the *Ecclesiastical History* and revised it, was becoming a leading figure in the Church who was well aware of media channels. Since the Church as an institution constantly pursued the means and instruments of mediating its message to different audiences, the writing of a "media history" by Eusebius becomes even more understandable.

Another introductory remark should be made. In the following I will employ a tripartite division of the public sphere in the cities of the Roman Empire.[13] First is the "inner public sphere," which includes the institutions that emerged during the three first centuries within the Christian community (church, assembly, synod, common prayer group, school, cemetery, discussion groups). Second is the "outer public sphere," which includes pa-

---

sity Press, 1984), 35: "During most of the period I speak of, from around A.D. 100 to 312, Christians as such avoided attention. The fact is well known and easily illustrated. They can hardly be blamed for that, out of common prudence." As we shall see, not every media channel was initiated by Christians; some, such as martyrdom, were forced on them by the Roman authorities, and they made good use of them for publicity purposes.

12. James Curran, "Communications, Power and Social Order," in *Culture, Society and the Media,* ed. Michael Gurevitch et al. (London and New York: Methuen, 1982), 216.

13. I use here the famous terminology of Jürgen Habermas, *The Structural Transformation of the Public Sphere: An Inquiry into a Category of Bourgeois Society,* trans. Thomas Burger (Cambridge, Mass.: MIT Press, 1989), but I adapt it to the world of antiquity. On Habermas, see Craig Calhoun, ed., *Habermas and the Public Sphere* (Cambridge, Mass.: MIT Press, 1992).

gan institutions such as the public bath, amphitheater, market, and gymnasium. In certain instances we can even speak of an additional, third division which may be called the "institutional public sphere." There, the Roman and local authorities manifested their power, in the Roman senate, city assemblies, magistracy, and army.

I wish to emphasize that I am not writing a comprehensive work on the issue of historiography as a medium of mass communication, nor a detailed study of the historiography of Eusebius. Rather, I am offering here an analysis of Eusebius's aims and methods in the *Ecclesiastical History* that takes us beyond the investigation of his use of sources.[14] My conclusions may be developed later by others and applied to other works of ancient historiography in more detail. Since my purpose is limited, and my approach new, I will spare my readers a long and fatiguing summary of research on Eusebius's historiography, merely referring them to the main scholarly studies in footnotes and in passing when necessary. Two bibliographical recommendations should be made here: Robert M. Grant's concise monograph *Eusebius as Church Historian* is a fine introduction that may be consulted by scholars or the general reader. Grant tackles the *Ecclesiastical History* through themes such as martyrology, canonicity, attitude towards Jews, and heresy. Timothy D. Barnes's *Constantine and Eusebius* is a more elaborate study that is excellent for beginner and scholar alike, with a full bibliography.[15]

14. The investigation of how Eusebius used his sources has been undertaken often. See, e.g., E. Schwartz, "Eusebios von Caesarea," *Real-encyklopädie der classischen Altertumswissenschaft*, vol. 6, part 1 (1907), cols. 1370-1439; Richard Laqueur, *Eusebius als Historiker seiner Zeit* (Berlin and Leipzig: W. de Gruyter, 1929); B. Gustafsson, "Eusebius' Principles in Handling His Sources, as Found in His 'Church History,' Books I-VII," *Studia Patristica* 4 (1961): 429-41.

15. Some scholars deal with the *Ecclesiastical History* as typical of Eusebius's "historical" thinking, in line with his *Demonstratio Evangelica* and *Praeparatio Evangelica*; see, for instance, Glenn F. Chesnut, *The First Christian Histories: Eusebius, Socrates, Sozomen, Theodoret, and Evagrius*, 2d ed. (Macon, Ga.: Mercer University Press, 1986), Chaps. 3-7. In contrast, I regard the *Ecclesiastical History* as representing an altogether different genre. On Eusebius's historiography, see also Laqueur, *Eusebius als Historiker seiner Zeit*; Vincent Twomey, *Apostolikos Thronos: The Primacy of Rome as Reflected in the Church History of Eusebius and the Historico-apologetic Writings of Saint Athanasius the Great* (Münster: Aschendorff, 1982); Monika Gödecke, *Geschichte als Mythos: Eusebs "Kirchengeschichte"* (Frankfurt am Main: P. Lang, 1987); Friedhelm Winkelmann, *Euseb von Kaisareia: Der Vater der Kirchengeschichte* (Berlin: Verlags-Anstalt Union, 1991); Harold W. Attridge and Gohei Hata, eds., *Eusebius, Christianity and Judaism* (Detroit: Wayne State University Press, 1992).

According to E. Schwartz and others, the *Ecclesiastical History* was a careless and untidy work.[16] I will claim, on the contrary, that Eusebius was a subtle writer who knew exactly what he was doing. This estimate is strengthened by the fact that the Church historian was aware of the concept of linear history but intentionally did not pursue this mode. He used, of course, a chronological framework for the ten books of the *Ecclesiastical History*, but even when a linear progression is evident, it is interrupted by frequent flashbacks, ruminations, and many other matters that hamper the flow of events (a practice reminiscent of Herodotus, but still unlike him). In short, his grand historical framework is linear, but the details are not.

Eusebius's basic linear approach is a result of his theology of history, which can be sketched on the basis of the *Ecclesiastical History* together with the *Demonstratio Evangelica* and the *Praeparatio Evangelica* as follows: Christianity was not a new phenomenon (it did not begin with Jesus under Augustus). It had already been established at the creation of the world through the existence of the Logos.[17] The patriarchs, who were pious non-Jews, were already Christian through the manifestation of the Logos.[18] But the whole of mankind underwent a terrible decline. It was Moses who saved the wayward Jews from Egypt and gave them the Law to keep them going until the reemergence of Christianity. During the Mosaic period the real Christian faith was hidden, and Moses' laws were "images and symbols" (*eikōnes kai symbola*) that suited only the Jews of Palestine. But the Jews did not fulfill the first covenant and so were punished. Moreover, since they did not acknowledge Jesus as their Messiah, but killed both him and John the Baptist, they suffered destruction. The surviving remnant of the Jewish people became the new elect, and from them sprang the apostles of Jesus. Thus since Judaism — the inferior form of Christianity — was destroyed (except for this remnant), Christianity took over and en-

16. Schwartz, "Eusebios von Caesarea"; also Timothy D. Barnes, *Constantine and Eusebius* (Cambridge, Mass.: Harvard University Press, 1981).

17. For the notion of God's "control over the whole fabric of history" in Eusebius's writing, see Chesnut, *First Christian Histories,* Chap. 3.

18. For the Logos as a force behind the history of humankind and the concept of history in Eusebius's theological writing, see Chesnut, *First Christian Histories,* Chaps. 4-5, and Arthur J. Droge, "The Apologetic Dimensions of the Ecclesiastical History," in *Eusebius, Christianity and Judaism,* ed. Attridge and Hata, 492-509. See also the survey of Raffaele Farina, *L'impero e l'imperatore Cristiano in Eusebio di Cesarea: La Prima teologia politica del Cristianesimo* (Zurich: Pas Verlag, 1966), esp. 36-74.

compassed all the Gentiles in the world, as it was destined to do according to the Jewish prophets. It was no coincidence that Jesus appeared when Augustus created the Principate and founded a new Roman Empire.[19] However, during the succeeding years, the evil demons acted against Christianity through the "bad" emperors, and the final victory of Christianity ensued when Constantine founded a new Christian Kingdom.[20] This is the story in brief. We will see in the following that although the grand picture is linear, the details within this general framework are not.

At all events, Eusebius even wrote a *Chronicon*. There the linear concept is expressed in parallel columns (only one after Jesus, namely, the history of Christianity running parallel to the history of the Roman Empire).[21] Hence the question should be asked: Why in fact did he abandon the strictly linear presentation of history in the *Ecclesiastical History*? Was he really that negligent? Or was he working on a different kind of historical genre, hardly known until then? To me, this last possibility seems the more likely. We should note also that Eusebius wrote Books 1-7 of the *Ecclesiastical History* first, and only later added Books 8-10. His chronological scope extends from Jesus (although he also briefly refers to biblical history in Book 1) to Constantine. Eusebius himself edited Books 1-7 several times but did not deem it necessary to alter them drastically, whereas he changed Books 8-10 several times before they reached their present form.[22] When in later years he made slight revisions, the changes were minor, and when he deliberately shortened his *Martyrs of Palestine* in order to incorporate it

19. For Eusebius's conviction that the rise of Augustus and Christ were linked by God's providence, see Chesnut, *First Christian Histories*, 76-79.

20. For the alliance of Christians and the Roman Empire and the concept of progress in Eusebius's writings, see Wolfram Kinzig, *Novitas Christiana: Die Idee des Fortschritts in der Alten Kirche bis Eusebius* (Göttingen: Vandenhoeck & Ruprecht, 1994), 517-68. On good and bad emperors, see Chesnut, *First Christian Histories*, 80ff.

21. Alden A. Mosshammer, *The "Chronicle" of Eusebius and Greek Chronographic Tradition* (Lewisburg, Penn.: Bucknell University Press, 1979); and William Adler, "Eusebius' *Chronicle* and Its Legacy," in *Eusebius, Christianity and Judaism*, ed. Attridge and Hata, 467-91.

22. For these issues, see Barnes, *Constantine and Eusebius*, 149-50 and passim; Chesnut, *First Christian Histories*, Chap. 6. Before the beginning of the persecution in 303 C.E., Eusebius edited most of Books 1-7. In ca. 313 came the second edition, namely, Books 1-7, 8 (including the short recension of the *Martyrs of Palestine*), and 9. In ca. 315 he published the third edition, Books 1-10.7 (including a rewritten Book 8). In ca. 325 he issued a fourth edition, which included Books 1-10, and in 326 he made some minor editorial changes.

in the *Ecclesiastical History* he was well aware of the end product. This would indicate that he was content with what he had done (contrary to Schwartz's view), because he had the opportunity to change it completely during his various editorial recensions. Moreover, Eusebius had read some of the great historians of antiquity and was familiar with their genres of historical writing; yet he chose to write differently.

In the following chapters, I will attempt to show why Eusebius's *Ecclesiastical History* depicts a process that can be described as a "media revolution" in early Christianity. In particular I shall focus on his methods of presenting this revolution. I will demonstrate that he worked like a modern reporter and editor in using journalistic methods to describe the spread of Christianity. In this sense he was himself a media revolutionary. For instance, his history treats time as our newspapers do: sometimes presenting episodes that took place during a few hours, sometimes summarizing events that transpired over the course of several months or even years. Eusebius wrote along different lines than those of Thucydides or Polybius, because relevance was his main concern. Moreover, the notion of objectivity was almost alien to his writing. Sections of his history can be viewed as three-dimensional accounts that reflect reality, perceived reality, and fiction.

Since modern media scholars consider historiography a medium addressed to the masses, we can — with reservations — apply some of the results of media performance research to ancient historiography in general and to the *Ecclesiastical History* in particular. A fundamental observation about the modern media, that they "usually assert the principle of their own right to determine, in their publication policy, what is in the interests of their audience and, indirectly, of society,"[23] can and should be applied to Eusebius's work in his history. He definitely decided what the interests of his public were.

According to Denis McQuail,[24] whose work is based on earlier research, there are several different versions of the self-perceived social role of the media. He enumerates the following:

> Neutral *observer*, transmitter and interpreter of events of significance in society — the role of public *informant*. A second version is that of *participant* or *advocate*, involving the aim of engaging in political and social

23. Denis McQuail, *Media Performance: Mass Communication and the Public Interest* (London: Sage Publications, 1992), 84.
24. Ibid., 85.

life and having a purposeful influence on events. This may include an *altruistic* element . . . an impulse to speak up for society's victims, minorities and underdogs. A third kind of involvement is as critic, adversary, *watch-dog* of any sphere of public life. Fourthly, there is a widespread view that the media have a task as a platform or *forum* for the diverse voices of society, allowing the expression both of varied opinions and cultural streams. . . . Fifthly, there is a role of responsible *guardian* which is sometimes adopted in matters of public order and morals, culture or personal conduct . . . . This has been described as a 'sacerdotal' role. [25]

Although at first glance these observations describe only the modern scene, we may still use them as a starting point for the research methods we wish to apply to ancient historiography in general and to Eusebius's *Ecclesiastical History* in particular. For starters, we may ask whether the ancient historian was indeed a "neutral observer." Thucydides attempted to be one, but Eusebius certainly was not. He was perhaps an interpreter of events of significance in society and can be seen playing the role of a "public informant." With the second media role in view, we may say that Thucydides, Polybius and Eusebius were involved in political life, but to what extent their histories had a "purposeful influence on events" is hard to determine. Unlike the first two, Eusebius most certainly had an "impulse to speak up for society's victims . . . and underdogs" (the Christians at certain junctures of his history). Historiography can also be examined, in terms of the third media role, as critic, adversary, and watchdog. Josephus wrote his furious critique of the Zealots after the Great War was over, but it reflects the opinions that he and others held during the last stages of the war. Polybius became an ardent critic of Greek dependence on Rome before 168 B.C.E. Eusebius criticizes his adversaries — the heretics and the Jews. In the following we will examine whether his criticism had any effect on the "hard evidence" he relates in his *Ecclesiastical History*. In other words, did his criticism affect the data? The fourth role of the media, too, is of great importance and can be applied to ancient historiography. Eusebius created a forum for varied opinions, for example, those of

25. Ibid., 85-86, citing the research of Herbert J. Gans, *Deciding What's News: A Study of CBS Evening News, NBC Nightly News, Newsweek, and Time* (New York: Pantheon Books, 1979) and J. G. Blumler, "Producers' Attitudes towards the TV Coverage of an Election," in *The Sociology of Mass Media Communicators*, ed. Paul Halmos (Keele: University of Keele, 1969), 85-115.

the heretics. But one has to measure how pluralistic and fair he was in adducing the opinions of his opponents. Did he give the heretics a proportional role within his account? (For the sake of comparison, we may note that Josephus granted the various groups a more or less fair proportion of space in the *Jewish War,* although he deeply hated some of them). The fifth role of the media may also be applied to the *Ecclesiastical History.* Eusebius wrote a "sacerdotal" report, since he — unlike Thucydides — was actually "working" for a certain group, the Catholic orthodoxy, and he made constant attempts to be a guardian of its ethics.[26]

Standards of Media Performance

Let us now examine some criteria or standards for judging media performance that we can use in our approach to ancient historiography. For the sake of precision, it will be useful to quote McQuail and others verbatim and at some length. Applying modern media performance scholarship to ancient historiography modifies our understanding of this particular medium. On the one hand, the ancient texts take on a different meaning when set against a comprehensive group of media factors, since we can then see more clearly how partial and incomplete their media performance actually was. On the other hand, since we know so little about the behavior of ancient texts as communicative factors within the society, we can perhaps fill in some gaps with the aid of modern scholarly study of the dynamics of communicative media performance in modern societies. The combination of our knowledge about the ancient texts with some of the conclusions of modern media studies will then help us better understand the nature of ancient historiography.

Diversity

In his *Media Performance: Mass Communication and the Public Interest* Denis McQuail says that diversity in mass media involves meeting the fol-

26. That Eusebius represented the Catholic Church has been argued by almost every scholar dealing with the *Ecclesiastical History.* So, for instance, Barnes, *Constantine and Eusebius;* Gödecke, *Geschichte als Mythos;* and Twomey, *Apostolikos Thronos.* Cf. W. Den Boer, "Some Remarks on the Beginning of Christian Historiography," *Studia Patristica* 4 (1959): 348-62.

lowing standards. First, the media should reflect in structure and content the realities of the societies in which they operate. Second, minorities should have equal access to the media. Third, the media should provide a forum for every variety of point of view within the society. Fourth, the media should provide choices of content that satisfy the needs of the various audiences in the society. This is an ideal picture of how diversity in the media should look. Since diversity "is so general and can have so many different formulations and expressions,"[27] I will offer only some general observations concerning the term, showing how problematic it is in reality.

McQuail explains how scholars of media performance describe diversity in modern mass media: "Progressive social change is linked in several ways to diversity. Innovation, creativity and originality in all fields of social and cultural life are unlikely to exist without diversity within a society and also over time."[28] But, says McQuail, "Most of the research cited [in the problem of diversity] has been guided by an expectation of finding much 'distortion' and only limited diversity of structure, content or audience. Both expectations have generally been met. Nearly every group or area of human activity can be shown to be either incorrectly represented statistically or misrepresented, according to some objective indicator." However, according to W. Schultz, quoted by McQuail,[29] since the media are participants in society and have to meet the wishes of their audiences and clients, one cannot expect a "pure reality," but rather only a "media reality." Moreover, diversity, as well as other factors to be examined here, is dependent on the role of time in the media coverage. McQuail notes that "a cross-section at a moment of time (for instance, the news of a day or a week) will yield a different result from a sample of the same size taken over a year, and will need to be judged by different standards. Some attention may also have to be given to *cumulative* diversity. Thus, over time, the *range* of attention is likely to widen (more and different events in the news, for instance)."[30] Another important observation concerning diversity is that "in practice, a statistically correct picture is no more likely to be recognized or accepted as true by its audience than is a highly skewed version. Content that is sent is never the same as content received. Meanings will be added and changed, gaps and contexts filled in. There is evidence that au-

27. McQuail, *Media Performance*, 181.
28. Ibid., 143.
29. W. Schulz, "Mass Media and Reality" (paper presented at the Sommatie Conference, Veldhoven, Netherlands, 1988).
30. McQuail, *Media Performance*, 170.

diences do not accept what they see as a single literal truth nor do different audience members experience the same 'reality' as it is represented in the media."[31] Further, "Between the 'picture of reality' offered and the 'actual reality,' there is usually a third variable of 'perceived reality' which has some independence from the other two because it is self-constructed. This could also be a third dimension for diversity analysis."[32]

Five major factors can be gleaned from these negative results of media scholarship and applied to Eusebius's *Ecclesiastical History*:

1. failure to reflect diversity faithfully;
2. distorted picture of a group or section in society;
3. discrepancy between statistical "truth" and the presentation of reality;
4. faulty use of time that creates disproportionate pictures of diversity; and
5. distinction of "picture of reality," "actual reality," and "perceived reality."

The historiography of ancient times will look different than it does in traditional analyses if one examines it against the background of these factors. We will encounter some of them in detail in later chapters. Here I will say only that in most parts of the *Ecclesiastical History* there is clearly a gap between the statistical truth and the presentation of "reality." For instance, from Eusebius we get the impression that Christianity spread majestically throughout the world from the outset, but we know that this is far from the truth. Eusebius had no intention of including in his descriptions, and in the right perspective, everything that happened. He also used the time factor very loosely, sometimes reporting at length about events that took place in a few hours and sometimes giving one sentence to events that transpired over a whole year or even several years (without informing his readers). He produces a distorted account of other groups in his society, and even distorts the correct proportions of events in his own inner public sphere as against the outer public one. Hence one can say that Eusebius lacked a real sense of diversity, but he did express what I will call later "limited" diversity (cf. Chapter 2).

31. T. Liebes and E. Katz, "Patterns of Involvement in TV Fiction," *European Journal of Communication* 1, no. 2 (1986): 151-72.

32. McQuail, *Media Performance,* 170.

Did other historians of antiquity meet the standard of diversity? It would be interesting to examine Thucydides, for example, to see whether he was more diverse than Eusebius. In fact he answers to some of the elements we have mentioned above and certainly makes more of an attempt to reflect his reality than Eusebius does.[33]

Concerning diversity of audience, we can already at this early stage cite a short example demonstrating how an audience can react differently to the same show and how this diversity is represented by Eusebius. The martyrdom of James figures in *Hist. Eccl.* 2.23, where Eusebius reproduces the account he found in Hegesippus. The important sentences for our analysis are the ones about the audience assembled at the event:

> So the Scribes and Pharisees mentioned before made James stand on the battlement of the temple, and they cried out to him and said, "Oh, just one, to whom we all owe obedience, since the people are straying after Jesus who was crucified, tell us what is the gate of Jesus?" And he answered with a loud voice, "Why do you ask me concerning the Son of Man? He is sitting in heaven on the right hand of the great power, and he will come on the clouds of heaven." And many were assured and glorified at the testimony of James and said, "Hosanna to the Son of David." Then again the same Scribes and Pharisees said to one another, "We did wrong to provide Jesus with such testimony . . . . So they went up and threw down the Just. (2.23.12-16)

From Eusebius's representation of this episode we can see how different segments of the audience perceived the events in different ways (in line with the helpful distinction made by Liebes and Katz, mentioned above). Some participants who were altogether opposed to Christianity (mainly the Pharisees) are presented as viewing the occurrence at face value, since they did not wish to see it, or rather perceive it, in a different manner. Eusebius depicts them as taking the performance of James at face value (as a result of their communal ethos, but this can also be seen as a presentation of an alternative "perceived reality"). Another section of the participant public were willing, according to Eusebius, to accept innovations (they were not preconditioned by the strict Pharisaic attitude). They were "assured" (*plērophoreō*) by his dramatic act to receive James as a holy man. Hence they actually represent a "perceived reality" of what

---

33. Cf. his wonderful description of the circumstances leading to the futile conquest of Sicily by the Athenians in Books 6–7, and its aftermath.

happened. They do not take the events at face value as the former group did. But we also have the "media reality" of Eusebius himself, which is different from the two other realities. His own "picture of reality" is shaped by the story of Jesus and Satan on the pinnacle of the temple (Matt. 4:5). We may also detect here some facts of the "actual reality," or "statistical reality" in McQuail's words (for instance, the mere fact that James was killed, as is shown independently by Josephus, *Ant.* 20.200).[34] The "perceived reality" of the audience of Eusebius is impossible to detect.

Be that as it may, Eusebius in this account reflects some kind of limited diversity. But does he demonstrate other aspects of diversity? We shall see in the following chapters that the posing of this question is in itself an important part of the study of ancient historiography. As McQuail says, "If we can measure the information in media content, and if we can categorize items of information in a relevant way, it follows that we can also measure the (internal) *diversity* of texts."[35]

Objectivity

I find it refreshing to read modern research on objectivity, a term that has ceased to be used at all among scholars of ancient history. For some decades now it has been dismissed whenever it arises. Positivism in particular was unacceptable during the period when deconstruction was most in vogue. I hope to show that the criterion of objectivity can and should be placed again on the research agenda of ancient historiography. Let us start here with some observations of McQuail, who summarizes recent scholarship on this issue.

In his *Media Performance: Mass Communication and the Public Interest,* McQuail notes that "in the pre-television era, objectivity was often considered an old-fashioned virtue which offered a standard against which the sensationalism and the political bias of popular mass newspapers could be judged" (p. 183) and that "in part, it is the routinization of the

---

34. *Hist. Eccl.* 2.23.21-24. For the difficulties of the passage in Josephus, see Emil Schürer, *The History of the Jewish People in the Age of Jesus Christ (175 B.C.–A.D. 135),* vol. 1, rev. and ed. Geza Vermes and Fergus Millar (Edinburgh: T & T Clark, 1973), 430-41.

35. Denis McQuail, *Mass Communication Theory: An Introduction* (London: Sage Publications, 1994), 250.

objectivity norm which has attracted the fire of critics, who found the new pretence (as they saw it) of offering undiluted truth about the world more misleading than the old kind of diverse partisanship and propaganda" (p. 184). He adds that

> Glasser (1984), for instance, argued that objectivity is an ideology and itself a form of *bias:* against the watch-dog role of the press; against independent thinking; against genuine responsibility (which would involve taking responsibility for the consequences of reporting). . . . News research has persistently cast doubt on the possibility of real 'neutrality' in reporting . . . . Even supposedly objective news of the highest professional calibre has not escaped attack, when fundamental differences of interests and values are involved.

We shall see in the following chapters how true some of this is concerning Hellenistic historiography in general and Eusebius in particular. Six points made by McQuail (drawing on the work of J. H. Boyer) to clarify the meaning of objectivity will be useful for our purpose:[36]

1. balance and even-handedness in presenting different sides of an issue;
2. accuracy and realism of reporting;
3. presentation of all main relevant points;
4. separation of facts from opinion, but treating opinion as relevant;
5. minimizing the influence of the writer's own attitude, opinion or involvement;
6. avoidance of slant, rancour or devious purpose.

Whereas Thucydides and even Polybius merit a high score in their ability to comply with these criteria (or some of them), Eusebius's *Ecclesiastical History* is more problematic. The reasons are not difficult to detect, and here we can again draw upon McQuail's discussion of objectivity. For instance, Eusebius, like modern mass media, selected and presented information "to please consumers and to attract attention, thus emphasizing form more than content." Moreover, Eusebius more than Thucydides or Polybius was in the habit of giving summaries of the most important

---

36. McQuail, *Media Performance,* 184, citing T. L. Glasser, "Competition and Diversity among Radio Formats: Legal and Structural Issues," *Journal of Broadcasting* 28, no. 2 (1984): 127-42; and J. H. Boyer, "How Editors View Objectivity," *Journalism Quarterly* 58 (1981): 24-28.

points "just as the news medium as a whole is organized to give a clear indication of priorities . . . a clear division (of location and definition) is usually observed between fact on the one hand and opinion or interpretation
on the other."[37] Eusebius had his priorities (the theological themes mentioned above), and he set up an inner hierarchy within them. In the *Ecclesiastical History* he usually does not deviate from them (unlike Herodotus,
for instance, whose digressions are sometimes more extensive than his
main theme, the Persian wars; it seems that Herodotus did not work with a
strong notion of priorities). If one attempts to separate Eusebius's opinions from his "facts," the "facts" turn out in many instances to have a
smaller percentage of space devoted to them.

McQuail also discusses objections to making objectivity a criterion
for judging the standards of mass media:

> First, that objectivity is impossible and it makes little sense, in conse-
> quence, to measure it; secondly, that it is undesirable and should not be
> treated as a positive performance norm. . . . the impossibility of com-
> plete objectivity has been argued on several grounds. One is that the un-
> avoidable process of news *selection* must also entail subjective judge-
> ment, of which journalists themselves may be unaware. . . . Another is
> that all events and reports of events which are candidates for treatment
> as news have to be placed in wider frames of reference which give them
> evaluative meanings. Thirdly, the omissions, gaps and silence which are
> unavoidable may also be eloquent, reflecting implicit (and subjective)
> judgements about relevance and assumptions about society and its val-
> ues. Fourthly, and most broadly, it is quite clear that news is always pro-
> duced within a context of numerous and powerful external and internal
> pressures . . . which are almost bound to deflect journalism from any
> ideal goal of recounting "truth."

Later McQuail goes on to say that "perhaps the most fundamental objec-
tion is the view that there *is* no objective reality "out there" to report on:
the best we can expect is no more than different versions of a multifarious
set of impressions. No account of reality can be uniquely correct or complete, except in the most trivial instances." Further, "we have no neutral
language with which to provide an objective account of reality, even if we
accept that this exists. . . . The argument for the undesirability of objectivity is linked to its impossibility, since it is misleading to offer something

37. McQuail, *Media Performance*, 185.

17

which cannot be delivered."[38] Moreover, "in the most critical view of objectivity, the practice is viewed as actively serving, whether willingly or not, the interests of agents or an established order and as reinforcing a consensus which mainly protects power and class interests."[39]

McQuail himself recognizes that the very nature of news makes objectivity a relative factor:

> News, we are often reminded . . . is still a narrative of people and events, with elements of drama, myth and personalization as well as of fact . . . these features are embedded in the history . . . and in the current practice of news . . . and are likely to influence how news is "read" by its audience and also *why* it is read in the first place.[40]

> It is hard . . . to see how objectivity can ever be more than relative — a position taken in relation to other positions and established on the balance of available evidence. Much news and related kinds of information is, of its nature, no more than a response to, or reflection of, the claims and doings of established power, which are themselves often bizarre, irrational and certainly not disinterested. There is another sense in which an emphasis on balance as such and on finding the middle way between (often) just two opposed positions can itself give rise to bias.[41]

From here McQuail proceeds to offer a typology of bias that distinguishes two basic variables: "hidden" or "open," on the one hand; and "intended" or "unintended," on the other.[42] The cross-classification of these two variables yields four main types of non-objective or biased news performance. First, there is *partisanship,* an open and intended bias that is "normally identified in the structure of news media by its form (editorial leading article, opinion column, forum or access slot, letter, paid advertisement). In such cases, the convention is to separate partisan from objective sections." Second, there is *propaganda,* a hidden and intended bias that is "more difficult to deal with, partly because the intention *is* concealed. It can often appear in the form of objective news, for instance, as informa-

38. Ibid., 187-88.
39. Ibid., 188, referring to Gans, *Deciding What's News.*
40. McQuail, *Media Performance,* 189.
41. Ibid., 192.
42. Ibid., 193-95, following P. Golding, "The Missing Dimension — News Media and the Management of Social Change," in *Mass Media and Social Change,* ed. Elihu Katz and Tamas Szecsko (London: Sage Publications, 1981), 63-81.

tion (or 'disinformation') supplied to news media by spokespersons, public relations sources, interest or pressure groups; or 'pseudo-events' staged to gain media coverage or attract an audience. . . . The most problematic feature of propaganda, defined like this, is the near impossibility of identifying it in the news output in any certain or systematic way." Third, there is *unwitting bias,* an "open, but unintentional, bias in the *selection* of topics, events and news angles" that can usually be recognized in "systematic patterns of preferential attention or avoidance which are not justified by any statistical reality, but where there is no reason to suspect propagandist purpose." Fourth, there is *ideology,* defined as "hidden but unintended bias, embedded in texts" and stemming from the enduring values of the newsmakers themselves. Moreover, notes McQuail,

> it is important to stress that both 'news performance' and its assessment take place in cultural settings which define and limit both. Ideas of what is fair and reasonable in the way of objectivity may vary from one society to another and even from one theme or issue to another, depending on the overall balance of view in the society. . .we should not lose sight of the fact that 'news' is not simply facts, but a special form of knowledge (Park, 1940), which is inextricably compounded of information, myth, fable and morality.[43]

The problem of objectivity in ancient sources is usually tackled *ad rem* and *ad hoc.* In McQuail we have a systematic analysis, based on the behavior of media texts, that may be useful in our research since it not only raises new questions but also enables us to find new directions in the study of ancient historiography. We will see in the following chapters that Eusebius worked as a reporter on a small scale and was "employed" by a strong organization (the Catholic Church) whose communications web was established all over the Roman Empire. He was not a parochial reporter but gathered material from the whole world and wrote a universal history (or rather a history of "universes," to use quantum mechanics language) that encompasses a great part of the East. He was not an objective writer; indeed, objectivity does not appear to have been high on his list of priorities. Eusebius himself seems, unlike Thucydides, not even to have attempted to write an objective narrative. It is quite obvious that he made a

---

43. McQuail, *Media Performance,* 202-3, citing Robert E. Park, "News as a Form of Knowledge," in *On Social Control and Collective Behavior: Selected Papers,* ed. Ralph H. Turner (Chicago: University of Chicago Press, 1967), 32-52.

conscious selection of news in an extremely "subjective" manner and placed his material in wide frames of reference. Later we will detect many gaps in his history, silences "reflecting implicit (and subjective) judgements about relevance." He worked, we know, under enormous stress from outside pressures, such as difficulties with the Roman authorities (during times of persecution) and with heresies and heretics, and he even had to come to grips with his own orthodox "organization" (in the Arian controversy). Moreover, Eusebius was a great dramatist; his narratives about people can be seen as a strange mixture of facts, fiction, and idealization. Then, too, his writing was imbued with the values of the society in which he acted, values that are sometimes hidden in the text and sometimes easy to detect. His language is far from "objective," since his rhetoric is not neutral, and this can be seen as well in cases other than those concerned with his enemies, the heretics. His history is a patchwork of imaginative information, stories (both apocryphal and real), polemical attacks, hard information, and so on. In short, much of the *Ecclesiastical History* looks more like a modern newspaper than a linear, Thucydidean history.

Relevance

McQuail discusses the standard of relevance within his section on objectivity, but for my purposes it will be useful to treat it independently.[44] In *Media Performance* he says,

> although [relevance] seems to be a matter of common sense, it turns out to be a complex and slippery term. . . . relevance is thus the key term in assessing the quality of news selection. It is a standard which can be applied at different levels in media content: at that of general subject or topic choice (e.g. international v. local news, or crime v. political news); at the level of event or 'story' (some events are more 'newsworthy' than others); within particular 'stories', when selection has to be made among component elements in news editing . . . much the same criteria of relevance apply in the first two levels, although the third (internal relevance), the question of what contributes to adequate *comprehension* on the part of the audience plays an additional role. What makes the relevance standard most difficult is the problem of establishing the 'significance' of news topics or events. We may take the common-sense view

44. Cf. also McQuail, *Mass Communication*, 145-48.

that significance refers to what matters most, what touches people's lives most deeply. However, this leaves open the question of significance for *whom*, about *what* and according to *whose* judgement.

Moreover,

> in practice, relevance judgements are made by news media, on a continuous basis, without agonized introspection, according to established convention and routine, in response to numerous pressures and cues. . . . Much of this work has been described and analysed within the tradition of 'gatekeeper' research, which has tried to explain systematic patterns in the outcomes of news selection.[45]

The standard of relevance can shed light on much of our analysis of ancient historiography. Again, we historians of antiquity think we know what relevance means, but here we find a discussion based on the behavior of media texts over many decades. Alongside the other criteria mentioned, study of this aspect may help us in one of our most puzzling problems, identifying Eusebius's audience. It should be said at once that Eusebius, unlike Thucydides, was constantly preoccupied with the notion of relevance. He regarded his history as germane to an important purpose and directed it toward a well-defined audience. He did not hide his desire to produce a relevant history of Christianity. The concept of relevance was of course not alien to Thucydides, Ephorus, and Polybius, but it played a limited role and was kept low in the scale of priorities in their historical writing.

Let us examine some of the standards or criteria of relevance and then cite an example from Eusebius himself to demonstrate our case. McQuail examines three: absolute (normative) standards, real world indicators, and the audience as guide.

Absolute (Normative) Standards

McQuail remarks that "the view that significance can be judged according to some independent, 'absolute' standard . . . depends upon having faith either in a grand theory or ideology or on considerable confidence in the judgements of experts," and he adds that "comparison with the views of

---

45. McQuail, *Media Performance*, 198, citing Pamela J. Shoemaker, *Gatekeeping*, Communication Concepts 3 (Newbury Park, Calif.: Sage Publications, 1991).

independent experts on what is more or less significant might seem a more viable option, but these views are likely to represent a partial and elite view of the world rather than what might concern the average newspaper reader."[46] This criterion shows how important it is to ask new questions about historiography, since one is obliged to make a special study of the issue of relevance when tackling an ancient historical text. We will see that when we compare Eusebius with other historians of antiquity on the basis of external or absolute standards of relevance, his historiography comes out looking different. He, unlike many others, was *bound* by the strict standards of the orthodox Catholic Church. Thus it is not enough to say that Eusebius was partial or one-sided; one has to take the criterion of relevance into serious consideration in order to describe his stance. The guidelines of the Church can be discovered behind many sections of the *Ecclesiastical History*, guidelines that were significant in an absolute and normative sense (some were formulated at Nicaea in 325).

Real-World Indicators

According to McQuail, "By this criterion, news is more relevant, the more it corresponds to the reality as measured by independent records of the reality — in official statistics, other sources, etc." The problem is that there is "too much reality to 'reflect,'" and that "versions of the 'real world' of everyday life in society are normally mediated through institutional sources (political, economic, judicial, etc.) which seek to establish (often competing) priorities and *agendas* which they would like to see in news."[47] Thus, this criterion cannot take us very far. If we apply it to the *Ecclesiastical History*, we might be left with little real history in the sense of "news" that reflects aspects of "real life." However, the real-life criterion can show us a great deal about the role of relevance in Eusebius.

The Audience as Guide

McQuail thinks that this criterion is the most promising empirically, since "if what is significant is what affects most peoples' lives most deeply most often, then it is the people themselves (the media public) who ought to know." He adds, "If measures of audience interest or demand are used as

46. McQuail, *Media Performance*, 199.
47. Ibid., 199.

the main criteria of relevance, the outcome is unlikely to correspond with the views of experts or with 'real world' statistics, or even with any of the various institutional agendas. Nevertheless, this standard of relevance is readily applicable, since much is known (or knowable) about audience interests."[48]

How then can we apply this criterion to Eusebius or any other historian of antiquity? Since we cannot measure audience interest in antiquity, we may assume that the text itself reveals the nature of the audiences. Thus it is clear that Thucydides was less preoccupied with his audience than was Eusebius. The former wrote his history for people to remember what happened in the Peloponnesian War regardless of what they would have wished to have happened. The audience that Polybius had in mind was elitist; he wrote a *pragmatikē historia* intended to be a textbook for politicians, generals, and other high officials.[49] Josephus Flavius wrote his *Antiquities* for a wide Graeco-Roman audience because he wanted to demonstrate that the Jews were much older than most people in the region, that they had a long and venerable history to present and were therefore superior in status.

Where then does Eusebius stand in this respect? We shall see in later chapters that his rhetoric, his imagery, his manner of telling stories, and his narrative, as well as his methods of popularizing highly theological matters, show quite clearly that most of what he wrote was meant for a "simple" audience, not for an elite of intellectuals of any kind. Hence one can say that Eusebius kept his ears open to reactions and wished to accommodate his audiences' interests. He wrote about matters that a specific identifiable audience wanted to know about. Who were these simple people for whom he had to write in simplistic terms? Probably Gentiles and Jews who were interested in Christianity, people who were still hesitating about crossing the frontier into the domain of Christianity, as well as the hoi polloi of Christian believers who had constantly to be reminded of the Catholic organization and its correct *(orthos)* views.[50] It seems that Eusebius was aware of the interests of his audience while writing the *Ecclesiastical History* and that he wrote his *Demonstratio Evangelica* for a totally different part of society. Moreover, his "historical" accounts are meant to

---

48. Ibid.

49. See Walbank, *Polybius;* Arthur M. Eckstein, *Moral Vision in the Histories of Polybius* (Berkeley: University of California Press, 1995).

50. On the audience of Eusebius studied from a different angle, see Gödecke, *Geschichte als Mythos,* 27-31.

impart specific lessons about the realities that he and his audience encoun-tered during their time and in their immediate environment (martyrdom, heresy, relations with the Roman authorities, canonical authority, ethics, etc.). Thus we can frequently detect his reaction to his specific audience, just as we can with other historians of antiquity. Eusebius's writing, im-bued as it is with various religious and institutional interests, makes his history relevant for a defined segment of his society. His history therefore does not necessarily correspond to the "real world." It does not even cor-respond to the interests of the superpower of his day, the Roman Empire, or to those of the aristocrats in his own society, who had other agendas.

How do modern journalists cope with the selection of news and the satisfaction of standards of relevance? According to McQuail, they apply *timeliness* and *topicality* as "news values." This means that they prefer big events or topics that are immediate in impact and close to home either cul-turally or geographically.[51] With Eusebius, we cannot say that he is narrat-ing immediate news (although to a theologian any news can be considered immediate). But he certainly relates his news according to topics (in con-trast to the methods employed by Dionysius of Halicarnassus, Josephus Flavius, and Livy). Moreover, he also applies the criterion of narrating only crucial matters of a time and place close to his own culture. Hence his nar-rative of "news" would be considered "biased."

Sensationalism and Impartiality

We will deal in more detail with the issue of sensationalism in Chapter 2. McQuail defines sensationalism as the "'human interest', personalization or other 'entertainment' characteristics of news" and notes, "The more that news has such features, the more it may be thought to be lacking in 'information value', and thus unlikely to be relevant to information needs, however immediately *interesting* it may be to audiences."[52] This factor is of major significance in Eusebius. We shall see in various cases that sensa-tionalism — the reporting of shocking events and amazing phenomena — often occurs in the *Ecclesiastical History* at the expense of more serious or mundane coverage providing solid information (contrast, for instance, Polybius, Book 4).

51. McQuail, *Media Performance*, 199-200.
52. Ibid., 200.

Media scholars evaluate the sensationalism vs. impartiality factor by applying two subcriteria, "balance" and "neutrality." On both these counts, Eusebius would fail the test. Impartiality "requires the reporter (or news channel) to maintain a distance, not to take sides in matters where there are two or more points of view or different valuations," while "balance" involves "*selection* or *omission* in respect either of facts which may imply values or of expression of points of view on the supposed 'facts' by the parties involved. . . . It can be taken to require either *equal* attention to the main protagonists . . . or attention proportionate to the varying significance of the actor's involvement in an event. . . . Attention can be balanced in terms of measurable space or time in news. . . ."[53] Eusebius, in contrast to someone like Polybius, is not a balanced historian, and we will have repeated opportunities to substantiate this judgment.

The second subcriterion is neutrality, which refers chiefly to "the use of potentially evaluative words, images and frames of reference and also of different styles. When assessing neutrality, we look for *connotation* rather than *denotation* (as in the case of balance)."[54] Our study will show that, in comparison with Thucydides, neutrality was not Eusebius's strongest point.

Measuring Objectivity

As we return to the measuring of objectivity, media performance studies again offer us systematic methods based on the behavior of texts in real life. Let us now deal with the subcriteria:

Factualness

It is refreshing to see that scholars of media speak about facts without all the heavy connotations and inhibitions that historians usually have (in particular those too deeply impressed by deconstructionist theories). McQuail says that a "fact" "is clearly different from a subjective opinion or a comment and it should, in principle, be verifiable by reference to reliable sources or to other independent accounts." He suggests a method of examining "the separation of facts from comment" by dividing the text into

---

53. Ibid., 201.
54. Ibid., 201; cf. Fiske, *Introduction to Communication Studies*, 85-87.

units of analysis, and isolating the facts in these sections.[55] Aspects of factualness are:

1. Information value. There are three indicators to measure information value. First, "density," "the proportion of all relevant points given"; second, "breath," "the number of *different* points as a proportion of the total possible"; and third, "depth," "the number of facts and motives accompanying and helping to explain the basic points."[56]
2. Readability. This measure relates to information "richness." "News texts with a relatively low incidence of facts are likely to have a high degree of redundancy and to convey little information. However, they are, in general, easier read and to understand."
3. Checkability. This indicator measures "the degree to which the 'facts' offered are (in principle) 'checkable' . . . or supported by a named source and relevant supporting evidence. The higher the proportion of verifiable units of information in a text, the more factual it may be considered."[57]

Accuracy

McQuail emphasizes that accuracy is linked to the problem of credibility and suggests some methods to measure accuracy.[58] Here I will mention only those that can be applied to historiography in antiquity.

1. Verification of facts against a "reality" record. This means checking "points in a text against an external, reliable, version of the same information (or with the original source). There are too many possible kinds of error to apply a uniform approach. Blankenberg for instance, listed 14 categories of error, including omission; under and

---

55. McQuail, *Media Performance*, 205.

56. Ibid., 206, citing K. Asp, "Mass Media as Molders of Opinion and Suppliers of Information," in *Mass Communication Review Year Book*, vol. 2, ed. C. Wilhoit and C. Whitney (Beverly Hills: Sage Publications, 1981), 332-54.

57. McQuail, *Media Performance*, 206, citing W. L. Taylor, "Cloze Procedure: A New Tool for Measuring Readability," *Journalism Quarterly* 30 (1953): 415-33. One may note, for instance, the readability of Aristotle's *Athenaion Politeia* 14-18 as against 29-30.

58. McQuail, *Media Performance*, 207-10.

over-emphasis; misspelling; faulty headings; misquotes; incorrect ages; names, etc.[59]

2. Source or subject perception of accuracy. This refers to checking "with persons or organizations which are the subjects or sources of news. . . . Use of this method has indicated that, while most errors are trivial, the ones perceived to be most significant by those directly affected are more often matters of difference of interpretation or of alleged misrepresentation, than of indubitable fact. . . ."[60] In his *Analysis of Newspaper Content*, McQuail compared different newspaper accounts of the same stories on the same days in terms of their coverage of facts and figures; he concluded that "the rather high degree of intermedia difference which emerged said more about the different possibilities of presenting factual information than about the accuracy performance of the newspapers."[61]

3. Eyewitness comparisons. Under this heading, McQuail discusses a "complex variant of research which has been developed as a general strategy for recording the way in which news media 'construct' their own reality, especially as a result of their distinctive working procedures. . . . The results confirmed that the media may be more influenced by their own organizational (and technical) logic and the logic of the 'story' or 'script' based on earlier events, than by actual 'reality' as it occurs."[62]

4. Credibility. According to McQuail, "The research literature suggests that, in general, credibility has most to do with trust in the *source* on grounds of its fairness, good faith and lack of bias."[63]

5. "Internal" accuracy. Here McQuail refers in particular to the inconsistency between the headline and the substance of the story that follows.[64]

Now, historians of antiquity know some of these methods, but they would rarely apply all of them as a comprehensive system of research to one single text.

59. Ibid., 207, citing W. Blankenberg, "News Accuracy: Some Findings on the Meaning of the Term," *Journalism Quarterly* 47 (1970): 375-86.
60. McQuail, *Media Performance*, 208.
61. Denis McQuail, *Analysis of Newspaper Content* (London: H.M. Stationery Office, 1977).
62. McQuail, *Media Performance*, 208-9.
63. Ibid., 209.
64. Ibid., 210.

Completeness

McQuail claims that the completeness or fullness of a news story can be assessed in much the same way as accuracy. The criterion of completeness has two aspects: "*internal* completeness (all the essential facts of a given story) and *external* (all the essential stories, which may be measured in much the same way as diversity or relevance). There is a third dimension which may sometimes be relevant — that of cumulative completeness over a long-running story. News media are sometimes criticized for not "finishing" stories and they have no obligation to do so."[65]

This brief review of media performance standards will suffice for the moment. In later chapters I will employ many of the methods developed by media performance scholars. Here I should add that various historians in antiquity used to work with assistants. It is difficult to assess whether Eusebius did this, although he was aware of the fact that one could have assistants to help one gather material (cf. Book 6 concerning Origen). But even if he worked alone both in the library and in gathering material from written sources and informants, his *methods* of collection and writing can be evaluated in line with the criteria we have reviewed above. Having these in mind, we will get a refined picture of Eusebius's methods.

Let me give an example of how one can analyze a text with the help of our criteria. In Book 5 of the *Ecclesiastical History,* we are told that during the great persecution in Gaul a man called Alexander,

> a Phrygian by race, and a physician by profession, who had lived in Gaul for many years and was known to almost every one for his love toward God and boldness of speech (for he was not without a share of the apostolic gift), stood by the judgement-seat and by signs encouraged them to confession, and seemed to those who were standing by as though he were in travail. But the crowd, angry that those who had formerly denied were confessing again, howled at Alexander as though he were responsible for this. The governor summoned him and asked him who he was, and when he said "a Christian," he flew into a rage and condemned him to the beasts. And the next day he went into the arena together with Attalus; for to please the mob the governor had given Attalus back to the beasts. They passed through all the instruments of torture which were prepared in the amphitheatre, and endured a great contest. Finally they

65. Ibid., 210.

28

too were sacrificed. Alexander uttered neither groan nor moan at all, but conversed with God in his heart, and Attalus, when he was put on the iron chair and was being burned and the reek arose from his body, said to the crowd in Latin, "Lo, this which you are doing is to eat men, but we neither eat men nor do anything else wicked." And when he was asked what name God has, he replied, "God has not a name as a man has." (5.1.49-52)

Can we at all measure the objectivity of this text? Let us use some of the criteria mentioned earlier, not necessarily in the same order. Concerning the account's "factualness" — its information value, readability and checkability — we can say that it does not add much information to what we know of other martyrs in Gaul (or elsewhere for that matter), except for the name of Alexander, and the fact that he was a Phrygian and a physician. If, for instance, we compare this piece of "history" to any occasional narrative in Thucydides (for instance, in Book 8), or Josephus's *Jewish War*, we will notice that the density, breadth, and depth are considerably lower in this passage from Eusebius. Hence by criterion of factualness, Thucydides would be high up on the scale; Eusebius, extremely low. The readability of Eusebius's text is easy and its redundancy high, since this story repeats so many elements that we find in various other martyrdom stories both in Eusebius and elsewhere.[66]

Concerning "checkability," we cannot verify this story at all, but this is a problem with many ancient texts. However, Eusebius quotes this story verbatim, along with others, from a letter written by the churches of Lyons and Vienne to their brethren in Asia Minor (5.1.2-3). This letter confers a relatively high degree of credibility on the information.

And what about "accuracy"? The "reality record" of this text can be affirmed, because it is highly probable that these martyrdoms really took place in the seventies of the second century in Gaul. Moreover, there are probably not too many factual errors, but we can assume that there are many omissions, since the letter from Lyons and Vienne itself did not intend to tell a complete story. The text also presents, no doubt, a "perceived" reality, since the martyrdom of Polycarp was a well-known precedent, especially in Gaul. Thus much of the picture we get here is perceived through

66. See Chapter 3 below. Cf. Marsha Witten, "The Restriction of Meaning in Religious Discourse: Centripetal Devices in a Fundamentalist Christian Sermon," in *Vocabularies of Public Life: Empirical Essays in Symbolic Structure*, ed. Robert Wuthnow (London and New York: Routledge, 1992), 19-38.

the imagery and ideas we find in the *Martyrdom of Polycarp*. Moreover, although we get some of the details of the surrounding world, such as the reaction of mob and crowd, much of this looks like stereotypical description, and we miss a great deal. The *Ecclesiastical History* lacks details that we have in the *Martyrdom of Perpetua and Felicitas*.[67] We miss details relating to the Romans and their strategies, and others as well. Thus this depiction lacks completeness even in the details that we would expect in such a drama. Take, for instance, the siege of Amphipolis narrated by Thucydides or the Roman siege of Jerusalem recounted by Josephus.[68] In the latter we find less reconstructed, perceived reality, are given many more details that are necessary to the description, and therefore get a much fuller and more complete description. The level of redundancy in Josephus is low. In contrast, Eusebius presents the story of Alexander not necessarily in order to adduce a complete account, or a balanced one, but to offer a readable and relevant story from the orthodox Catholic point of view.

The issue of relevancy will be tackled in later chapters, but here I will note that the high proportion of narratives dealing with martyrs in the *Ecclesiastical History* is not accidental — even though in the three hundred years covered by the work, the actual periods of persecution add up to a maximum of thirty years. Stories about martyrs were significant and relevant at the time Eusebius was writing and editing because the encounter with martyrdom had again become acute and interesting. Eusebius grants martyr stories so great a "timeliness" and "topicality" that the ten books of the *Ecclesiastical History* give the impression that martyrdom went on much longer than it did in reality. This is understandable, since martyrdom was the real news at the time; it was "newsworthy".

Hopefully I have said enough in this chapter to indicate that applying standards of evaluating modern media performance to ancient historiography can allow us to put ancient historical texts in a framework of relativity and thereby enable us to assess one historian's quality against another's. At the very least, adapting the methods of modern media studies can shed new light on the methods and aims of Eusebius's *Ecclesiastical History*.

---

67. Cf. Patricia Cox Miller, *Dreams in Late Antiquity: Studies in the Imagination of a Culture* (Princeton: Princeton University Press, 1994), Chap. 6.

68. Thucydides 4.102-7; Josephus, *The Jewish War*. See Doron Mendels, *The Rise and Fall of Jewish Nationalism*, 2d ed. (Grand Rapids: Eerdmans, 1997), Chap. 12.

CHAPTER 2

Sensationalism and the Social Order

The Case of Paul of Samosata

Paul of Samosata, the bishop of Antioch from 260 to 272 c.e. who came to be regarded as a heretic, knew better than many of his generation how to exploit the outer public sphere in order to enhance his ideas. This we learn from his adversaries, the orthodox bishops. Eusebius's relatively great emphasis on this particular heretic (*Hist. Eccl.* 7.29.1–30.19) shows how important he was for the historian's purposes. The heretical views of Paul were no doubt disturbing, although Eusebius himself was close to them during the Arian debate. But even more disturbing to the Church Fathers and to Eusebius (who in this case just relates the "news") was the heretic's behavior. This, at any rate, is the impression that we get from reading Eusebius's presentation. As he sometimes does, Eusebius quotes the formal decision of the Fathers, who in this case gathered in Antioch for the synod of 268-69 c.e.[1] Their decision figures in the shape of a letter addressed to the bishops of all the provinces and to Dionysius bishop of Rome and Maximus bishop of Alexandria (according to Jerome *De Viris Illustribus* 71

---

1. *Hist. Eccl.* 7.27-30. Lawlor and Oulton place the council "not later than" 268 (*Eusebius, Bishop of Caesarea: The Ecclesiastical History and the Martyrs of Palestine,* vol. 1 [London: SPCK, 1927], 256-57); cf. Fergus Millar, "Paul of Samosata, Zenobia and Aurelian: The Church, Local Culture and Political Allegiance in Third-Century Syria," *Journal of Roman Studies* 61 (1971): 1-17. According to later sources there were either seventy or eighty bishops at the synod, including many who had traveled great distances.

it was composed by Malchion). We may assume that the letter originally included some theological discussions concerning Paul's heretical views, in line with *Hist. Eccl.* 7.30.6, 11, but most of this was omitted in the *Ecclesiastical History*; hence we are left only with "the externals of Paul's conduct."[2] Probably Eusebius's sensitivity to the question of Paul's heresy at the time he was writing Book 7 is one of the reasons for his silence concerning theological matters.[3] Thus we are left with much more "interesting" information containing many sensational details about the social behavior of Paul and the anger of the Church Fathers.

What exactly made them so angry? It has been suggested that they were Origenists who were exasperated by Paul's disdain for Origen's theology;[4] that they represented the Greek stratum of society as against Paul, the native Syrian;[5] and that they just hated his bad moral behavior.[6] It has also been claimed that Eusebius's account of Paul amounts to a caricature of a pagan rhetorician.[7] Finally, we should not forget that to the Church Paul was an infuriating heretic. Scholars dealing with this theological rift have had to rely on later, problematic sources.[8] In the following I will at-

2. Millar, "Paul of Samosata," 10.

3. The theological matters can probably be found in Leontius of Byzantium. Cf. Charles Joseph Hefele, *A History of the Christian Councils from the Original Documents to the Close of the Council of Nicaea, A.D. 325*, vol. 1, 2d ed., trans. and ed. William R. Clark (Edinburgh: Clark, 1883), 123. Cf. also Theodoret, *Haereticarum fabularum compendium* 2.8. For an extensive survey of research on Paul of Samosata, see Lorenzo Perrone, "L'enigma di Paolo di Samosata: Dogma, chiesa e società nella Siria del III Secolo: prospettive di un ventennio di studi," *Cristianesimo nella storia* 13, no. 2 (1992): 253-327.

4. So H. C. Brennecke, "Zum Prozess gegen Paul von Samosata: Die Frage nach der Verurteilung des Homoousios," *Zeitschrift für die Neutestamentliche Wissenschaft* 75 (1984): 274-75, although he himself does not agree with the view. The view is rejected by Wolfgang A. Bienert, *Dionysius von Alexandrien: Zur Frage des Origenismus im 3. Jahrhundert* (Berlin: de Gruyter, 1978).

5. This notion has been successfully refuted by Millar, "Paul of Samosata," and J. Burke, "Eusebius on Paul of Samosata: A New Image," *Kleronomia* 7 (1975): 8-20.

6. So F. W. Norris, "Paul of Samosata: Procurator Ducenarius," *Journal of Theological Studies*, n.s., 35 (1984): 50-70.

7. V. Burrus, "Rhetorical Stereotypes in the Portrait of Paul of Samosata," *Vigiliae Christianae* 43 (1989): 215-25.

8. Adolf von Harnack, "Die Reden Pauls von Samosata . . . ," *Theologische Literaturzeitung* 50 (1925): 227-32; Friedrich Loofs, *Paulus von Samosata: Eine Untersuchung zur altkirchlichen Literatur und Dogmengeschichte* (Leipzig: Hinrichs, 1924); Gustave Bardy, *Paul de Samosate: Étude historique* (Louvain: "Spicilegium sacrum lovaniense" bureaux; Paris: E. Champion, 1923); and Henri de Riedmatten, *Les actes du procès de Paul de Samosate: Étude sur la christologie du IIIe au IVe siècle* (Fribourg: Editions St-

tempt to explain the anger of the Church Fathers from a different perspective, by arguing that what they resented was the "media revolution" that Paul had started. Let us first consider some aspects of his behavior.

The letter cited by Eusebius in 7.30.2-17 generally and abruptly says that Paul "departed from the canon, and has turned aside to spurious and bastard doctrines," and then more specifically that "though he was formerly poor and penniless, neither having received a livelihood from his fathers nor having got it from trade or any occupation, he has now come to possess abundant wealth, as a result of lawless deeds and sacrilegious plunderings and extortions exacted from the brethren by threats" (7.30.6-7). This description is followed by details of his scandalous behavior. From this statement it is quite clear that Paul came from a poor family and that he was a self-made man. He made his money during his office as bishop. But how exactly did he make his money? According to the letter of the distinguished Church Fathers, it was by "lawless deeds and sacrilegious plunderings and extortions exacted from the brethren by threats" (7.30.7). We get more details about Paul's wealth: "He deprives the injured of their rights, and promises to help them for money, yet breaks his word with these also, and with a light heart makes his harvest out of the readiness of persons engaged in lawsuits to make an offer, for the sake of being rid of those that trouble them." The letter concludes this section — which starts with the statement that "we are under no obligation to judge the actions of him . . ." — with the accusation that "he considers that godliness is a way of gain" (7.30.7).

Paul, to judge from his other deeds, probably acted in line with numerous non-Christian figures who strove for influence and power in Antioch at the time. As a result, he became one of the *plousioi* of the city, part of a well-defined upper social class. Having private means, he could act independently and pay for his expensive public relations and extravagant behavior. This was a clever move on the part of a man who wished to conquer the outer public sphere as well as the institutional one for his own purposes.

However, possessing great wealth was apparently not enough if one wished to have a power base in a city at the time. Being a bishop gave Paul

Paul, 1952). See also Brennecke, "Zum Prozess gegen Paul von Samosata"; E. Scheidweiler, "Paul von Samosata," *Zeitschrift für die neutestamentliche Wissenschaft* 46 (1955): 116-29; and J. H. Declerck, "Deux nouveaux fragments attribués à Paul de Samosate," *Byzantium* 54 (1984): 116-40.

some power, but it was limited to the Christian congregation and to his associates (the inner public sphere). An obvious weakness of the bishop's office was that it left the holder exposed to imminent persecutions by the secular authorities. Paul thus set up a political link with Zenobia, the queen of Palmyra; but he needed a formal public office as well, or as the letter expresses it, "he sets his mind on high things." Such an office, though, was most probably not granted to him. Thus he was "clothing himself with worldly honours and wishing to be called *ducenarius* [a high-ranking official with a salary of 200,000 *sestertii*], rather than bishop"; he "struts in the market-places, reading and dictating letters as he walks in public, and attended by a bodyguard, some preceding, some following, and that too in numbers" (7.30.8). Whether Paul was a real procurator or just imitated one,[9] what matters is that the external trappings of the office of *ducenarius* were, according to the account, important to him. The Fathers, of course, did not like his showing off in public places, and they complained: "the faith is ill thought of and hated because of his conceit and the overweening pride of his heart" (7.30.8). Hated by whom? Probably people in the outer public sphere. As a bishop, Paul had no natural access to the outer public sphere of the city, which he desperately craved. By posing as a *ducenarius* he could penetrate the public sphere quite freely, and according to the Fathers he caused damage to the orthodox Church by this kind of publicity.

But this is not the whole story. Although the letter repeats that the Fathers did not judge him for his behavior, it nevertheless goes to great lengths detailing

> the quackery in church assemblies he himself devised, courting popularity and posing for appearance' sake, and thus astonishing the minds of the simpler folk, with the tribunal and lofty throne *(bēma men kai thronon hypsēlon)* that he prepared for himself, not befitting a disciple of Christ, and the *secretum (sēkrēton)* [the private chamber of a magistrate] which, in imitation of the rulers of the world, he has and so styles. Also, he smites his hand on his thigh and stamps the tribunal with his feet; and those who do not applaud or wave their handkerchiefs, as in a theatre, or shout out and jump up in the same way as do the men and wretched women who are his partizans and hearken in this disorderly fashion, but who listen, as in God's house, with orderly and becoming reverence, — these he rebukes and insults. (7.30.9)

9. For my purpose here it does not matter, but see the discussion in Millar, "Paul of Samosata," and Norris, "Paul of Samosata: Procurator Ducenarius."

From this colorful description we learn that Paul convened church assemblies, and that in them he appeared on a *bēma* and chaired the session from a *thronos* in order to impress *(phantasiokopōn)* the "simpler folk."[10] He communicated with the *demos* by means of these external acts, "courting popularity," a well-known expression in Hellenistic historiography to denote contacts with the populace.[11] The impression that we get here is that Paul was not only an extraordinarily colorful and eccentric figure, but an extremely noisy one as well. He caused commotion around him both in the market (moving around and dictating), and in the assemblies, where he stamped with his feet and demanded the applause of the audience. The letter explicitly says that his followers behaved in a "seditious fashion" *(stasiōtais)*.

Thus the letter describes Paul as one who attempted, in the terms of our study, to enter the outer public sphere by employing sensational means. In simpler words we would say that he wanted to attract people's attention (as rhetoricians did at the time),[12] and thus expand the Christian congregation. But why would a bishop need all this? No doubt Paul was an able man, since his heresy was seen as a formidable menace to the Church. But he was also a talented media manipulator, since he managed to remain bishop of Antioch for more than ten years even while keeping to his heretical ideas. He also managed to gain an important political ally in the person of Zenobia.[13] Hence the answer to the above question can be found in the nature of Paul's acts. Specifically, in addition to the power base he created (being now a *plousios*, a wealthy person, and a *ducenarius*), he engaged in behavior alien to the contemporary Church. He behaved, as the Fathers themselves observe, in a theatrical manner. By his gestures and the nonverbal aspects of his speech,[14] Paul of Samosata wished to achieve a very specific purpose, namely, to impress the audience and link it to him by other

---

10. For *thronos*, see Millar, "Paul of Samosata," 13.

11. See Doron Mendels, *Identity, Religion and Historiography: Studies in Hellenistic History* (Sheffield: Sheffield Academic Press, 1998), Chap. 2.

12. Burrus, "Rhetorical Stereotypes."

13. Millar, "Paul of Samosata."

14. See the list of presentational codes in M. Argyle, "Non-verbal Communication in Human Social Interaction," in *Non-verbal Communication*, ed. Robert A. Hinde (Cambridge: Cambridge University Press, 1972): bodily contact, proximity, orientation, appearance, head nods, facial expression, gestures, posture, eye movement and eye contact, nonverbal aspects of speech. Cf. also John Fiske, *Introduction to Communication Studies*, 2d ed. (London: Routledge, 1990), 68-70.

than intellectual media channels (a theological sermon, for instance). He knew very well that spiritual talk was not suited to the kind of audience he was approaching ("simple people"). Moreover, by transmitting "noises" that were familiar codes of high officials within the outer public sphere, he caught a large public that was altogether deaf to the intellectual discourse of bishops. Paul constructed a three-dimensional message comprised of colorful scenery, a great deal of noise and rhythm, and some verbal content. In other words, his performance within the outer public sphere was sensational because nobody expected such behavior from a bishop. We will see later what this means in terms of media performance.

The letter goes on to tell us about Paul's attitude regarding the "interpreters of the Word who have departed this life," towards whom he behaves in an "insolent and ill-bred fashion in the common assembly, and brags about himself as though he were not a bishop but a sophist and charlatan" (7.30.9). In other words, Paul openly went against the canon and its "right" (orthos) interpreters, thereby undermining the authority of the main propagandistic charter common to all members of the orthodox network. Following this line he put a stop to the psalms

> addressed to our Lord Jesus Christ, on the ground that they are modern and the compositions of modern men, but he trains women to sing hymns to himself in the middle of the church on the great day of the Pascha, which would make one shudder to hear. Such also is the kind of discourse that he permits the bishops of the neighbouring country and towns, who fawn upon him, and the presbyters as well, to deliver in their sermons to the people. (7.30.10)

His congregation sang psalms to him and uttered his praises while he encouraged them to say that he was an "angel from heaven" (7.30.11), and he altered the traditional church ceremony on the grounds that it was a recent innovation — yet another instance of sensationalism in going against the conventional codes of behavior. These acts made him so powerful that he influenced surrounding bishops to act likewise. Moreover, he shifted the attention of his congregation from the figure of Jesus Christ (who was human anyhow, according to his theology), to the holy figure of the "angelic" bishop. It seems that he took a bit too seriously Ignatius of Antioch's admonition to respect bishops as though they were Jesus Christ himself (e.g., *Epistle to the Trallians* 3:1).

Then comes the description of the *subintroductae*. These mysterious women, who apparently were sisters in the church of Antioch and lived in celibacy beside the priests,[15] are assigned a very obscure (and suspicious) role in the Fathers' letter:

> And as to the *subintroductae*, as the Antiochenes call them, his own and those of the presbyters and deacons in his company, with whom he joins in concealing both this and the other incurable sins . . . yea, he has even made them rich, for which cause he is the beloved and admired of those who affect such conduct . . . and we are not ignorant of this: how many have fallen through procuring *subintroductae* for themselves, while others are under suspicion; so that even if it be granted that he does nothing licentious, yet he ought at least to guard against the suspicion that arises from such a practice, lest he cause someone to stumble, and induce others also to imitate him. For how could he rebuke another, or counsel him not to consort any further with a woman and so guard against a slip, as it is written, seeing that he has sent one away already, and has two in his company in the flower of youth and beauty, and even if he go away anywhere, he brings them around with him, living all the while in luxury and surfeiting? Wherefore, though all groan and lament in private, so fearful have they become of his tyranny and power, that they dare not accuse him. (7.30.12-15)

The latter reaction is obviously attributed not only to women, but to all pious Christians within the inner public sphere. According to the letter, Paul was excommunicated chiefly as a consequence of his behavior, with Domnus appointed bishop in his stead (7.30.17).

The account ends with the statement by Eusebius himself that, even though Paul was excommunicated, he "refused on any account to give up possession of the church-building." Matters were finally settled, though, with the intervention of the emperor Aurelian (7.30.18-19).

A Rival Media Revolution

To return now to the question posed above: why were the Church Fathers so angry? In other words, why did they draw this picture of Paul as it appears in their letter, and why did they give it an enormous amount of publicity, sending it to be read in all the provinces? First, let us be fair to Paul of Samosata. As far as we know, he did not get an equal opportunity to pre-

15. Millar, "Paul of Samosata," 17.

sent his case to the world. Paul received all this negative publicity from the dominant institution of which he was part because he refused to play according to its prescribed rules and code of behavior. His behavior as bishop is presented by Eusebius (who shortened the original letter, and apparently took out difficult theological passages) as a media revolution launched against the Church. Paul indeed acted against the media patterns that the Church had already created, by forming his own framework and channels of communication. The essence of his revolution (besides his heretical ideas, which perhaps were less revolutionary in the context of so many other heretics in this line from Marcion onward) was his deviation from the media patterns of the third-century Church. Later Catholicism, in fact, adopted many of these "externals" to promote Christianity.[16]

The Church based its media systems on the assumption that the Logos was everywhere and that the light of God was spread over the world through different agents and channels, some of whom were not even aware that they were Christian missionaries.[17] Yet most of the missionizing was performed by God's "formal" agents — the bishops, synods, lower clergy, and later also monks — by means such as teaching (as Eusebius shows in *Dem. Evan.* 1.6[21]; 1.8[29]). Communication was channeled through different media such as sermons, prayers, and social work, but also through dramatic acts such as martyrdom and aggressive propaganda against heretics.

Modern media research has shown that communication is performed through symbols:

> It is assumed that evaluative direction is always implicit in the choice of words and phrases in any kind of text, and that such direction is open to decoding . . . . Methods of analysis vary from the common sense to the arcane, but all share an assumption that any culture organizes meaning and allocates values, by means of symbols, in a consistent way so that what counts as positive or negative can be readily deciphered by those who share the culture (the relevant language or 'interpretative' community).[18]

16. Peter Brown calls Paul of Samosata "the Christian bishop of the future" (*The Body and Society: Men, Women, and Sexual Renunciation in Early Christianity* [New York: Columbia University Press, 1988], 192).

17. This Logos theology is to be found throughout the *Demonstratio Evangelica*.

18. Denis McQuail, *Media Performance: Mass Communication and the Public Interest* (London: Sage Publications, 1992), 230.

In the synodical letter excerpted at length by Eusebius we see Paul using symbols easily decodable by non-Christians in the outer public sphere. But these very same symbols were interpreted negatively by the Church Fathers and by those orthodox Christian folk who feared and resented Paul's "tyranny and power": Paul exploited the poor (instead of helping them), behaved like a secular ruler (instead of a spiritual one), dressed extravagantly (instead of modestly), had dubious relations with women (instead of avoiding the very appearance of evil), and acted raucously (instead of expressing holiness through silence). In short, the media symbols that Paul reflected in his behavior and language went against the symbols that the Church had adopted for many years prior to his appearance. Yet Paul's "evaluative direction" gained a great deal of success among his audiences, including sectors of the inner public sphere and its leadership (other bishops and presbyters). In other words, Paul was a media revolutionary because during this period the symbols of the Catholic Church radiated simplicity within the inner public sphere. As examples of this simplicity, we could note the unpretentious buildings of the churches (often just private houses), the plain garments of the clergy, the silent assemblies of prayer, the celibacy so widely practiced, the call to endurance (martyrdom), and the help for the poor. Paul, by contrast, demonstrated that Christianity needed much more than the conventional media performance in order to enlarge the community. He therefore created colorful "jingles" and other media devices that were noisy and verbally different from the regular church rhetoric.

The latter can be interpreted in line with the observations of Karen A. Cerulo:

> variations in symbol syntax represent different communication strategies, that is, different methods of conveying a message. . . . With regard to political symbols . . . we could determine which symbol structures are most stimulating to populations at large or specific blocks of voters. Such knowledge would also be valuable to market research. Advertisers could determine how to structure jingles or graphic displays in order to stimulate the desired results. Finally, classifying symbol structure could offer important information to the therapeutic domain.[19]

19. Karen A. Cerulo, "Putting It Together: Measuring the Syntax of Aural and Visual Symbols," in *Vocabularies of Public Life: Empirical Essays in Symbolic Structure,* ed. Robert Wuthnow (London and New York: Routledge, 1992), 111-29.

In the historical realm, Cerulo claims that her research demonstrates that

> the nature of a nation's modernization experience is linked to the structure of the symbols it adopts. Leaders of rapidly modernizing nations adopt embellished symbols while those in gradually modernizing nations favor basic symbols. In essence, these findings suggest that different communication strategies are called for by varying sociopolitical conditions, socioeconomic conditions, and periods of historical development.[20]

We can use this description as a background for the analysis of Paul's media revolution. Paul had many supporters in Antioch and elsewhere (as we hear from the letter itself). His media strategies, attractive to certain segments of both the inner and outer public spheres, competed with the institutional media performance of the Church itself. It is quite plausible that what really distressed the Church Fathers was that Paul adopted "embellished" (or downright alien) symbols through which Christianity gained a great deal of popularity. In other words, he was more successful than the orthodox Church in marketing the merchandise of Christianity.[21] Paul understood something the Fathers and Eusebius did not: the basic symbols of orthodox Christianity were no longer effective in an Antiochene society that was changing. Thus, the more Christianity wished to make converts, the more it had to reach out to the outer public sphere by modifying its media performance. From the letter it becomes clear that, even though the new media strategies went against the grain of some of the more traditional members of the inner public sphere, those Christians still remained reluctantly within the congregation, groaning against Paul's tyranny and power. By his new media performance, Paul gained many supporters for the Christian cause from the outer public sphere without really losing his supporters within the inner one.

Paul even succeeded in winning the support of many Christians within the inner public sphere by selling them new media symbols to accommodate the changing times. For instance, it was not enough to say that the bishop was a holy figure, a vague and amorphous symbol. Paul transformed the symbol into a more vivid one, making the bishop an "angel of heaven" who could be seen in reality. This went well with his

---

20. Ibid., 125-26.

21. That Paul was successful we can learn from the anxiety the Fathers express concerning the (to their view) bad image that Paul reflected in the outer sphere.

claim that Jesus was a more earthly figure than orthodox doctrine laid down.

In short, if we analyze the words and behavior of Paul and the reaction of the Church Fathers as related in Eusebius's account, we may conclude that the Fathers felt threatened less by Paul's theology than by his revolutionary media performance. Eusebius's presentation itself reflects his keen awareness of the media assets that the Church possessed as a world organizational network.

This leads us into the problem of order in third-century Christian society. In his *Media Performance* Denis McQuail broadly defines *order* as "the principle (and value) of social cohesion and social harmony: whatever has to do with the binding together of society, the interdependence of its members, the organization of their activities, the shared awareness of belonging and of a common identity in group, community, and society." He goes on to distinguish between the social and the cultural domains, even though the boundary between the two is rarely firm. Social order has to do with "control (relations of power and compliance) or with solidarity (mutual attachment and cooperation)," whereas cultural order concerns "meanings and symbols."[22] Speaking of social order in particular, McQuail notes that

> in most societies, social institutions exert a 'bias' in favour of 'normality' and of social harmony, with which 'good order' is usually identified. This bias favours the existing hierarchy of social status and of economic reward. There is also a 'bias' in society [that favours] approved values towards cooperation rather than conflict. A consensus on some 'fundamental values' of the society is usually presumed (though it does not go completely unchallenged). . . . Often, the result has been to highlight those aspects of the media which appear *disruptive* of the established order — especially representations of conflict and violence, 'bad news', deviance, discontent, crime, scandal. . . .[23]

I cannot see any real obstacle to applying some of these conclusions to our study of Paul of Samosata (indeed, a broader application of them might have far-reaching effects on the study of ancient history in general). The

---

22. McQuail, *Media Performance*, 237.

23. Ibid., 238. See also Nancy Signorielli and Michael Morgan, eds., *Cultivation Analysis: New Directions in Media Effects Research* (Newbury Park, Calif.: Sage Publications, 1990).

Fathers present Paul of Samosata as disrupting the established social order in Antioch. Their letter is strongly biased in favor of "good behavior" within the Christian community and assumes a strict and clear perception of "good order." To put it differently, the Fathers sent a letter to all the communities implying what the right order of the Church should be and reaffirming the values that their organization, the Church, had adopted.[24] Like our modern mass media, the letter highlights the disruptive factors of what it reports. The Fathers are "biased" towards good order. Within the inner public sphere of Antioch and its environment, then, Paul of Samosata attempted such a perfect media performance that, to use McQuail's words, he was trying to avoid openly "undermining established authority" [the Catholic Church] even while attempting to "promote innovation and change and to reflect the shifts of social norms and values."[25]

But here we have to pause and ask ourselves: why does Eusebius present Paul as so sensational? Compared to other accounts of heresies in the *Ecclesiastical History*, this account is not redundant. It is both interesting and sensational. According to McQuail, "'sensationalism' often comes down to a high degree of personalization, emotionalism and dramatization in content. It also entails distinctive forms of presentation designed to gain audience attention: use of large headlines, photographic illustration, much film material, sound and dramatic music, etc."[26] The Church Fathers, of course, could not exploit such devices, but they did dramatize the content of their letter and place emphasis on the sounds and gestures of Paul. People reading this letter aloud could have been quite amused or shocked. We would have expected the Church Fathers to issue only the theological decision of their synod, but they present the heretic as a sensational creature caring solely about media performance. This in itself shows that media performance was essential to the maintenance of their own position as leading figures of a world organization.

---

24. Letters were important communication vehicles in late antiquity since they were addressed to whole communities, read aloud, copied, and distributed all over the Christian world. On the publication and circulation of early Christian literature, see Harry Y. Gamble, *Books and Readers in the Early Church: A History of Early Christian Texts* (New Haven and London: Yale University Press, 1995), 82-143.

25. McQuail, *Media Performance*, 240.

26. Ibid., 233, citing John P. Robinson, Mark R. Levy, et al., *The Main Source: Learning from Television News.* (Beverly Hills: Sage Publications, 1986).

Eusebius and Media Performance

Let us now analyze Eusebius's work as an historian by employing the criteria that modern researchers use to evaluate the standards of modern media performance. Whereas in Chapter 1 I discussed only some general statements, here I will attempt to show in more detail how various results of media studies can help us in the understanding of ancient historiography.

Diversity

Diversity in modern mass media research is a complex term,[27] and I shall apply only those conclusions that may help us in the case of Paul of Samosata. Eusebius may be viewed here as a media channel who took upon himself the task of passing on the most important matters concerning the history of Christianity. Does he fulfill the requirements of diversity within this scope (and within the organization in which he operates, namely, the orthodox Catholic Church)? Does he reflect all sources, messages, and audiences equally, as well as all political, geographical, and sociocultural nuances of all streams within the Church? It is quite clear that he does not. We have already noted in Chapter 1 that he does not tell us about the history of Christianity in the West and that he leaves enormous gaps in the history of the Eastern churches. But let us go back to Paul of Samosata. Since we have no other sources for this case — something that can also happen in the mass media today (for instance, the explosion of the TWA carrier over the coast of Long Island in July 1996 remains an enigma since the only source we have is the fact of explosion and death, and some oral evidence from people who claim to have seen the explosion itself[28]) — we must apply the criteria to the description as we have it in Book 7 of the *Ecclesiastical History*. (Some other scattered evidence does not give us much additional information, except for the theological aspects.)

Diversity includes some subcriteria. First, we can ask whether Eusebius is diverse in terms of his topics and themes, namely, does he write for different segments of society? Does he have several audiences in mind?

27. See McQuail, *Media Performance*, 141-81.
28. Cf., for instance, *Newsweek*, International Edition, 29 July 1996, 11-15; 5 August 1996, 40-44. We now have the remains of the carrier as well.

By eliminating the theological arguments from his own summary para-graphs and from his excerpts of the letter sent by the Fathers to the prov-inces (omission is in itself an important device in modern mass media), he reveals a very specific purpose. We have already seen that he wanted the message to get through to an audience that was not interested in (or did not have the ability to understand) theological speculations, a trait that is common to much of his *Ecclesiastical History*.

This subcriterion of diversity, namely, the representation of seg-ments of society within a certain text, should be examined throughout Eusebius in order to reach a general conclusion concerning his audience or audiences. Yet we can attempt now to arrive at a partial conclusion based on the case of Paul of Samosata. The audience Eusebius had in mind was not given to theological speculations but was sensitive about the order within the organization of the Church. The target audience was thus com-posed of good Christians, who were already part of the congregation, and perhaps pagans who were potential converts to Christianity but who re-sisted the Christian model that Paul proposed. If we take several sections of society in general at that period concerning which we have some infor-mation and set Eusebius's description against this background, we can say that he lacks diversity concerning pagan society and is well aware that he lacks it. His text is not diverse whether we think of the outer public sphere or the inner one. At any rate, our problem in researching audiences in an-tiquity still remains that of measuring not only their diversity, but also the content of communication as received by them.[29]

According to a second subcriterion of diversity, "innovation, creativ-ity and originality in all fields of social and cultural life are unlikely to exist without diversity within a society and also over time. *Equality* also presup-poses diversity (and vice versa), since diversity is a relativizing concept, op-posing any claim to dominance or to cultural superiority."[30] Although a modern situation is being described, it is legitimate to note that heretics of all sorts and kinds within Christianity were creative and innovative, as was Paul of Samosata. But from the outset Christianity adopted cultural as-pects from its surroundings (as is made clear, for instance, in Clement of Alexandria's *Stromateis*) but formed, in its own estimation, a superior cul-tural and theological orthodoxy that attempted to dominate every aspect of life within its boundaries (the inner public sphere). It looked down on

29. Cf. McQuail, *Media Performance,* 158.
30. Ibid., 143.

the pagans of the outer public sphere who did not show any willingness to convert. Social equality within the community was one of the greatest ideas of Christianity, but orthodoxy excluded the concept of intellectual pluralism within the Church. We know that during the centuries before Paul of Samosata, the orthodox Church attempted to crush all diverse opinions concerning Jesus Christ and other aspects of the faith. One powerful method of doing so was the skilled use of "limited" diversity. Around 200 C.E. Irenaeus presented the various theologies of heretics but then proceeded to demonstrate the superiority of orthodoxy, or rather, of what was shaping up to be mainstream Christianity.[31] To use the arguments of Walter Bauer in his *Orthodoxy and Heresy,* some of which remain valid, we actually discover in certain quarrels of orthodoxy with heretics a minority claiming that it alone is orthodox (or mainstream) and crushing any attempt at diversity within the organization.

We shall see in Chapter 4 that this minority succeeded in certain instances because of its media performance, a subtle and aggressive communication energy that was channeled through a very rigid and powerful organizational network. No group, including the most powerful of the heretics, could compete with it. Simon Magus is not a very good example since he arrived on the scene at an early stage of Christianity when it was not yet organized. Paul of Samosata is, and Eusebius's methods are an expression of exactly these organizational methods. However, there existed a limited diversity in orthodoxy that made it possible to present partial and selected information about an adversary within the Catholic Church. Since the Church was not pluralistic, such diversity was used only in order to crush members who were so audacious as to hold unorthodox opinions. Thus, to use P. Jacklin's terminology,[32] Eusebius does not reflect "representative diversity" in the sense of "representative diversity when the 'structure' of diversity in communications corresponds to the structure of diversity in society."[33] By society we mean here the Christian congregation.

We have seen up to now that in terms of media performance, we find in Eusebius a limited (or, rather, unequal) diversity, even concerning the Christian inner sphere. We also witness a lack of what McQuail calls

---

31. In his *Adversus Haereses;* cf. Johannes Quasten, *Patrology,* vol. 1 (Westminster, Md.: Christian Classics, 1986-92), 288-92.

32. P. Jacklin, "Representative Diversity," *Journal of Communication* 28, no. 2 (1978): 85-88.

33. McQuail, *Media Performance,* 144.

"equality of access," which is "the ideal form of diversity . . . in which *all* relevant candidate groups or interests have an equal share of access to media channels or receive equal attention in the media."[34] Paul of Samosata did not get a chance to state his case within the final decision of the synod that excommunicated him, nor did he get a fair chance in Eusebius, although he had created "a small, wealthy or powerful" minority.[35] Salust and Livy, by contrast, show more diversity in their respective audiences.[36] Eusebius reflects a very minimal kind of diversity of pagan society, and a very limited one of his own Christian society.

A third subcriterion of diversity concerns quantity versus quality. The quantity of reportage does not always match its quality and vice versa.[37] In the letter of the Church Fathers, the amount of publicity Paul receives is impressive, while his successor Domnus, who is the positive figure, gets only a few sentences in the letter and in Eusebius's commentary: "We were compelled therefore . . . to appoint another bishop in his stead for the Catholic Church [choosing] by the providence of God, as we are persuaded, Domnus the son of the blessed Demetrian, who formerly presided with distinction over the same community; he is adorned with all the noble qualities suitable for a bishop . . ." (7.30.17).

A fourth subcriterion of diversity relevant to the case of Paul of Samosata is the amount of attention and substance given him within the letter.[38] This is a relative issue. I have just noted that although Paul of Samosata was popular and his heresy spread in many regions around Antioch, he receives a lot of negative attention, whereas his successor, a positive figure in the eyes of the Fathers and of Eusebius, gets very little. But the question is also a horizontal one; we have to compare what kind and amount of attention Eusebius gives other heretics. We will see in Chapter 4 that neither the amount of attention nor the substance of content that Eusebius bestows on heretics necessarily reflects the lack or abundance of his sources; rather, it represents a media method that may even go back to the strategies of the organization itself, namely, the orthodox Catholic Church.

Does Eusebius, like Thucydides, take note of the "statistical" reality of the world he describes? The application of this fifth subcriterion is com-

34. Ibid., 147.
35. The phrasing belongs to McQuail, *Media Performance*, 148.
36. See for instance, my *Identity, Religion and Historiography*, Chap. 12.
37. McQuail, *Media Performance*, 149.
38. Ibid., 163.

plex,[39] but we can cite many instances in the *Ecclesiastical History* where he does not care a bit about "statistical" reality. Interesting examples are his short announcements or "advertisements," where he simply states that the Church grew stronger and spread all over the world (based on Matt. 28:19). But he never informs us what proportion the Christians formed at any given time within Gentile society, although he probably had at least some numerical information. Given the nature of Eusebius's account, no one can estimate the real strength of the Church on the eve of Constantine's victory at the Milvian Bridge, or earlier. No reference to statistical reality concerning this crucial fact can be found anywhere in Eusebius's *Ecclesiastical History* (or in his *Vita Constantini*).

To get back to our text, we can only guess at the statistical reality in the case of Paul of Samosata. It seems that the fierce negative reaction of the Church Fathers and of Eusebius can give us some clue concerning Paul's influence, but this is an estimate based on a typical speculation of a modern ancient historian. If we apply this particular subcriterion of diversity, the letter of the Church Fathers in itself does not give us any information about how many people were impressed by Paul of Samosata's behavior. How many Gentiles joined his group? Was his movement at all noticeable in the city of Antioch? How strong was his influence on neighboring regions? Eusebius merely says that "Such also is the kind of discourse that he permits the bishops of the neigbouring country and towns, who fawn upon him, and the presbyters as well, to deliver in their sermons to the people" (7.30.10). Even when the Fathers do express something approaching a statistical figure, it turns out on close examination to be worthless. For instance, it is said that Paul was attended by a bodyguard, "some preceding, some following, and that too in numbers" (7.30.8). How many? Who were they? Other historians of antiquity made considerable efforts to present a statistical reality (Thucydides on battles and Polybius on certain topics; Herodotus and Josephus also wish to present numbers — not always very accurately — to show how perfect they are as historians).[40] Hence in the case of Paul of Samosata we are left with what W. Schulz would call a "media reality" (not necessarily equal to reality itself).[41] I suspect that there was a hidden motive behind this obscurity:

39. Ibid., 169-70.
40. Cf., for instance, the wonderful description of the battles in Sicily given by Thucydides, Books 6-7, passim.
41. W. Schulz, "Mass Media and Reality" (paper presented at the Sommatie Conference, Veldhoven, Netherlands, 1988).

both the Church Fathers and Eusebius knew that real numbers would jeopardize their media efforts altogether. Since Christianity was still a relatively small movement, it seemed better to be general and obscure rather than specific and clear (in particular when their "advertisements" were designed to convey how numerous and flourishing they were).

Another, sixth subcriterion of diversity has to do with time and cumulative diversity.[42] What length of time does the letter against Paul cover? Does the "range of attention" widen over time, that is, is there more publicity as a consequence of later events in a sequence of events? The letter may describe a period of up to ten years.[43] At any rate, it does not describe events that transpired in a day or a few months, but over a long period. This means that although the letter and the space allotted to it by Eusebius are relatively impressive (compared with his coverage of the heresy of Basilides, for instance), the letter's content is very concise. In fact, its account of Paul is not a linear historical one, but a summary of the sensational aspects of his career. Thus we get very little information, and the little we do get is extremely condensed when compared, for instance, with Eusebius's description of Polycarp's martyrdom, which yields a lot of information concerning events that took place in a few hours, or perhaps days. But there, as we will see, we are confronted with the difficult problem that the account is "constructed." In the case of Paul of Samosata, we can assume that his heretical behavior received more attention around the year 269/70 C.E., and thus the description is more reflective of those last years than the earlier ones of Paul's bishopric. This can be supported by Eusebius's coverage of the years leading up to the synod of 269/70 C.E. In *Hist. Eccl.* 7.29.1-2 Eusebius indicates that Paul managed to conceal his heresy over many years. This apparently means that his behavior was then still acceptable.

Objectivity

I have already discussed some aspects of objectivity. Here we will look briefly at the case of Paul of Samosata. J. H. Boyer's six points can easily be

---

42. McQuail, *Media Performance*, 170.

43. Lawlor and Oulton, *Eusebius*, 2:255, hold that Paul's term of office was eight years. One should remember that either one or two synods concerning Paul were held at Antioch in the mid-sixties.

applied to Eusebius's account, because the decision of the synod of Antioch in 269/70 c.e. was communicated through two channels: the letter of the Fathers, and the account in Eusebius, which was accessible to many readers.[44] The stenograms of Malchion "which we know to be extant even to this day" (*Hist. Eccl.* 7.29.2) included only the disputations between Malchion and Paul of Samosata. But even with only these sources available, we can apply some of the aspects of objectivity listed in Chapter 1. Let us see how the six points of Boyer apply to this case.

1. Are the letter and Eusebius's summary excerpts of it balanced and evenhanded in presenting different sides of the issue? The answer is no. The letter does not intend to be balanced (and this is to be expected when a strong institution wishes to get rid of one of its members who may threaten its ideological existence). If Eusebius had been a Thucydides, he might have written a balanced account (as in the Melian dialogue recounted in Book 5, for instance). He could have treated Paul's popularity and own views in detail, and dealt with many other "positive" aspects of the case.

2. Can Eusebius be credited with accuracy and realism in his reporting? Only partially. It seems likely that we get a real picture of at least one aspect of Paul. As we have seen above, his sensational side is depicted in a realistic and accurate manner (if we leave out some of the caricatured facets). But the lack of balance jeopardizes even the little accuracy we have.

3. Does Eusebius present all the relevant points about Paul of Samosata (as Thucydides does about the Mytilene affair in Book 3 of the *Peloponnesian War*)? He indeed adduces many matters that are relevant to his own stance, but he excludes all the points of dispute that were available to him, such as the stenograms of Malchion, fragments of which we still have in later sources.[45] Also, he concludes his account of the synod of 264 c.e. by saying that "when all, then, were coming together frequently on different occasions, arguments and questions were mooted at each meeting, the Samosatene and his party attempting to keep still concealed and to cloak what was heterodox" (7.28.2), but he does not report what was actually said.

4. Does Eusebius distinguish between facts and opinion, treating opinion as relevant? His accounts of the synods of 264 c.e. (7.27.1-2;

44. J. H. Boyer, "How Editors View Objectivity," *Journalism Quarterly* 58 (1981): 24-28.

45. Hefele, *History of the Christian Councils,* 1:121; Perrone, *"L'enigma di Paolo di Samosata,"* 321.

7.28.1-4) and of 269/70 c.e. (7.30.1-19) are very concise (he gives the lists of participants, but nothing on the disputes over Paul's heresy), and as we shall see in a moment the rhetoric is quite neutral, with some exceptions.

5. Does Eusebius minimize "the influence of the writer's own attitude, opinion or involvement" — his own and that of the Church Fathers whose decision he cites verbatim? The answer would have to be no.

6. Does Eusebius avoid slant, rancor, or devious purpose? In this particular case he is milder than in his usual accounts of heretics. He does not, however, miss any opportunity within his reports of the synods concerning Paul to insert a negative expression such as "this person espoused low and mean views as to Christ . . ." (7.27.2), or later describing Paul as a "spoiler of the flock of Christ," or, in the letter, calling his heresy a "deadly doctrine" (7.30.3).[46]

We are thus left with the strong impression that objectivity was not Eusebius's main concern in dealing with Paul of Samosata. He made a subjective choice of what he related, even among the comparatively many sources that were available to him. He put the case of Paul within a wider frame of reference (Gentile background), giving it an "evaluative meaning." It cannot be read as an isolated case. Also, many omissions and silences show that the description cannot be considered as objective. If we take into consideration the enormous pressures on Eusebius himself when writing and editing Book 7 (persecutions, the start of the Arian controversy), we can understand why he was not objective in this particular case. Eusebius's sympathy for the theology of Paul of Samosata may explain why he treats Paul somewhat more mildly than he does other heretics.

46. τῆς θανατηφόρου διδασκαλίας.

CHAPTER 3

Martyrdom as Media Asset

T he public martyrdom of Christians during the second to fourth centuries was seen by Eusebius (and presumably also by the Church itself) as an important media asset. In martyrdom, Christianity enjoyed a
golden opportunity to advertise itself and to enter the public sphere on a
grand scale. When the Roman authorities locked martyrs in dark cells far
from the public eye, Eusebius regarded such an act as a serious blow to the
publicity efforts of the Church. In the following we will see that Eusebius's
"media reality" (which may roughly coincide with some of the actual reality) was accepted because of the special methods he employed when he reported on martyrs. These methods may be better understood if studied
against the background of research on modern media performance. As already observed in Chapter 1, martyrdom was a dynamic kind of media
channel that was new to pagans. It had a shocking effect, was aggressive in
its message, and was similar in many different parts of the Roman Empire.
This created the correct impression that a worldwide organization stood
behind it. Ironically, it was the Romans who created the framework for this
media channel, and it was this channel that challenged the existing traditional media channels of the Roman Empire within the public sphere. Before we start our examination of Eusebius's treatment of martyrdom in the
Ecclesiastical History, let us first remind ourselves what the public sphere
means. It is here understood as a three-dimensional realm: (1) the forums
in which the public manifested its presence, such as the market place, public bath, prison, amphitheater, shop, and assembly (the outer circle);
(2) public institutions in which the authorities manifested their power,

such as the magistracy, the army, and the senate (the institutional circle); and (3) Christian institutions that gradually, over the course of the second and third centuries, gained a place in the outer circle, such as churches, assemblies, burial societies, and private schools (the inner circle).[1]

Stephen and Paul

In Book 2 of the *Ecclesiastical History,* Eusebius says that with the martyrdom of Stephen,

> there arose the first and greatest persecution of the Church in Jerusalem by the Jews. All the disciples, with the single exception of the Twelve, were scattered throughout Judaea and Samaria . . . but they were not yet in the position to venture to transmit the word of faith to the Gentiles, and announced it only to Jews. At that time Paul was still ravaging the Church, entering into the houses of the faithful, dragging out men and women, and handing them over to prison. (2.1.8-9)

Eusebius naturally uses Acts as a historical source and takes Acts 8:3 at face value, saying that people were put in prison at that stage of persecution. Then he proceeds to Paul's martyrdom, which is not described but only hinted at in Acts. He says that when Paul arrived in Rome for the second time (not described by Luke in Acts), he "suffered martyrdom under Nero" (2.22.2). This piece of information is corroborated by 1 Clement 5. He continues by saying that

> during this imprisonment he wrote the second Epistle to Timothy, indicating at the same time that his first defence had taken place and that his martyrdom was at hand. Notice his testimony at this point: "At my first defence . . . no man was with me, but all deserted me (may it not be laid to their charge), but the Lord stood by me and strengthened me that the preaching might be fulfilled by me and all the Gentiles might hear, and I was delivered from the lion's mouth." (2.22.2-3; like Daniel, we might add)

It is quite clear that Eusebius here interprets 2 Timothy 4:16-17 in the con-

---

1. The inner public sphere was sometimes no more than a secret gathering place of the Christians, as Justin says to Rusticus during the inquiry (Herbert Musurillo, *The Acts of the Christian Martyrs* [Oxford: Clarendon, 1972], 49-51).

text of a supposed martyrdom of Paul. He emphasizes that Paul was alone and that even his friends were not with him, but Paul thought that the publicity of his plight could be helpful: "the Gentiles might hear." It would be a "waste" of his martyrdom if it remained a private matter. On the occasion of the so-called first defense, even Paul's biographer Luke was not present (2.22.6). Eusebius describes Paul's desire for martyrdom as a spiritual act in the apostle's own words, drawn again from 2 Timothy: "the Lord will deliver me from all evil and save me for his heavenly kingdom . . . for I am already offered up and the time of my release is at hand" (2.22.5-6). Eusebius is very cautious here since Luke in Acts does not tell us about a martyrdom of Paul. Thus he says that "Paul's martyrdom was not accomplished during the sojourn in Rome which Luke describes" (2.22.7), but later, when Nero became a reckless criminal, the apostles were "attacked along with the rest." Eusebius does not describe Paul's martyrdom itself but treats it as a spiritual and very private matter far away from the public eye. Although Eusebius knew 1 Clement, he does not use Clement's information about Paul's martyrdom. 1 Clement 5 says: "Owing to envy, Paul also obtained the reward of patient endurance, after being seven times thrown into captivity, compelled to flee and stoned."

James the Just

A change in the publicity issue emerges from Eusebius's description of the martyrdom of James the Just. We have encountered him in Chapter 1, but we shall examine this affair here in more detail. Eusebius introduces James at the outset as the "brother of the Lord" and bishop of Jerusalem, and he tells the story in a narrative that differs widely from the narratives concerning later martyrs. The story goes as follows:

> They brought him into the midst and demanded a denial of the faith in Christ before all the people, but when he, contrary to the expectations of all of them, with a loud voice and with more courage than they had expected, confessed before all the people that our Lord and Saviour Jesus Christ is the son of God, they could no longer endure his testimony, since he was by all men believed to be most righteous. . . . The manner of James's death has been shown by the words of Clement already quoted, narrating that he was thrown from the battlement and beaten to death with a club, but Hegesippus, who belongs to the generation after the Apostles, gives the most accurate account of him speaking as follows in

his fifth book:[2] ". . . Now, since many even of the rulers believed, there was a tumult of the Jews and the Scribes and Pharisees saying that the whole people was in danger of looking for Jesus as the Christ. So they assembled and said to James, 'We beseech you to restrain the people since they are straying after Jesus as though he were the Messiah. We beseech you to persuade concerning Jesus all who come for the day of the Passover, for all obey you. For we and the whole people testify to you that you are righteous and do not respect persons. So do you persuade the crowd not to err concerning Jesus, for the whole people and we obey you. Therefore stand on the battlement of the temple that you may be clearly visible on high, and that your words may be audible to all the people, for because of the Passover all the tribes, with the Gentiles also, have come together.'" (2.23.2-11)

James took this precious opportunity and testified about Jesus, with the result that "many were convinced and glorified." His rhetoric on this occasion was simple and clear-cut, and not necessarily very anti-Jewish. The Scribes and Pharisees said to one another "we did wrong to provide Jesus with such testimony, but let us go up and throw him down that they may be afraid and not believe him" (2.23.14). After they threw him down, they decided to stone him. While they were stoning him, he was praying for them. Then, we are told, "a certain man among them, one of the laundrymen, took the club with which he used to beat out the clothes, and hit the Just on the head, and so he suffered martyrdom" (2.23.18). And here comes a very interesting note: "And they buried him on the spot by the temple, and his gravestone still remains by the temple. He became a true witness both to Jews and to Greeks that Jesus is the Christ, and at once Vespasian began to besiege them" (2.23.18). Eusebius adds that "it seems that James was indeed a remarkable man and famous among all for righteousness, so that the wise even of the Jews thought that this was the cause of the siege of Jerusalem immediately after his martyrdom" (2.23.19).

The story is told in such a way that the issue of publicity becomes central. Eusebius evidently believes that Christianity can be promoted by publicity and counterpublicity. Enemies can be a wonderful publicity asset (ultra-Orthodox Jews in modern Israel get enormous media exposure

2. For Hegesippus, see H. J. Lawlor, "The *Hypomnemata* of Hegesippus," in his *Eusebiana: Essays on the Ecclesiastical History of Eusebius, Bishop of Caesarea* (Oxford: Clarendon, 1912), 1-107; T. Halton, "Hegesippus in Eusebius," *Studia Patristica* 17 (1982): 688-93.

from their constant disputes with other Jews; the war of rhetoric that ensues brings many issues to the fore). Hence the martyrdom of James is depicted as a media event of a dynamic nature; the whole scene takes place in the public sphere, near the Temple, on the Passover, and among all the familiar public Jewish symbols. (The public sphere is here not yet distinguished from other spheres as it will be in our discussion of the development of Christianity at a later stage). According to Eusebius's account, James gained by using publicity whereas the Pharisees lost by using it. This publicity had three manifestations. First, the speech uttered by James from the Temple battlement was such an obvious promotion for Christianity that the Pharisees themselves, says Eusebius, declared "We did wrong to provide Jesus with such testimony." Second, the pushing of James from the battlement, and his stoning and killing in public, are important since by this shocking death Eusebius believes that James "became a true witness both to Jews and to Greeks that Jesus is the Christ." A true witness has to be a *public* one. Third, James's grave became a famous site for pilgrimage. One of the severest punishments the Romans imposed during persecutions was the prohibition on visiting cemeteries.

In this story we find the first steps of an elaborately narrated Christian martyrdom. This martyrdom, though, is performed not by the Roman authorities but by Jews in Jerusalem. We do not yet find many of the elements typical of martyrdoms of the second century, when the Romans performed them and made an institutional spectacle of them (in an amphitheater or court),[3] and when descriptions of the terrible torture undergone by the martyrs received a lot of precious space from the Church historian. But one element is already accentuated here: publicity is essential for an ideal martyrdom. This can be learned also from the pictures (real or perceived) that Eusebius uses to describe James's public performance: James is put into the "midst" *(eis meson);* he speaks to all people in a loud voice, amid the tumult of the crowd; he persuades the crowd; and he stands on the battlement of the Temple to be clearly seen and heard by all the people. The gathering is of all tribes and Gentiles; many are convinced; his gravestone still remains near the Temple; and his act of "testimony" is a public act. Eusebius is thus aware that publicity is gained by challenging a big crowd in the open, by creating a spectacle with a theatrical performance, and by doing all that while generating a lot of noise accompanied

3. D. Potter, "Martyrdom as Spectacle," in *Theater and Society in the Classical World,* ed. Ruth Scodel (Ann Arbor: University of Michigan Press, 1993), 53-88.

by sharp, vivid gestures. Thus Christians learned how to exploit the public sphere for the promotion of their ideas, or at least this is what Eusebius perceives as one of the causes for Christianity's growing popularity. Without being able to examine what the "cognitive learning effects" were on audiences at the time,[4] we can say that the spectacle of martyrdom was more effective in bringing the Christian message to a large audience than were learned lectures or books. Martyrdom was, in effect, a major "source of information" about Christianity.

Ignatius

The martyrdom of Ignatius represents a further step in Christian awareness of the value of publicity.[5] In Book 3 of the *Ecclesiastical History*, Eusebius narrates that Ignatius, bishop of Antioch, was

> sent from Syria to Rome to be eaten by beasts in testimony to Christ. He was taken through Asia under most careful guard, and strengthened by his speech and exhortation the diocese of each city in which he stayed. He particularly warned them to be on their guard against the heresies which then for the first time were beginning to obtain, and exhorted them to hold fast to the tradition of the Apostles, to which he thought necessary, for safety's sake, to give the form of written testimony. Thus while he was in Smyrna where Polycarp was, he wrote one letter to the church at Ephesus . . . and another to the church at Magnesia on the Meander . . . and another to the church in Tralles. . . . In addition to these he also wrote to the church at Rome, and to it he extended the request that they should not deprive him of the hope for which he longed by begging him off from his martyrdom. It is worth while appending a short extract

4. J. M. McLeod et al., "On Understanding and Misunderstanding Media Effects," in *Mass Media and Society*, ed. James Curran and Michael Gurevitch (London: Arnold, 1991), 245.

5. For Ignatius in general, see William R. Schoedel, *Ignatius of Antioch: A Commentary on the Letters of Ignatius of Antioch* (Philadelphia: Fortress, 1985). On Ignatius as martyr, see Karin Bommes, *Weizen Gottes: Untersuchungen zur Theologie des Martyriums bei Ignatius von Antiochien* (Cologne: Hanstein, 1976); Y. Sato, "Martyrdom and Apostasy," in *Eusebius, Christianity and Judaism,* ed. Harold W. Attridge and Gohei Hata (Detroit: Wayne State University Press, 1992), 623-27; and Rodney Stark, *The Rise of Christianity: A Sociologist Reconsiders History* (Princeton: Princeton University Press, 1996), 180-81.

from this in support of what has been said. He writes as follows: "From Syria to Rome I am fighting with wild beasts, by land and sea, by night and day, bound to ten 'leopards' (that is, a company of soldiers), and they become worse for kind treatment. Now I become the more a disciple for their ill deeds, 'but not by this am I justified.' I long for the beasts that are prepared for me; and I pray that they may be found prompt for me; I will even entice them to devour me promptly; not as has happened to some whom they have not touched from fear; even if they be unwilling of themselves, I will force them to it. Grant me this favour. I know what is expedient for me; now I am beginning to be a disciple. May I envy nothing of things seen or unseen that I may attain to Jesus Christ. Let there come to me fire, and cross, and struggles with wild beasts, cutting, and tearing asunder, rackings of bones, mangling of limbs, crushing of my whole body, cruel tortures of the devil, may I but attain to Jesus Christ!" (3.36.3-9).

Ignatius wrote these words during the first half of the second century, but his wishful thinking is an anticipatory list of many of the methods that would be used later in the century in other martyrdoms. It is interesting to note that only some of these devices are mentioned in the extant letters of Ignatius (see his *Letter to Romans*). Probably Eusebius was not faithful to his sources here but borrowed some of the tortures contained in descriptions of later martyrdoms. In other words, he constructed Ignatius's martyrdom, using associations familiar to his own fourth-century audience. In later martyrdoms, the nature of the torture has a public significance. Moreover, at the time, the Romans were not too sensitive about the effects of the media channels they freely offered the Christians: they let Ignatius write and send his letters; they let him publicize his ideas throughout the provinces and in Rome; and they let him speak freely to the dioceses in each of the cities through which he was led. It seems that they were not really worried about his media performance since it remained within the limits of the inner public sphere. We hear from Eusebius and from Ignatius's letters themselves that Ignatius used these media opportunities to deal with many burning church issues such as heresy, the position of bishops, and martyrdom. Yet, it is Ignatius's media performance itself that Eusebius chooses to emphasize.

Nevertheless, we are not treated to the familiar scenes typical of the martyrdom of Polycarp half a century later. Before going into this, we

57

should ask why Ignatius was so eager to suffer all the dreadful tortures he enumerates. He himself says that the beasts are a testimony for Jesus (*To the Smyrnaeans* 4 and elsewhere). It is quite clear that he wished to imitate Jesus, but is that all he had in mind? Or, is that all Eusebius had in mind? Why did Eusebius add a list of well-known "later" tortures? If Ignatius was really the first model martyr, it is possible, since these tortures were performed in the outer public sphere only in later times, that Eusebius put in Ignatius's mouth the wish to be publicly martyred, in line with the martyrdoms Eusebius himself depicts in his account of the latter part of the second century. Ignatius, or Eusebius, evidently thought that media performance in the inner public sphere alone was not sufficient to witness to the truth claims of Christianity; to be effective, martyrdom had to take place in the outer public sphere, in the style of the martyrdoms of Polycarp and the Christians of Lyons and Vienne.

Polycarp

In an article entitled "Social Theory and the Media," J. B. Thompson conveniently summarizes an idea advanced by Michel Foucault in *Discipline and Punish: The Birth of the Prison:*

> The societies of Antiquity and of the Middle Ages were societies of spectacle: the exercise of power was linked to the public manifestation of the strength and superiority of the sovereign. It was a regime of power in which a few were made visible to many, and in which the visibility of the few was used as a means of exercising power over the many — in the way, for instance, that a public execution in the market square became a spectacle in which a sovereign power took its revenge, reaffirming the glory of the king through the destruction of a rebellious subject.[6]

In line with this idea, we shall see that the Romans wished to demonstrate their power against the Christians in a crowded theater. But what actually happened in this power struggle is that, as Brent Shaw has shown, the martyrs emerged victorious because of their endurance.[7] Let us now examine

---

6. J. B. Thompson, "Social Theory and the Media," in *Communication Theory Today,* ed. David Crowley and David Mitchell (Cambridge: Polity, 1994), 42.

7. B. D. Shaw, "Body/Power/Identity: Passions of the Martyrs," *Journal of Early Christian Studies* 4, no. 3 (1996): 269-312.

the next martyrdom in the *Ecclesiastical History*, the "classical model" martyrdom of Polycarp.[8]

Eusebius emphasizes the sweeping publicity that the martyrdom of Polycarp received from the outset by being described in a document that was sent out to other churches. In *Hist. Eccl.* 4.15.1-3, he says that the story of Polycarp is "still extant in writing. The document purports to be from the church of which he was the leader, and gives to the neighbouring dioceses the following account of what happened to him." Eusebius uses parts of this letter, known to us as the *Martyrdom of Polycarp*, in his narrative.

The publicity of the act of martyrdom is enhanced by Eusebius's mention of other martyrs who were persecuted at the same time as Polycarp. Their sufferings highlight the publicity of martyrdom performed in the outer public sphere:

> for they say that those who were standing around were astounded (*kataplesso*) when they saw that at one time they were torn by scourges down to deepseated veins and arteries, so that the hidden contents of the recesses of their bodies, their entrails and organs, were exposed to sight. At another time they were stretched on seashells and on sharp points, were taken through all kinds of punishment and torture, and finally were given to be eaten by wild beasts. (4.15.4)

About the martyr Germanicus, Eusebius says, "At his glorious death the whole crowd was amazed (using *apothaumazo*) at the God-loving martyr for his bravery, and at the courage of the whole race of Christians, and be-

---

8. For an extensive philological, literary and theological study of Polycarp's martyrdom, see Gerd Buschmann, *Martyrium Polycarpi: Eine formkritische Studie: Ein Beitrag zur Frage nach der Entstehung der Gattung Märtyrerakte* (Berlin: de Gruyter, 1994). See also J. W. Van Henten, "The Martyrs as Heroes of the Christian People: Some Remarks on the Continuity between Jewish and Christian Martyrology, with Pagan Analogies," in *Martyrium in Multidisciplinary Perspective*, ed. M. Lamberigts and P. van Deun (Leuven: Leuven University Press, 1995), 304-13; Theofried Baumeister, *Genese und Entfaltung der altkirchlichen Theologie des Martyriums* (Bern: Peter Lang, 1991), 31ff. (text and commentary); W. H. C. Frend, *Martyrdom and Persecution in the Early Church: A Study of a Conflict from the Maccabees to Donatus* (Oxford: Blackwell, 1965), Chap. 10; B. Dehandschutter, "The Martyrium Polycarpi: A Century of Research," in *Aufstieg und Niedergang der Römischen Welt*, vol. II.27.1, ed. Hildegard Temporini (Berlin: de Gruyter, 1993), 485-522. On martyrdom in Eusebius, see Robert M. Grant, *Eusebius as Church Historian* (Oxford: Clarendon, 1980), Chap. 10; and Victor Saxer, *Bible et hagiographie: texte et thèmes bibliques dans les actes des martyrs authentiques des premiers siècles* (Bern: Lang, 1986), Chap. 3.

gan to howl out together, 'Kill the atheists! Let Polycarp be sent for'"
(4.15.6). It should be emphasized that the public display of cruelty had a
special significance in ancient societies; through it, the authorities manifested their power. Also, the amazement was not positive, as one might
think; it was a negative reaction and demonstrated the power of the multitude in the decision-making of the Roman authorities concerning the
Christians. If the crowd did indeed shout "Let Polycarp be sent for," and if
in fact a "great uproar arose at this cry," then Polycarp was apparently a famous person among the Gentiles. But most probably it was the letter
quoted by Eusebius that wished to show how famous Polycarp was within
the outer public sphere. Be that as it may, this section of the story demonstrates the role of the multitude in the act of martyrdom.[9] This multitude,
in fact, incites the authorities (who are Roman officials) to carry on with
the act of public martyrdom. Against this background, the letter also adduces the story of "a certain native of Phrygia named Quintus" who "seeing the beasts and the other threats, was overcome in his mind and weak-
ened and finally abandoned his salvation" (4.15.7). Why would Eusebius
— as he also does elsewhere — adduce such a case? Here we touch upon
the issue of relevance, which will be tackled later in this chapter: the so-
called lapsed had important informational value for Eusebius's own generation.

It should be emphasized that the multitude is perceived here as being
on the receiving end of a media event. Through this multitude who participate in the event, information concerning Christianity was evidently
spread en masse and very fast, in particular when martyrdom was still a
fresh phenomenon for the public.[10] Moreover, the power of the populace
is perceived as one of great importance, since it was this body that helped
the authorities come to a decision concerning the acceptance of Christianity by society in general. Society in the outer public sphere "voted" against
the new religion.

Later, when Polycarp is brought into the arena, "the uproar in the
arena was so great that no one could even be heard" (4.15.17). Polycarp receives great exposure and plays his role in a subtle and wonderful manner;
he becomes, in effect, a media celebrity. We also hear from the letter that

9. This topic is, unfortunately, ignored by Elias Canetti, *Masse und Macht*
(Frankfurt: Fischer Taschenbuch, 1980), and J. S. McClelland, *The Crowd and the Mob:
From Plato to Canetti* (London and Boston: Unwin Hyman, 1989).

10. The urban setting of martyrdom is emphasized by G. W. Bowersock, *Martyrdom and Rome* (Cambridge: Cambridge University Press, 1995), Chap. 3.

among the multitude were Christians who heard a "voice from heaven" saying: "Be strong, Polycarp, and play the man" (4.15.17). Polycarp challenges the Roman authorities (the representatives of the institutional public sphere) in front of the multitude, the majority of whom are antagonistic toward the martyr, a man of eighty-six years. But Polycarp also provokes the multitude.

The letter, which is cited verbatim at this point (although with abbreviations), conveys a dialogue between Polycarp and the proconsul that symbolizes a contest for the visibility of power before an enormous audience. The proconsul begs Polycarp to remember his age, to "swear by the genius of Caesar," and to repent. He advises him to declare "away with the Atheists." Polycarp seizes the opportunity and makes a theatrical gesture: "with a stern countenance [he] looked on all the crowd in the arena, and waving his hand at them, he groaned and looked up to heaven and said: 'Away with the Atheists'" (4.15.19). The dialogue goes on, and Polycarp even makes a bold attempt to act as a missionary: "I am a Christian. And if you wish to learn the doctrine of Christianity fix a day and listen" (4.15.21).

For the audience gathered in the theater, this is a real challenge, as well as a grand and stimulating show. The proconsul surprisingly gives Polycarp the opportunity to proselytize in the full theater, saying to him: "persuade the people." Polycarp, aware that the crowd is hostile and that the media performance in the theater might turn against him since he would be shown up publicly as powerless, replies: "You I should have held worthy of discussion, for we have been taught to render honour, as is meet, if it hurt us not, to princes and authorities appointed by God; but as for those, I do not count them worthy that a defence should be made to them" (4.15.21-22). Polycarp knows that at this juncture a verbal media performance would be futile. Now he can only win the attention of the spectators by performing a shocking gesture. Thus he first antagonizes them by saying that they are not worth talking to (which is a very useful media device) and then presents silent endurance through a terrible but dramatic public martyrdom. When the proconsul threatens him with wild beasts, Polycarp says, "Call for them, for change of mind from better to worse is a change we may not take" (4.15.23). Then the proconsul threatens him with fire, and Polycarp, who welcomes this threat with great pleasure, adds, "Why are you waiting? Come, do what you will." The letter describes Polycarp as being "filled with courage and joy, and his face full of grace," whereas the proconsul is "astounded." As in our modern media, the facial expression and the body language are accorded great importance. Then the proconsul sends his herald "into the midst of the arena to announce three times, 'Polycarp has confessed that he is a Christian'" (15.25-26).

This entire scene is interesting in that the tension caused by the competition over the public sphere mounts from one moment to another. The show becomes more and more exciting for the audience. It should be noted that in contrast to the familiar cases of criminals and gladiators,[11] martyrs were granted the floor to speak out and air their views before the authorities and the populace. This custom was very wisely exploited by the martyrs, who, according to Eusebius, considered their exposure an important asset for the promotion of Christianity. The Logos, according to Eusebius (at various points in the *Demonstratio Evangelica*), is embedded in every creature in the inhabited world *(oikoumenē);* hence, martyrdom had the potential to arouse some of the people in the audience to react positively. We see a link being forged between the Roman authority and the audience when, at the herald's announcement,

> all the multitude of heathen and Jews living in Smyrna cried out with uncontrollable wrath and a loud shout: "This is the teacher of Asia, the father of the Christians, the destroyer of our gods, who teaches many neither to offer sacrifice nor to worship." And when they said this, they cried out and asked Philip the Asiarch to let loose a lion on Polycarp. (4.15.26-27)

By the end of the story, Polycarp emerges as the real victor of the contest. When the Asiarch refuses to release a lion against Polycarp, because "he could not legally do this as he had closed the sports," the people again shout "with one mind that he should burn Polycarp alive. . . . These things then happened with so great speed, quicker than it takes to tell, and the crowd came together immediately, and prepared wood and faggots from the workshops and baths and the Jews were extremely zealous, as is their custom, in assisting at this" (4.15.27-29). The crowd here takes the decisive action, rather than the proconsul; it is not only very noisy and full of movement, but makes the physical preparations for burning the old man. What does this mean?

The wording of the letter assigns blame for Polycarp's martyrdom to the multitude. In this presentation, we see a power struggle within the

11. See Thomas E. J. Wiedemann, *Emperors and Gladiators* (London and New York: Routledge, 1992).

outer public sphere involving not only the Roman proconsul (who was reluctant to act fiercely) and the martyr, but also the crowd.[12] In fact, three
entities struggle for the upper hand in the public sphere. This power struggle is created by a media event of such impact that it intensifies the existing
tensions between powers within the public sphere into a striking public
scene.[13] It becomes quite clear from the presentation that, although the
Christian martyr was burnt to death, he won the game not only because he
showed endurance,[14] but in particular because he succeeded in advancing
the Christian cause from a low priority within the public agenda to a very
high one, at least for a short period. He succeeded in this because his performance had, as we would say, a high "rating." The drama comes to a climax when the crowd spills out over public institutions such as baths and
workshops in order to collect the faggots. Then Polycarp goes to the pyre
and shows his outstanding endurance by his refusal to be nailed. They
bind him; then he prays and finally is burned (4.15.33).[15] Yet his body
"could not be consumed by the fire"; so he is stabbed with a dagger, and an
extraordinary thing happens: "there came out much blood, so that the fire
was quenched, and all the crowd marvelled that there was such a difference between the unbelievers and the elect" (4.15.38-39). The letter explains that the "elect was he, indeed one, the wonderful martyr, Polycarp."

Thus the presentation underscores that by his act of martyrdom
Polycarp "conquered" the outer public sphere, at least in terms of the attention Christianity received on this occasion. Both the letter and Eusebius
give the impression that the audience and the Roman authorities could not
stay passive but reacted out of fear that the Christians would conquer the
public sphere. Polycarp himself was aware that he could not achieve his
aim by mere words or theological speculations, so he chose a shocking media performance. A negative analogy in our day would be the actions of
terrorists, who unfortunately get more attention through shocking deeds
than idealistic speeches.[16] We will discuss later the positive and negative ef-

12. McClelland, *The Crowd and the Mob,* does not deal with martyrdom at all; he
discusses Tacitus and moves on to Procopius.
13. See Potter, "Martyrdom as Spectacle," who deals with martyrdoms outside
the *Ecclesiastical History.*
14. Shaw, "Body/Power/Identity."
15. See A.-G. Hamman, *Das Gebet in der Alten Kirche* (Berlin: Lang, 1989), 84-
87.
16. See Alex P. Schmid and Janny de Graaf, *Violence as Communication: Insurgent
Terrorism and the Western News Media* (London and Beverly Hills: Sage Publications,

fects that a shocking act may have on an audience; here we may simply cite two examples, one ancient and one modern: the death of Agrippa I, who collapsed in a full theater (Acts 12:12-22; Josephus, *Antiquities* 19.343-50), and the assassination of Yitzhak Rabin, who was struck down in the middle of a peace demonstration.[17] The fact that Celsus, writing around 170 C.E., complained that Christianity was a revolutionary movement *(stasis)* shows that the new religion was making an impact on society as a whole (*Contra Celsum* 3.5).

The aftermath of Polycarp's martyrdom is no less interesting for our purposes. The Roman authorities recognized the attention that the Christians were enjoying in the inner as well as the outer public sphere, and how impressive Polycarp's performance was even in anti-Christian eyes. Thus in order to save face they "took care that not even his poor body should be taken away by us, though many desired to do so" (4.15.40; here Eusebius writes in the first person, in imitation of the narrator in Acts). Then the centurion burnt the body,[18] and the Christians came and collected the bones and buried them in order to come and "celebrate the birthday of his martyrdom." In other words, the Romans showed awareness of a successful media performance, and they did not want it to become complete and enduring. But the Roman authorities partially lost this battle, since within the inner public sphere, as the letter says, "the Lord will permit us to come together according to our power in gladness and joy, and celebrate the birthday of his martyrdom, both in memory of those who have already contested, and for the practice and training of those whose fate it shall be" (4.15.44). A memorial set up in the midst of the inner public sphere no doubt also radiated towards the outer one, even if only in limited proportions. This presentation of Polycarp's burial is reminiscent of the burial of James near the Temple. Here we have examples of the Christian use of static media channels.

The case of Polycarp was, to use media performance terminology, "constructed." It has been shown by scholars of media performance that in

---

1982); Richard W. Schaffert, *Media Coverage and Political Terrorists: A Quantitative Analysis* (New York: Praeger, 1992); and Gabriel Weimann and Conrad Winn, *The Theatre of Terror: Mass Media and International Terrorism* (New York: Longman, 1994). Of course, I am not identifying martyrdom as a form of terrorism, but only comparing the media effect of both phenomena on the public sphere.

17. "Death of a Peacemaker," *Time*, International Edition, 13 November 1995, 16-29.

18. Tatian says that the flesh of Christians was burned in order to prevent the resurrection of the body (*Oratio*, 6).

certain cases the media construct their own reality, and that in certain events the media "may be more influenced by their own organizational (and technical) logic and the logic of the 'story' or 'script,' based on earlier events, than by actual 'reality' as it occurs."[19] Various studies have shown that news commentaries on General McArthur's return to New York after his dismissal in Korea, as opposed to the information received from points along the procession route, were more in the line of a script written in advance than an expression of what was actually happening. It was a scenario "'defined' in advance, effectively 'pre-structured' by the media."[20] It was the very uniqueness of the McArthur story, though, that made it a significant media event. To cite another example, which we will discuss later, reports of terrorist attacks contain many standard topoi and repetitive themes that are due in part to the ideology or bias of reporters and to the simple fact that in reality terror attacks of a certain nature contain many recurrent events.

Yet, the letter describing Polycarp's martyrdom was of course not prestructured, but it did construct a script of events that, in many of their details, did not occur in reality, since we know that such details are taken from well-known biblical stories.[21] But here we must make a distinction between what classical philologists and historians call topoi (similar themes) and elements taken from the reporters' environment that make them construct the story as it stands now. The uniqueness of the Polycarp story, like that of General McArthur, makes it a media event worthy of reporting. In contrast to the traditional literary analysis of such texts, we wish to show what the media value of the construction was — in other words, why the story was constructed in a certain way in order to be "marketable" to a certain audience. Literary critics will usually look for the topoi and argue in consequence that the text does not reflect historical reality. The topoi they find are the ones embedded in previous literature.[22] By using the results of media studies, however, we can look for the social and cultural codes that our reporter has called upon in order to transmit the story to an actual receiver of his own time. What were his considerations in constructing the text as he did? We can thus make some observations concerning the audience that was meant to decode the communicative message transmitted by a given text. In our analysis, the story of

19. Denis McQuail, *Media Performance: Mass Communication and the Public Interest* (London: Sage Publications, 1992), 208-9.

20. Ibid., 208.

21. So, for example, Van Henten, "Martyrs as Heroes."

22. Buschmann, *Martyrium Polycarpi;* and Van Henten, "Martyrs as Heroes."

Polycarp becomes a multidimensional media event rather than a "flat" recitation of events imbued with literary themes derived from previous sources. How does this work?

Traditional literary analysis of the Polycarp story has highlighted many familiar topoi, such as Polycarp's reception of the soldiers who come to fetch him from his hiding place, which is recounted as a conflation of Abraham's reception of the three angels and the arrest of Jesus in Gethsemane. Polycarp's prayer and entrance into the city are, of course, reminiscent of Jesus' entry into Jerusalem: "now when he at last finished his prayer, after remembering all who had ever even come his way, both small and great, high and low, and the whole Catholic Church throughout the world, the hour came for departure, and they set him on an ass, and led him into the city" (4.15.15). The mild interrogation of the proconsul and the blood pouring out of Polycarp's wound would be further examples of narrative details that adopt the topoi of Jewish and Christian literature written well before the martyrdom of Polycarp.[23] With only these topoi, the story would have been easily decoded by Christians in the inner public sphere, who were familiar with the New Testament. But neither the letter nor Eusebius refers to these topoi explicitly; instead, they make a completely new event out of the story of Jesus' Passion. That is, Eusebius takes the Passion story and reconstructs it within a contemporary setting, as a media event in the arena. He employs methods that modern media performance would not be ashamed of. Many constructed elements made Polycarp's martyrdom more marketable within the inner Christian public sphere of the second century, but it was also a unique story that had media value for pagans and Jews in the outer public sphere.

Viewed as a whole, literary topoi plus contemporary elements (including novelistic elements) taken from the second-century scene turn Polycarp's martyrdom into a constructed media story.[24] The cultural and moral codes transmitted are therefore unique and differ from the Passion accounts of the New Testament Gospels and from other earlier stories. The intensive search for literary topoi is thus somewhat superfluous, because a later generation of thoughts and codes is reflected. The elements include:

23. Van Henten, "Martyrs as Heroes," 306ff.

24. The story of Polycarp's martyrdom is not just a recitation of topoi from stories like those in Daniel 3, 2 Maccabees 7, or the Passion narratives in the Gospels. Even though it has elements of the Passion story, there is no reason to doubt that Polycarp himself really wished to imitate Jesus. Hence the topoi have a factual basis, and Polycarp's martyrdom remains unique because it has many new elements.

- publicity on a grand scale: appearance in the arena;
- bold confrontation with pagans and Jews in a public setting;
- the option presented the martyr of denying the faith;
- various kinds of public torture;
- death on the pyre as the materialization of a dream;
- blame directed at the Roman authorities and their active role;
- the secondary role of the Jews (in contrast to the primary role they play in the Gospel passion narratives);
- the great age of the martyr (in contrast to the relative youth of Jesus);
- the martyr's contempt for the mob and his elitist approach to mission;
- the distinctive discourse of the martyr (not simply a rehash of Pilate's interrogation of Jesus);
- the real burial place (Polycarp's body did not disappear; his bones were buried).

All of these narrative elements, and others, make the Polycarp tale a completely new media story (as distinguished from media event) that had a media value for a variety of audiences in the second century and later. Accounts of terror attacks in Israel today are repetitive and have as many topoi in common as do martyr stories from antiquity. However, the topoi or themes that recur in contemporary media accounts can be shown to reflect reality. Thus topoi can reflect reality, because events of a certain nature happen in similar patterns. Sometimes these patterns are the result of the intentional imitation of a certain model.[25]

Who then are the addressees of the story of Polycarp's martyrdom?

25. I have analyzed with my students the narratives of terror attacks in Israel during the years 1995-97. We studied accounts in four major Israeli newspapers (Ha'aretz, Ma'ariv, Yediot Aharonot, and the Jerusalem Post). The results were surprising. We discovered that although we were analyzing separate incidents, the media related them in a similar manner, giving headlines and articles filled with the rhetoric of blood, martyrdom, and sacrifice (of the victims). The basic structure of the accounts was the same: the attack, the closure of the region, the arrival of help, the arrival of the religious unit to collect the bodily remains of people killed in the attack, the live television coverage of the event, the commotion of people trying to help and of groups shouting "Kill the terrorists!" or "Kill the Arabs!", and the appearance of the prime minister or some other important official. Then came mention of the reaction of the United States, followed by stories of individuals who were either killed or miraculously survived. Usually we also found a summary of former incidents of the same nature with the numbers of victims, and little maps and street plans.

The answer would have to be not solely Christians, but also not just the hoi polloi of pagan society. The story was probably aimed at an audience that would have appreciated such a drama and that would not automatically have resisted its Christian flavor. It seems that when the letter was composed, the common people were still resistant to the Christian mission, and Christians like Polycarp made attempts to win the more elevated sections of society by intellectual persuasion in line with what Polycarp says to the proconsul: "You I should have held worthy of discussion" (4.15.22). The story is constructed in such a way that Christian social and moral codes, as well as the more general ones, can be easily decoded (martyrdom as well as steadfastness; Christian mimesis of Jesus as well as having a "fun show"). Hence the account was directed toward segments within both the outer public sphere and the institutional one. When published and circulated in the outer public sphere (that is, when read aloud by many), the Polycarp story likely had an effect comparable to that which the event itself had in the theater during its occurrence. Thus, the martyrdom of Polycarp was transformed from a media event into a media text with a missionary purpose or, in modern terminology, a marketing value.

If we combine this last observation with Eusebius's theological understanding of the Christian mission, we can easily move on to a more specific conclusion. Eusebius believed that the society outside the Christian inner sphere was potentially ready to accept the Christian mission since the Logos is present everywhere in the world.[26] Hence this potential audience was ready and capable of decoding the message sent through the story of Polycarp's martyrdom without needing to know about Christ's Passion (or, for example, the story of Hananiah, Mishael and Azariah told in the book of Daniel). In other words, the moment the Polycarp media event became an independent media story (in its new constructed form, independent of the Passion narratives and other biblical stories), its media value was created for audiences of the second or fourth centuries.

We should mention here that the remainder of the letter, unfortunately heavily abbreviated in the *Ecclesiastical History*, contained a great deal of information. (Eusebius evidently collected much of it in a fuller version in his *Acts of the Martyrs*.) In *Hist. Eccl.* 4.15.46-48 we read that

> in the same document concerning [Polycarp] other martyrdoms are appended which took place in the same Smyrna at the same time as the

26. See H. Berkhof, *Die Theologie des Eusebius von Caesarea* (Amsterdam, 1939).

martyrdom of Polycarp, and among them Metrodorus, who seems to have been a presbyter of the Marcionite error, was given to the fire and put to death. A famous martyr of those at that time was Pionius. The document concerning him gives a full account of his special confession, his boldness of speech, the instructive apologies for the faith and popular addresses before the people and magistrates, as well as the correction and comfort to those who had succumbed to temptation in the persecution, which he addressed during his imprisonment to the brethren who visited him, in addition to this the tortures which he underwent, added to pain, nailing, the enduring of the flame, and, after all his marvellous deeds, his death; and to it we will refer those interested, for it is included in the martyrdoms of the ancients collected by us. There are also memoirs extant of others who were martyred in the city of Pergamon in Asia, Carpus and Papylas, and a woman, Agathonice, who died after many glorious confessions.

We learn from this passage that there were many more public martyrs, but Eusebius's decision as an "editor" was to narrate in detail only the martyrdom of Polycarp. Why? Polycarp was already considered a celebrity in the early Church during his own lifetime. Apparently even the Gentiles knew him, or at least Eusebius (and his source) thought that they knew him. Eusebius's decisions are reminiscent of those of modern media editors. Unlike Thucydides or Josephus, who have the ambition — not always fulfilled — to narrate everything within their scope of history, Eusebius makes his selection only in line with what he decides is relevant for his audience. He refers the more intellectually interested group of readers to his *Acts of the Martyrs* and claims that what he narrated in his history is sufficient for his general audience, mentioned above. In the *Ecclesiastical History* he usually relates all the most significant events and makes a selection of celebrities who were well-known in their own time (figures such as John the Apostle, Ignatius, Polycarp, and Justin). In other words, his history in general, as we shall see later, cannot meet the standards of "measuring objectivity" since it is incomplete, unbalanced, lacking in complete factualness and accuracy, and so on. However, it is full of relevance and extremely sensational. In contrast, Thucydides, Polybius, and Josephus would receive high scores among ancient historians when examined according to these criteria.

To conclude this section on Polycarp, a few summary observations are in order. On the one hand, the narrative is unbalanced and leaves out less famous martyrs (who apparently were no less brave than Polycarp), and it eliminates events that Eusebius judged superfluous. On the other hand, it is rich with news value; it is sensational, dramatic, and marketable to a diverse audience since it is extremely readable (as compared with accounts in Polybius and other ancient historians). The story contains some redundancies and familiar topoi, but it is related within a constructed framework that removes much of its factuality. The story of Polycarp is nicely put together to serve a particular media purpose. What we do not know, of course, is whether in the short term it achieved its purpose.

Justin Martyr

Justin Martyr, too, was a "celebrity."[27] Eusebius allots him considerable space just after his account of Polycarp and other martyrs mentioned in that letter (*Hist. Eccl.* 4.16-18, much of it connected to Justin). However, although Eusebius talks about Justin's martyrdom, he does not elaborate on it as he did in the case of Polycarp; he says only that Justin was "adorned with divine martyrdom when the philosopher Crescens . . . instigated the plot against him, for Justin had often defeated him in debate in the presence of hearers, and finally bound on himself the trophies of victory by his martyrdom for the truth of which he was the ambassador" (4.16.1). Later Eusebius says that "according to his own prophecy, he was caught by Crescens and suffered martyrdom," and he quotes Tatian (*Against the Greeks*) to the effect that "Crescens, who lurked in the great city . . . was himself so afraid of it [death] that he intrigued to inflict death on Justin, as though it were a great evil, because Justin by preaching the truth convicted the philosophers as gluttons and impostors" (4.16.7-9; 4.29.1, 3). Then we hear stories, through a quotation from Justin himself, about martyrs who were "privately" martyred by the Romans (as opposed to being executed publicly). For instance, Eusebius mentions one Ptolemy, who was imprisoned by the centurion and "tortured . . . for a long time in the jail" (4.17.9). Eusebius notes these stories about the "private" martyrs and comments that "to this Justin naturally and suitably adds the words which we quoted above, 'so I expect myself to suffer a plot from one of those named,' etc." (4.17.13).

27. For Justin in general, see Frend, *Martyrdom and Persecution*, Chaps. 9-10 passim.

70

This is interesting from our point of view since Eusebius believes that Justin, like the figures he mentions, was not publicly martyred, as was Polycarp. Justin appears in the *Ecclesiastical History* among the "private" martyrs of the sort mentioned in the Polycarp letter and by Tatian and Justin himself. Justin was martyred in 165 during the period of the martyrdoms at Lyons, as well as that of Polycarp himself, but is included in the *Ecclesiastical History* without all the shocking details we heard about in connection with the latter. Was that merely because Eusebius had no sources depicting Justin's martyrdom? This is hard to believe, since he goes on at length about a dissipated woman who was not at all a celebrity (4.17.2-8). Yet she can be considered a media asset for the Church historian: she was an extremely relevant example in a "real-life" demonstration of the phenomenon of conversion. She left a dissipated husband, and though herself dissipated, converted to Christianity. If Eusebius knew all this, could he not have acquired sufficient information about Justin's martyrdom? The answer seems clear: Eusebius would relate a martyrdom in great detail when he could find enough material that depicted it as a public show.[28] For him this was the real revolution launched by Christianity during those days. By contrast, he was extremely brief in his descriptions of martyrdoms that were less public, sometimes just mentioning such martyrs by name (Publius in 4.23.2-3 and Sagaris in 4.26.3). He would produce an elaborate account, as with the dissipated woman, if he was convinced that the circumstances leading to a "private" martyrdom were of relevance and public interest for other reasons. The story of the dissipated woman as well as that of Crescens and Justin are meant for an audience that is Gentile with a conversion potential.

The Martyrs of Lyons and Vienne

The martyrdom at Lyons and Vienne in Book 5 of the *Ecclesiastical History* is an important case for our study.[29] In many instances, Eusebius, like our

---

28. Even if *The Martyrdom of Saint Justin and his Companions* was available to Eusebius, the public exposure and publicity are absent from all three recensions. Justin was beheaded, as a Roman citizen, with his companions or drank hemlock in 165 c.e.

29. For detailed studies, see Jean Rougé and Robert Turcan, eds., *Les Martyrs de Lyon (177): Colloque international du Centre national de la recherche scientifique, Lyon, 20-23 septembre 1977* (Paris: Editions du C.N.R.S., 1978). For letters at the time, see Pierre Nautin, *Lettres et écrivains chrétiens des IIe et IIIe siècle* (Paris: Cerf, 1961). For

modern media, not only quotes verbatim from his source but also takes care to mention its origin and exact provenance.[30] In this sense he was a revolutionary. Yet at other times we know that, even though certain sources were available to him, he did not quote them at all and did not even attempt to present them in abridged form.[31] Much other material existed (such as the *Acts of the Palestinian Martyrs*, transcripts of public disputes), but he chose to use none of it. Like the editors who control modern media, he had his reasons for selecting and organizing his material in a particular manner, and he did this more extensively than any serious historian of antiquity.

In a letter to their brethren in Asia and Phrygia quoted by Eusebius, the Christians of Lyons and Vienne in Gaul maintain, "We were not merely excluded from houses and baths and markets, but we were even forbidden to be seen at all in any place whatever" (5.1.5). Evidently, the authorities (although the letter does not identify them by title or name) did not want Christians to be seen in public places but tried to eliminate them altogether from the outer public sphere. This suggests that the Christians had been rooted within the outer public sphere beforehand. Although the letter warns us that it cannot relate all the sufferings of the blessed martyrs because they were more than can be narrated "accurately" (5.1.4), it gives us some useful information. After the above mentioned ban was placed on the Christians, and before their trial,

> they endured nobly all that was heaped upon them by the mob, howls and stripes and dragging about, and rapine and imprisonment and stoning, and all things which are wont to happen at the hands of an infuriated populace against its supposed enemies and foes. Then they were dragged into the market-place by the tribune and by the chief authori-

---

women martyrs in the *Ecclesiastical History*, see Elizabeth A. Clark, "Eusebius on Women in Early Church History," in *Eusebius, Christianity and Judaism*, ed. Harold W. Attridge and Gohei Hata (Detroit: Wayne State University Press, 1992), 256-69; and in general Victor Saxer, *Bible et hagiographie* (Bern: Lang, 1986), Chap. 4.

30. See Arnaldo Momigliano, "Pagan and Christian Historiography in the Fourth Century A.D.," in *Essays in Ancient and Modern Historiography* (Oxford: Blackwell, 1977), 107-26. For Eusebius's treatment of this martyrdom in his various works, see Robert M. Grant, "Eusebius and the Martyrs of Gaul," in *Les Martyrs de Lyon (177)*, ed. Rougé and Turcan, 129-136.

31. Against B. Gustafsson, "Eusebius' Principles in Handling His Sources, as Found in His 'Church History,' Books I-VII," *Studia Patristica* 4 (1961): 429-41.

ties of the city, were indicted and confessed, and at last they were shut up until the coming of the governor. (5.1.7-8)

Even before the "regular" procedure, the populace was given opportunities to torment the Christians, unlike the case of Polycarp, where it became active only during the process in the arena. The description of the infuriated rabble is reminiscent of topoi in classical and Hellenistic literature (from Herodotus to Polybius) about the role of the mob.[32] It is important to note that a certain kind of (negative) interrelationship was created between populace and martyrs. At first there was no encounter, since the Christians were banned from public places in the outer public sphere; the next stage was that they were brought into this very same public sphere, but this time in order to enter into an extremely difficult and bloody struggle over getting the upper hand. It is quite clear that at first the mob and the Roman authorities get the upper hand. Yet the Christians manage to attract a great deal of attention. (Unlike private martyrs, or many dissidents in modern totalitarian states, who are put in dark cells; when they manage to clash in public with the authorities, they receive a great deal of media exposure. Tiananmen Square was a great asset for the opposition in China.)[33] The letter uses a well-known ploy of modern media as well, namely, communication of the circumstances in such a way as to arouse sympathy for the underdog (as in the case of Chinese dissidents or the Palestinians in the ongoing Arab-Israeli conflict), while insisting on the physical sufferings of the victims.

When the Christians were brought before the governor, "one of the brethren" named Vettius Epagathus intervened, and "asked to be heard himself in defence of the brethren to the effect that there was nothing atheistic or impious among us." The governor did not let him speak. Epagathus "was howled down by those around the judgement-seat, for he was a man of position, and the governor would not tolerate the just request which he had put forward but merely asked if he were a Christian himself" (5.1.9-10). This behavior is quite understandable: the governor did not want a distinguished man to make a public appearance in favor of the accused. In other words, he justifiably (from his point of view) did not want a speech

32. One thinks of the treatment of Jews in Nazi Germany, on which see Saul Friedländer, *Nazi Germany and the Jews: The Years of Persecution, 1933-1939* (New York: HarperCollins, 1997), Chap. 9.
33. On the showdown in Tiananmen Square, see the articles in *Time*, International Edition, 5 June 1989, 12-17, and 12 June 1989, 16-21.

praising Christianity to fill the public air. This policy of suppressing Christian publicity in the outer sphere was already evident on various occasions during the second century. It anticipates the more comprehensive policy adopted by the Roman authorities in the third century. In this case the governor gave preferential treatment to the howls of the mob that supported his policies. The picture drawn by the letter contains many dimensions, with a great deal of movement and sound.

At all events, the poor man "confessed in clear tones and was himself taken into the ranks of the martyrs" (5.1.10). When the governor "had publically commanded (dēmosia ekeleusen) that we should all be prosecuted," some heathen slaves who were afraid that they would be killed with the Christians accused them of performing "Thyestean feasts and Oedipodean intercourse" (5.1.14), and as soon as this "rumor spread, all men turned like beasts against us, so that even if any had formerly been lenient for friendship's sake they then became furious and raged against us, and there was fulfilled that which was spoken by our Lord" (5.1.14-15). We hear again of mob activities (no doubt with the consent of the Roman authorities, and betrayals of traditional "friendships" in some instances). The description of the clashes between populace and Christians is lively, and according to the letter these clashes worked to the benefit of the Christians. They received "negative" mob treatment, but a positive publicity asset resulted.

The account continues:

> the holy martyrs endured sufferings beyond all description . . . and all the fury of the mob and of the governor and of the soldiers was raised beyond measure against Sanctus,[34] the deacon from Vienne, and against Maturus, who was a novice but a noble contender, and against Attalus, a Pergamene by race, who had always been a pillar and support of the Christians there, and against Blandina, through whom Christ showed that things which are mean and obscure and contemptible among men are vouchsafed great glory with God because of the love towards him shown in power and not boasted of in appearance. (1.16-17).

We see again how the mob has an important role in the process of martyrdom since it assumes an active part in driving the authorities to act perhaps more harshly than they initially intended. The populace is dominant

---

34. For the following martyrs and their social status, see G. Thomas, "La condition sociale de L'Église de Lyon en 177," in *Les Martyrs de Lyon (177)*, ed. Rougé and Turcan, 93-106.

in the outer public sphere, provided it does things that are in line with the will of the Roman authorities. But being thrust into the midst of a mob also meant great publicity. It does not matter that this is a negative kind of publicity; it is publicity that penetrates and pervades the air for a long time.[35] Many terrorist groups in modern times have received extremely bad publicity, but the attention they did receive effectively placed them on the public agenda. In many instances, as the Palestinian case shows, in the course of time the bad publicity turned into sympathy that then resulted in a positive stance among the media (which began calling the Palestinians "freedom fighters" instead of "terrorists").[36]

Eusebius goes on to relate some cases of individual martyrs in Lyons and Vienne. They were "celebrities" in Gaul, the letter emphasizes. This highlighting of individuals is comparable to the presentations we find in our modern mass media. The letter uses this method in order to shock its audience and endow the description with realistic hues. When a disaster is described by our mass media, the report becomes effective when an anonymous mass turns into the personal. If 241 marines are killed in Beirut,[37] or a plane crashes somewhere in the world and we hear about hundreds of dead people, it is shocking; but not as shocking and dreadful as when we get stories about some of the deceased with names and personal histories attached.[38] (This is one merit of C. Lantzmann's *Shoah*, a film that for hours recites many personal stories against the background of the familiar number of six million.)[39] The methods employed by the letter are amazing when we examine them in line with methods to be found in our mass media. A picture penetrates when the detailed descriptions are of the most dreadful and horrific nature. Showing the shooting of a boy during the Vietnam war or the blood of persons shelled in a Sarajevo market is of greater media value than communicating the information that several thousand people were killed during a certain event. Our mass media create

---

35. Publicity also came through the decrees that were pronounced everywhere against Christians, as we hear, for instance, in Recension B.1 of the account of Justin's martyrdom: "impious decrees were posted against the pious Christians in town and country alike" (Musurillo, *Acts of the Christian Martyrs*, 47).

36. See the sources cited in note 16 above.

37. On the Beirut incident, see *Newsweek*, International Edition, 31 October 1983, 10-15.

38. On TWA flight 800, see *Newsweek*, International Edition, 29 July 1996, 11-18.

39. See Ron Burnett, *Cultures of Vision: Images, Media, and the Imaginary* (Bloomington: Indiana University Press, 1995), 160ff.

pictures that are unbalanced but that bring the most dreadful horrors into our homes. The more personal the stories are, the more horrific. Thucydides mentions thousands of people killed in Sicily in 413. This is an impersonal description. (Some historians before Eusebius's time were also aware of such techniques; Suetonius springs to mind.)

Thus we read many details of the tortures enacted against Sanctus, a famous person, and a brave one as well:

> For though the wicked hoped through persistence and the rigour of his tortures to wring from him something wrong, he resisted them with such constancy that he did not even tell his own name, or the race or the city whence he was, nor whether he was slave or free, but to all questions answered in Latin "I am a Christian . . ." and the heathen heard no other sound from him. For this reason the governor and the torturers were very ambitious to subdue him, so that when they had nothing left at all to do to him at last they fastened plates of heated brass to the tenderest parts of his body. His limbs were burning, but he continued himself un-bending and unyielding . . . . His body was a witness to his treatment; it was all one wound and bruise, wrenched and torn out of human shape . . . . For when the wicked after some days again tortured the martyr they thought that they might overcome him now that his body was swollen and inflamed if they applied the same tortures, seeing that he could not even endure to be touched by the hand. (5.1.20-24)[40]

But, of course, the martyr overcame his pain, and "he regained his former appearance and the use of his limbs, so that through the grace of Christ the second torturing became not torment but cure" (5.1.24). Because the public that attended the shows was presumably shocked, the elaborate descriptions in the letter (and in Eusebius) are given in order to shock the readers. The receivers of this medium get the horrible pictures transmitted directly into their homes, so to speak, as television spectators receive the horrific pictures transmitted to them daily. The relevance of the story also springs to mind since it shows that endurance pays in line with Christ's triumph (5.1.29). Steadfastness in public was a strategy of the Christian cause in the battle over the outer public sphere.

Some of the Roman governors evidently became aware of this strat-

---

40. For such "language of the body," see Averil Cameron, *Christianity and the Rhetoric of Empire: The Development of Christian Discourse* (Berkeley: University of California Press, 1991), 69ff.

egy at an early stage and wished to avoid the spectacle of Christianity gaining undue publicity in the outer public sphere. Thus

> when the tyrant's torments had been brought to naught by Christ through the endurance of the blessed saints, the devil thought of other devices, imprisonment in the jail in darkness and in the most horrible place, and stretching their feet in the stocks, separated to the fifth hole. . . . Thus most of them were strangled in the prison, being all those whom the Lord had chosen thus to depart manifesting his glory. Some were tortured so cruelly that it seemed impossible for them to live even if they had had every care, yet survived in the prison, bereft of human attention but strengthened by the Lord. (5.1.27-28)

This was yet another stage within the chain of suffering the martyrs underwent. But it shows what we are arguing: the dark jail became a syndrome signifying a worsening of the punishment methods employed against the martyrs. By tortures inflicted in prison, the authorities diminished the opportunities for public appearance and therefore for the promotion of Christianity.[41] The martyr disappeared altogether from the public eye, but not entirely from the outer public sphere. We have seen up to now that the struggle between the populace and the Roman authorities on the one side (in Polycarp's case, the people and the proconsul did not see eye to eye at the beginning, whereas during the media event itself they joined hands) and the Christian martyrs on the other took place in various institutions of the outer public sphere, such as the market, the governor's judgment forum, and then also in the prison (as demonstrated by a case that does not appear in Eusebius, the martyrdom of Perpetua and Felicitas, where we receive a rare picture of the inner scenes within a prison).[42] In all of these the

41. The publicity aspect of martyrdom is mentioned in passing by Clement of Alexandria, *Stromateis* 4.4.36: "These, we say, banish themselves without being martyrs, even though they are punished publicly."

42. This isolation from the public in prison brought about ideas that we find in Tertullian some decades before Eusebius. In his *Ad Martyras* he speaks about the benefits for Christians of their presence in prison: "The prison, indeed, is the devil's house as well, wherein he keeps his family, but you have come within its walls for the very purpose of trampling the wicked one under foot in his chosen abode (Chapter 1) . . . it is full of darkness, but ye yourselves are light; it has bonds, but God has made you free (Chapter 2) . . . meanwhile let us compare the life of the world and of the prison, and see if the spirit does not gain more in the prison than the flesh loses. . . . The prison does the same service for the Christian which the desert did for the prophet . . . (Chapter 2).

Christians showed that their presence within the outer public sphere could be challenged but not eliminated altogether.

Other individuals, too, underwent terrible sufferings. We read about Pothinus, who was brought by the soldiers

> to the judgement-seat; the local authorities accompanied him, and all the populace, uttering all kinds of howls at him as though he was Christ himself, but he gave noble testimony. When asked by the governor, Who was the God of the Christians, he said, 'If you are worthy, you will know.' And then he was dragged about without mercy, and suffered many blows; for those who were near ill-treated him with feet and hands and in every way, without respect even for his old age, and those who were at a distance each threw at him whatever he had at hand, and all thought that it would be a great transgression and impiety to omit any abuse against him . . . and he was thrown into prison scarcely breathing and after two days yielded up the ghost. (5.1.29-31)

This story demonstrates that the Christians did not give up, and that they fought for their hold in the outer public sphere. It seems as if most of the martyrs wished to appear in the most important institution of the outer sphere, the arena. This is clearly stated by the letter itself: "For they wove various colours and all kinds of flowers into one wreath to offer to the father, and so it was necessary for the noble athletes to undergo a varied contest, and after great victory to receive the great crown of immortality" (5.1.36). Athletes, one should remember, were first and foremost outstanding "actors" within the outer public sphere.[43]

Indeed, Maturus, Sanctus, Blandina, and Attalus were "led forth to the wild beasts, to the public and to a common exhibition of the inhumanity of the heathen *(eis to demosion kai eis koinon tōn ethnōn tēs apanthrōpias theama)*, for the day of fighting with beasts was specially appointed for the Christians" (5.1.37). We should remember Ignatius's desire to be led to the beasts since this was the opportunity to get an enormous audience in the amphitheater. From now on we are in the arena, and the letter informs us of various things that happened there to the above mentioned martyrs and to some others. For instance, it mentions Alexander, "a Phrygian by race and a physician by profession, who had lived in Gaul for

---

43. For ancient athletics, see M. I. Finley and H. W. Pleket, *The Olympic Games: The First Thousand Years* (New York: Viking, 1976); and *Lo sport nel mondo antico: ludi, munera, certamina a Roma* (Rome: Museo della Civilta Romana, 1987).

many years and was known to almost every one for his love toward God and his boldness of speech" (5.1.49). As before, only a few "celebrities" out of many are presented in detail. But throughout the whole description, the idea of publicity and the victory of Christian steadfastness in the fierce battle over the outer public sphere is emphasized. Hence

> Maturus and Sanctus passed again through all tortures in the amphitheatre as though they had suffered nothing before, but rather as though, having conquered the opponent in many bouts, they were now striving for his crown, once more they ran the gauntlet in the accustomed manner, endured the worrying of the wild beasts, and everything which the maddened public, some in one way, some in another, were howling for and commanding, finally, the iron chair on which the roasting of their bodies clothed them with its reek. Their persecutors did not stop even here, but went on growing more and more furious, wishing to conquer their endurance, yet gained nothing from Sanctus beyond the sound of the confession which he had been accustomed to make from the beginning. Thus after a long time, when their life still remained in them through the great contest, they were at last sacrificed, having been made a spectacle to the world *(theama genomenoi tō kosmō)* throughout that day as a substitute for all the variations of gladiatorial contests. (5.1.38-40)

Of Blandina it is said that after suffering terrible public tortures she "had overcome the adversary in many contests, and through the struggle had gained the crown of immortality" (5.1.42).[44] And then we hear that "Attalus was himself loudly called for by the crowd, for he was well known *(kai gar ēn onomastos)* . . . he was led round the amphitheatre and a placard was carried before him on which was written in Latin, 'This is Attalus, the Christian.' The people were very bitter against him . . ." (5.1.43-44). Later we hear that "the governor led them to the judgement-seat, making a show and spectacle of the blessed men to the mob." (5.1.47) The Phrygian Alexander and Attalus (who was brought back to the beasts since the governor wished to "please the mob") were tortured in the amphitheater. It is said that Attalus "when he was put on the iron chair and was being burned and

---

44. For a convenient survey of women martyrs, see S. G. Hall, "Women among the Early Martyrs," in *Martyrs and Martyrologies: Papers Read at the 1992 Summer Meeting and the 1993 Winter Meeting of the Ecclesiastical History Society,* ed. Diana Wood (Oxford: Blackwell, 1993), 1-21.

the reek arose from his body, said to the crowd in Latin, 'Lo, this which you are doing is to eat men, but we neither eat men nor do anything else wicked'" (5.1.52). Then we get all the dreadful details about the public torture of Blandina, and "the heathen themselves confessed that never before among them had a woman suffered so much and so long" (5.1.56).

The aftermath of the whole story is painful. The remains of the martyrs were not buried; the authorities "threw out the remains left by the beasts and by the fire, torn and charred, and for many days watched with a military guard the heads of the rest, together with their trunks, all unburied" (5.1.59). What is more, "the bodies of the martyrs, after having been exposed and insulted in every way for six days, and afterwards burned and turned to ashes, were swept by the wicked into the river Rhone which flows near by, that not even a relic of them might still appear upon the earth" (5.1.62). The authorities wished to eliminate any reminder of the martyrs from the outer public sphere. They knew what they were doing: a grave or some other vestige would have become a static media channel in the outer public sphere. They already knew that the Christians had a special relationship with static media channels, since the grave of a holy person very soon became a focal point for pilgrimage. There are more details, some of which Eusebius cites verbatim from the letter; others he decides not to include in his account (5.2.1). His methods of selection are sometimes more interesting than what he relates.

The martyrdoms of Lyons and Vienne as depicted by the letter present many important aspects of publicity and media performance:

1. The fact that the struggle over the outer public sphere was not fought merely in the arena but also in other public spheres shows that the Roman authorities were well aware that this struggle was taking place. According to Eusebius's presentation, they did all they could to eliminate and suppress the Christian martyrs alive or dead (comparable to the Nazis, who during the mid-thirties wished to eliminate the Jews from the public sphere).[45]
2. The martyrs are shown as being glad to be tortured in public. It is not accidental that Eusebius relates the public torturing process in elaborate detail. The bodies that are brought into the arena are intact and during the process are mutilated. The media value of such descriptions was to shock and horrify the audience, who only expected

45. See the excellent survey of Friedländer, *Nazi Germany and the Jews.*

a gladiator type of spectacle.[46] Mutilation is an important asset of the media performance, comparable to detailed reports concerning atrocities in our modern media. The dichotomy between the completeness of the bodies (and, in certain instances, the beauty as well) at the beginning of the show versus their repellent appearance towards the end is a media value factor. Its theological purpose is a different matter: the Christians showed the public that *sarx* (flesh) had no value in comparison to *pneuma* (spirit), and this made a great impression on pagans, who had a high esteem for the body and its various parts. These scenes, then, represent a carefully conceived strategy employed by Christians to conquer the outer public sphere at that time.

3. The presentation of the martyrdom of Lyons and Vienne is extremely theatrical.[47] It is full of conflicting noise and color: women and men naked in the arena facing a shouting mob; the private parts of men and women exposed; the roar of beasts and the struggle of naked humans against them. The very same animals depicted as hunted by aristocrats in mosaics of the Hellenistic and Roman periods (e.g., the mosaic of Constantine's palace in which two handsome youngsters hunt a lion, the king of animals, in Istanbul) are here subduing the poor Christians. However, the steadfastness of the martyrs in the arena actually signifies an impressive public manifestation of Christian power vis-à-vis the Roman authorities and the incited mob.

Eusebius's Editorial Decisions

Thus Eusebius presents martyrdom as a device to promote Christianity within the outer public sphere as well as the institutional one. What methods did Eusebius employ in order to deliver this kind of media performance of the martyrs? W. Lance Bennett identifies the four "information problems" of news in modern mass media as *dramatization, personalization, normalization,* and *fragmentation.*[48] Eusebius's accounts are charac-

46. Potter, "Martyrdom as Spectacle."

47. See in general K. M. Coleman, "Fatal Charades: Roman Executions Staged as Mythological Enactments," *Journal of Roman Studies* 80 (1990): 44-73.

48. W. Lance Bennett, *News, The Politics of Illusion,* 2d ed. (New York: Longman, 1988).

terized by *fragmentation* in that he makes a strict selection of his sources and intentionally does not quote all the available material. He, like a good modern journalist, abbreviates his sources and brings to his reader only the most interesting aspects he has found in them, those which have a "media value." Thus his stories usually lack past or future and are disconnected. He deals mainly with "celebrities" against the background of the anonymous masses. Thus he introduces short stories of individuals, and, as in our media, much of what he repeats becomes redundant and remains far from complete. Here we are confronted with the problem of *personalization*, which will become more evident in Book 8 of the *Ecclesiastical History*. Eusebius is more interested in persons than in processes and their causes. His decisions concerning the selection of stories show — as in the modern media — that he wished to present to his audience only the sensational and horrific side of the "news"; in this he shows himself to be gifted at *dramatization*. Eusebius uses a great deal of imagery to describe sound and movement. People in antiquity read aloud, and so the effects of sound and color became still more meaningful. Moreover, the source Eusebius quotes (the letter) is of such great value to him that he cites it verbatim; like modern journalists (and unlike ancient historians), he specifies his source to let it be seen as reliable. Like a journalist, he prefers at times to use an "official" source in order to present a "normal" account without being obliged to analyze it.

Hence, because of all these devices, Eusebius's description of martyrdom lacks completeness, is unbalanced or biased in "favor" of the martyrs, and is largely "constructed," that is, placed against familiar scenery and communicated with codes that can easily be deciphered by any reader, pagan or Christian. The lack of balance also comes to the fore in Eusebius's reluctance to relate the stories of the heretical martyrs (5.16.20-22; 5.18.6). In this he reflects the attitude adopted by the orthodox Church, that in reality orthodox martyrs wished to be separated from heretical ones (5.16.22). The criterion of relevance is operative in Eusebius's presentation of the martyrs of Lyons and Vienne, if only to judge from the space allotted to this event in Book 5. As in our modern media, the presentation of time is totally distorted. Comparable to a news report that allots only a few minutes to an event that went on for some time, the martyrdoms that took place over several hours receive considerable space in the *Ecclesiastical History*, while other persecutions, such as a ban on the Christians that may have covered several months, are treated very concisely. In the end we get a combination of actual reality (the places where the martyrdom happened in Gaul, the procedure employed by the Roman authorities, some of the names, and so on) with a great deal of "perceived" or "media" reality.

Eusebius himself makes it clear that he is working like a modern reporter; he claims that one can find the "real" accurate history of the martyrs elsewhere:

> what need is there to transcribe the list of the martyrs in the above mentioned document, some consecrated by beheading, some cast out to be eaten by the wild beasts, others who fell asleep in the jail, and the number of the confessors which still survived at that time? For whoever wishes can easily read the full account by taking the description which has been included in our collection of martyrs, as I said before. Such were the events which happened under Antoninus. (5.4.3)

Eusebius, like our modern media, aims at a popular and accessible presentation of his stories; thus, even when he touches on theological matters, he either avoids discussion or simplifies it. He leaves the more factual, objective presentation to other accounts that are generically different from his *Ecclesiastical History.*

As with our modern newspapers, reading Eusebius hardly gives a linear sense of time. We can read a newspaper that contains a great deal of information, and even if we do so every day and go back after a month or a year to the material we have read, we would still not be able to write a chronological history of that period (on most given themes). At most we would be able to arrange our material in a roughly linear order because newspapers have dates, but there would be no real sense of time. This is what we get when we read Eusebius's *Ecclesiastical History.* The general line is given by the reigns of Roman emperors and some lists of bishops. For instance, when Eusebius reaches the reign of Commodus, he briefly relates the martyrdom of Apollonius. Here he had an independent source, the *Acts of Apollonius.* We have an independent version of this text, but it is not very helpful, having been reedited after Eusebius.[49] He himself says that "the words of Apollonius before the judge and the answers which he made to the interrogation of Perennius, and all the defence which he made to the senate, can be read by anyone who wishes in the compilation which we have made of the ancient martyrs" (5.21.5). For our purpose it is interesting to note that he mentions Apollonius as a martyr in a period when things were more relaxed ("in the reign of Commodus our treatment was

49. Musurillo, *Acts of the Christian Martyrs,* no. 7.

changed to a milder one" [5.21.1]).[50] This martyrdom was therefore considered a real sensation by the historian. But he does not give a full account, even though one was available. He elaborates on this particular person, not only because Apollonius was an isolated case during a relatively peaceful time, but also because he was a "celebrity," "a man famous among the Christians of that time for his education and philosophy" (5.21.2). Eusebius, however, provides a relatively short account since he is aware that the more space he grants this elite individual, the more tedious his history will become for a general audience.

Eusebius's tendency to "construct" certain cases (e.g., that of Polycarp) suggests that he himself was aware that the more he went into detail, the more redundant his account would become. Thus Eusebius acted less as an historian and more as an editor with a hierarchy of priorities. His editorial decisions explain why his history appears careless, like a daily newspaper. If Thucydides had worked like Eusebius, he would have given us a long account of the battle at Melos but considerably shortened other battles reports on the basis of "editorial" judgment and an unwillingness to become redundant. Fortunately, Thucydides attempted to tell everything about the Peloponnesian War, and in a linear way. Be that as it may, throughout his *Ecclesiastical History* Eusebius makes selections and preferences, and he then writes in a hierarchical manner based on the priorities of what is important for his audience to know and what is not. For these reasons the historian only says laconically about Apollonius: "But the martyr, beloved of God, when the judge earnestly begged and prayed him to defend himself before the senate, made before everyone *(epi pantōn)* a most learned defence of the faith for which he was a martyr, and was consecrated by beheading as if by decree of the senate" (5.21.4). The emphasis on publicity here reflects a marked editorial preference.

Another editorial decision can be found in the presentation of the pupils of Origen, who was educated in a "zeal" for martyrdom (6.2.5). In his "Life of Origen" in Book 6, Eusebius relates in passing certain martyrdoms that took place in Alexandria at the time (204 C.E.), emphasizing again how public the persecutions were. His account is focused on the life of Origen. Thus he is not expected to elaborate on the various martyrs. He only says that Origen

---

50. On Apollonius, see R. M. Grant, "Eusebius and the Martyrs of Gaul," 131. Cf. Eusebius's mention of the martyrdom of Publius in *Hist. Eccl.* 4.23.

won for himself an exceedingly wide reputation among all those who were of the faith, by the kindly help and goodwill that he displayed towards all the holy martyrs, unknown and known alike. For he was present not only with the holy martyrs who were in prison, not only with those who were under examination right up to the final sentence, but also when they were being led away afterwards to their death, using great boldness and coming to close quarters with danger; so that, as he courageously drew near and with great boldness greeted the martyrs with a kiss, many a time the heathen multitude round about in its fury went near to stoning him. (6.3.3-4)

Then Origen was pursued by the authorities but managed to hide. We get only a glimpse of the publicity of the martyrdoms in Alexandria, but we may assume that since there were "unknown" people among the martyrs, Eusebius gives no more than a very general account. Also, his "main item" in Book 6 is something else: the "Life of Origen."[51] Therefore, he actually neglects most of the important "factual" history of the Church at the time and relates his main subject in an independent "documentary" about the great scholar.

Known martyrs receive more "broadcast time" by Eusebius than unknown ones. The known martyrs mentioned here are apparently Origen's students, who are mentioned by name: Plutarch, Serenus, and others (6.4.1–6.5.1). But in terms of ancient history, not much can be learned here about the "factual" reality. We get only very short pieces of information, one sentence for each of the students who were martyred. The account here is "one-dimensional" and "flat." Eusebius does not even mention the existence of other, more elaborate accounts that his readers could consult. The treatment here is comparable to secondary news items that receive little space, in line with the scale of priorities employed. However, Eusebius highlights one case of a woman martyr and presents her martyrdom more elaborately. Why was she more important than the others?

We have already seen that sensation and relevance rather than factual history were often Eusebius's main concern (e.g., in the case of Paul of Samosata). This is why he decided to tell us about a brave woman from Alexandria named Potamiaena (6.5). He may have had an accessible source, but as we have already seen, the availability of sources was not a sufficient reason for Eusebius to include an item or to ignore it. Potamiaena was a ce-

51. See in general Henri Crouzel, *Origen,* trans. A. S. Worrall (Edinburgh: T & T Clark, 1989).

85

lebrity, and Eusebius loved celebrities.[52] In both ancient and modern times, it is the media that create celebrities, and not vice versa. It is probable that Eusebius created some of the celebrities he mentions in his accounts. In her favor, Potamiaena was a pure woman, a virgin, both beautiful and clever. Above all she provided a perfect example because she was tortured in public: "No sooner had she spoken than she received the sentence, and Basilides, being one of those serving in the army, took her and led her away to death. And as the crowd tried to annoy her, and insult her with shameful words, he kept restraining them and driving away the insulters, displaying the greatest pity and kindness towards her" (6.5.3). According to the story, Potamiaena developed a good relationship with Basilides: "She on her part accepted his fellow-feeling for her and bade him be of good cheer, for that she would ask him from her Lord, when she departed, and before long would requite him for what he had done for her" (6.5.3). Then she was tortured in a way that Eusebius has not described until now: "Thus speaking [it is said], she right nobly endured the end, boiling pitch being poured slowly and little by little over different parts of her body from head to toe. Such was the contest waged by this maiden celebrated in song" (6.5.4-5). Although other women had already been mentioned by Eusebius, this case had a special "media value."

The martyrdom of Potamiaena reflects a turning point, which may be just a "perceived" or "media" reality, that is, seen (or intentionally transmitted) only by our historian. Until now we have observed in his *Ecclesiastical History* that martyrdom in public was important for demonstrating the presence of Christians in the outer public sphere. The public was hostile but also "amazed" during its encounters with the brave Christians. Martyrs became a great publicity asset for Christianity. But here for the first time we hear from Eusebius that at the turn of the century the missionary aspect of martyrdom was really working. Martyrdom in public was paying off.[53] It had indeed become an effective media method in converting people to Christianity. Martyrdom and mission went hand in hand

52. Eusebius says of her: "The praise of this woman is to this day still loudly sung by her fellow-countrymen" (*Hist. Eccl.* 6.5.1).

53. Tertullian observed this aspect many years before in his account of Perpetua and Felicitas: "ita omnes inde adtoniti discedebant ex quibus multi crediderunt" ("Thus everyone would depart from the prison in amazement and many of them began to believe"; Musurillo, *Acts of the Christian Martyrs,* 124). And even earlier, from Justin, we hear that it was the steadfastness of martyrs that brought him to convert to Christianity (*2 Apology* 12).

and thus became relevant for Eusebius to relate in detail.[54] He tells us about Basilides, the soldier mentioned above, who converted to Christianity three days after the martyrdom of Potamiaena, when she appeared in his dream "wreathing his head with a crown and saying that she had called upon the Lord for him, and obtained what she requested, and that before long she would take him to herself" (6.5.6). The soldier confessed and was beheaded. Eusebius adds that "it is related that many others of those at Alexandria came over all at once to the word of Christ in the time of the persons mentioned, because Potamiaena appeared to them in dreams and invited them." This marvelous demonstration probably represents more of a "perceived" picture of reality (that is, an apocryphal story) than a factual one.

Eusebius employs stories like this when he wishes to demonstrate a certain point of high relevancy. He was, we may say, a colorful reporter and as sometimes in our modern media, he occasionally dissociates himself completely from reality (as when, for instance, stories about the reappearance of Elvis Presley or UFO's are taken seriously by some media persons). In this case we actually get information, even if only perceived or invented, concerning so-called "behavioral effects." In an important aspect of mass media research, scholars look at the mass media as a "major source for behavioral modelling and for excitation."[55] Some of these studies may cast a new light on many of our observations concerning martyrdom as a media channel.

Eusebius's "editorial" decisions emerge very clearly also in his account of the martyrs of Decius's time. On the one hand, he gives a brief and dry report about the martyrdom of Origen and his students. On the other, he relates a vivid picture of martyrs in Alexandria through a letter of Dionysius of Alexandria to Fabian, bishop of Antioch (6.41-42).[56] In both accounts he is extremely partial. He chooses cases from all over the eastern Empire but does not present a "statistical reality" from all over the region. The first part of the account, the one dealing with Origen's students, is flat and extremely short. The reason for this is easy to see. He says generally in

54. In general for this aspect, see Hans von Campenhausen, "Das Martyrium in der Mission," in *Die Alte Kirche,* ed. Heinzgünter Frohnes and Uwe W. Knorr (Munich: Kaiser, 1974), 71-85.

55. McLeod, et al., "On Understanding and Misunderstanding Media Effects," 246.

56. For Dionysius of Alexandria, see Johannes Quasten, *Patrology,* vol. 2 (Westminster, Md.: Christian Classics, 1986-92), 101-9.

6.39.1 that during the persecution against the churches under Decius "Fabian was perfected by martyrdom at Rome" and that in Palestine, Alexander the bishop of Jerusalem confessed and died, apparently a natural death in prison, as did Babylas, bishop of Antioch. Origen was tortured, though apparently not in public, and died (6.39.5). All these martyrs are celebrities in the Church, but they do not receive the publicity that Polycarp or Potamiaena enjoy. Why? First of all, these particular cases seemed to Eusebius to be without "news value" because they were reminiscent of former martyrdoms. Secondly, martyrdom became commonplace in the middle of the third century; they were performed in a familiar manner and without significant public attention. They were no longer interesting to the Church historian's audience. Eusebius again reveals his priorities. Even the martyrdom of the great Origen gets but a short passage, which reveals nothing new, except for some novel methods of torture that Eusebius has not mentioned in previous cases:

> the nature and extent of that which he endured for the word of Christ, chains and tortures, punishments inflicted on his body, punishments as he lay in iron and in the recesses of his dungeon; and how, when for many days his feet were stretched four spaces in that instrument of torture, the stocks, he bore with a stout heart threats of fire and everything else that was inflicted by his enemies . . . [of all these matters] the man's numerous letters contain both a true and accurate account. (6.39.5)

Eusebius ingeniously highlights methods of torture that he did not recount in former martyrdoms. He wished to endow martyrdom, which by then had become a monotonous story, with some new exciting information, as a good modern reporter would do. The war waged in the former Yugoslavia had many dreadful events to offer to the media every day, but these events became so monotonous that the reports became shorter and shorter, even when the reporters had plenty of information available. Reports about the war shifted from the first page to the second in many leading newspapers in the West. Only when some "special" kind of atrocity came up did the editors decide that it should be regarded as first priority and given the appropriate space. In this respect the media distorted the "real" history of the war.[57] The average reader was left with general impres-

---

57. Compare the detailed accounts of the *Helsinki Watch Documentation of War Crimes,* to reports in newspapers in the West. See D. E. Williams, "Probing Cultural Implications of War-Related Victimization in Bosnia-Hercegovina, Croatia, and Serbia,"

sions. A similar method was adopted by Eusebius. He had access to Origen's account of his own martyrdom but spared his audience the complete story since it had become uninteresting, redundant, and evidently too theological. The only new and shocking details were the novel methods of torture, which Eusebius rehearses in detail. His audience would have identified with the old scholar just by reading about the physical (not spiritual) atrocities inflicted on him. The end product is a partial one that leaves the reader with only a general impression. Josephus worked differently in his *Jewish War*. He did not spare his readers the same details repeated over and over again in order for them to get a complete picture, even if his report became overly detailed and tedious.

Eusebius deemed it necessary nonetheless to intertwine in his narrative some extremely vivid "close-ups" from Alexandria. His account is taken from an eyewitness and celebrity, Dionysius, whose writings provided Eusebius with evidence for the martyrdoms that occurred during Decius's short reign. These vivid descriptions could attract the interest of his audience even if the accounts themselves dealt again with "boring" incidents. Eusebius's decisions about what should enter his history and what should be left out were determined by his concern for relevancy, not just the availability of sources. In what follows, we will examine some of his specific editorial decisions.

New Information

We have already seen that when Eusebius relates repetitive phenomena, he attempts to awaken the reader's interest — not always successfully — by eliminating the repeated material; in such cases he attempts to provide new information that he has not supplied before. Some examples may be cited from the "factual" aspects of Dionysius's letter to Fabius, bishop of Antioch (6.41-42). Most of the martyrs figuring here underwent tortures that we have not encountered so far in the *Ecclesiastical History*. In this respect Eusebius's decision to include this selection of martyrs seems justifiable. Like a modern media person, he affords space to new sensational information. For instance we hear of Metras, who refused to "utter

in *Communication in Eastern Europe: The Role of History, Culture, and Media in Contemporary Conflicts,* ed. Fred L. Casmir (Mahwah, N.J.: Lawrence Erlbaum, 1995), 277-311, esp. 291-98.

blasphemous words," so "they belaboured his body with cudgels, stabbed his face and eyes with sharp reeds, and leading him to the suburbs stoned him" (41.3). Or of Quinta, who was bound by the feet and "dragged through the whole city over the rough pavements, so that she was bruised by the big stones, beating her all the while, and bringing her to the same place they stoned her to death" (41.4), and the virgin Apollonia, whose teeth were broken by blows to her jaws and who, when threatened with being burned alive, leaped into the fire willingly (41.7). These are sensational pieces of information for the benefit of people who are tired of reading again and again about a martyr who was "merely" burnt or thrown to the beasts. Dionysius himself, referring later to the "common" martyrs during the persecution of Valerian, says laconically that "it is superfluous to recount by name our people, since they are numerous and unknown to you . . . some enduring scourging and fire, others the sword, conquered in the fight and have received their crowns" (7.11.20). Dionysius was a great storyteller, and Eusebius was more than delighted to incorporate his account into the *Ecclesiastical History*.

The Transformation of the Public Sphere

Eusebius relates a drastic change in Roman policies towards the Christians. This does not mean that such a change really occurred, but this is the impression that he wants his readers to get. As far as we can learn from Eusebius's descriptions, the persecutions that occurred before Decius were limited to a power struggle over the outer and institutional public spheres waged by the authorities, the populace, and the Christians. Whereas in earlier cases the Romans wished to eliminate the Christians from public institutions such as the market, the public baths, and the assemblies, we now hear of the wish to eliminate the Christians altogether, even from their own inner public sphere. As with Decius's period, there is more of an intrusion into the private domains of the Christians (cf. Dionysius of Alexandria, *Hist. Eccl.* 7.11.18-21).[58] From Eusebius we receive a "media reality" in which the mob becomes more violent and out of control. We hear of a real pogrom launched against Christians. The persecution started a

---

58. For the persecution under him, see Frend, *Martyrdom and Persecution,* 249-51; and G. W. Clarke, "Double Trials in the Persecution of Decius," *Historia* 22 (1973): 650-63.

year before the formal edict of Decius, when the mob was incited against Christians. Eusebius comments that Satan stirred and incited the heathen against the Christians. "Aroused by him and seizing upon all authority for their unholy deeds, they conceived that this kind of worship of their gods — the thirsting for our blood — was the only form of piety" (6.41.1-2). A pogrom took place in which the mob rushed into the houses of the holy in order to plunder them (41.5-6). Celebrities were expelled from Alexandria or barely escaped from the city and were lost in the desert (6.42.3, Chaeremon bishop of Nilopolis). In the interim a *stasis* (revolution) occurred among the city's factions, and the Christians were left alone for a while (6.41.8-9). In other words, the physical aspect of eliminating Christians from the public sphere as well as penetrating into their "private" inner sphere, seems in this account of Dionysius to be more predominant than what we encountered before. Further, whereas in the martyrdoms of the second century many Christians received a platform (within the existing institutions) from which they could state their views and demonstrate their physical endurance, in the mid third century this opportunity seems to have diminished or vanished altogether. In most instances even the torture of martyrs was no longer carried out in the vast public sphere of the arena. According to the *Ecclesiastical History*, Christians were hunted like simple brigands and were martyred without the dignity characteristic of the martyrdom of Polycarp. Whether this development was real or only perceived remains to be seen.[59]

Relevance

Eusebius does not usually tell stories about events that are not imbued with relevance and news value for his own audience. In this case, the relevance is twofold. First, through some of the examples cited by Dionysius of Alexandria, Eusebius was able to strengthen his case concerning martyrdom and mission. For instance, when a band of soldiers and an old man had taken their place before the court, "before anyone could otherwise

59. The acts of the martyrs in Musurillo taken with the long version of Eusebius's *Martyrs of Palestine* (Syriac) highlight the "perceived reality" that we find in the *Ecclesiastical History*. Potter, "Martyrdom and Spectacle," has examined some cases of martyrdom outside the *Ecclesiastical History;* he argues that in the third century the authorities were reluctant to put Christians to death as a spectacle because they did not like to see people from the upper classes undergoing such dreadful experiences in public.

seize them, they ran of their own accord to the prisoner's dock, saying that they were Christians . . . exulting in their witness, God spreading abroad their fame gloriously" (6.41.22-23). Eusebius's editorial comments are no less fascinating than his historical reportage. Second, Eusebius found in Dionysius's account a good presentation of the issue of *lapsi*, which is elaborately reported later on in his *Ecclesiastical History*. Dionysius was of the opinion that

> the divine martyrs, themselves among us, who now are assessors of Christ, and share the fellowship of His kingdom, and take part in His decisions and judge along with Him, have espoused the cause of certain of the fallen brethren who became answerable for the charge of sacrificing; and seeing their conversion and repentance, they judged it had the power to prove acceptable to Him who hath no pleasure at all in the death of the sinner, but rather his repentance. (6.42.5)

The Human Interest Story

Dionysius was an excellent writer who knew how to tell a good story, and Eusebius loved incorporating colorful human interest stories into his history. As in today's tabloids, so in Eusebius's work a personal story gets maximum attention. For instance, the story of the pursuit of Dionysius by the authorities plunges us into the midst of Alexandria from an angle that changes the perspective of events altogether.[60] This "moving picture" gets more space than events that happened over longer periods and that were more significant historically. We hear that Dionysius escaped, and he tells us the following:

> on a former occasion also, when the persecution under Decius was publicly proclaimed, that selfsame hour Sabinus sent a *frumentarius* to seek me out, and on my part I remained four days at my house, expecting the arrival of the *frumentarius;* but he went around searching everything, the roads, the rivers, the fields, where he suspected I was hidden or walking, but was holden with blindness and did not find the

60. Note the observation of Williams, "Probing Cultural Implications," 292, with reference to atrocities in Yugoslavia: "The revealing nature of personalized testimony becomes apparent as victims and eyewitnesses relate minute details of their experiences involving enemy assaults."

house [reminiscent of the story about Lot and Abraham in Sodom]. (6.40.1-9)

Dionysius at last was smuggled out of the city, but he came back later. Eusebius also tells us about Dionysius's appearance before the deputy prefect of Egypt in 258 (under Valerian) alongside some of his colleagues and "one of the brethren from Rome" (7.11.3). We will come back to this story in a later chapter, but here it will suffice to note that the authorities reached the firm conclusion that, in order to eliminate the Christians (and in particular their leaders) completely from the public sphere (in its three dimensions), they should not be granted permission to hold public assemblies, nor be allowed to visit cemeteries where some of their holy brethren were buried, but should simply be banished from the cities to remote places. (Recall, in contrast, that in Lyons and Vienne the Christians were persecuted but left in their own inner public sphere within the cities.) Eusebius quotes Dionysius himself:

> "Aemilianus, the deputy-prefect, said to them: 'I see that ye are at once ungrateful and insensible of the clemency of our Augusti. Wherefore ye shall not be in this city, but ye shall betake yourselves to the parts of Libya and [remain] in a place called Cephro. For this is the place I chose in accordance with the command of our Augusti. And it shall in no wise be permitted either to you or to any others either to hold assemblies or to enter the cemeteries, as they are called.'" (7.11.10; cf. also 9.2)

Eusebius presents us with an interesting piece of information concerning martyrdom and the public sphere: the Romans apparently came to realize that the availability of the public sphere for Christian activity — whether the agora, the public baths, the pyre, the arena, or the graves of martyrs — was becoming disastrous to Roman interests. In other words, the decision reached by the authorities was apparently a reaction to the success of the Christian mission within the public sphere. As in the case of the martyrs of Lyons and Vienne, when the Roman authorities thought that their manifestation of power within the cities was being challenged, they reacted fiercely.

But the Christians did not give up. They assembled secretly in the existing cities and conquered public spheres outside the traditional spaces. They became the greatest promoters of their religion. Dionysius says:

> But we did not abstain from even the visible assembling of ourselves with the Lord; nay, I strove the more earnestly to gather together those

93

in the city, as if I were with them, "being absent in body," as he [St. Paul] said, "but present in spirit," and at Cephro a large church also sojourned with us, some brethren following us from the city, others joining us from Egypt. And there God opened unto us a door for the world. And at first we were pursued, we were stoned, but afterwards not a few of the heathen left their idols and turned to God. Then for the first time was the word sown through our agency among those who had not formerly received it. (7.11.12-13)

The belief that the Christians were God's agents in every place, including public institutions, and that they were given the divine task to spread Christianity, is the point where the public sphere and theology meet.

The Valerian Persecution and Its Aftermath

When Eusebius reaches the persecution under Valerian, he is again concise and economical of space,[61] mentioning only cases that yield new information not provided before or that present some kind of a relevant lesson *(exemplum)*. He relates the persecution both through Dionysius's letters and in his own words. When he finds a description showing clearly that the Romans started to separate martyrdom from publicity, which was important new information, he gives it verbatim:

> For even to this day the prefect does not cease from putting to a cruel death, as I have said before, some of those who are brought before him, while others he mutilates with tortures, or allows to pine away in imprisonment and chains, giving his orders that no one is to go near them, and investigating whether any has been found so doing. (7.11.24-25)

Eusebius proceeds to give new information describing the behavior of martyrs from villages as opposed to those from cities. Here he mentions three names, Priscus, Malchus, and Alexander, and reports that

> It is said that these men, who were living in the country at first reproached themselves for their carelessness and sloth, because instead of

61. For the problems of this persecution, see Henri Gregoire, *Les persécutions dans l'empire Romain* (Brussels: Palais des Academies, 1950), 46ff.; Frend, *Martyrdom and Persecution,* 423-27; and Fergus Millar, *The Emperor in the Roman World: 31 BC–AD 337* (London: Duckworth, 1977), 568-70.

hastening to secure the crown of martyrdom, they were proving contemptuous of prizes, though the present opportunity was bestowing them upon such as yearned with a heavenly desire. But that when they had taken counsel thereon, they started for Caesarea, appeared before the judge and met the above-mentioned end. (7.12.1)

As fate would have it, Valerian was captured by the Persian King Sapor I, during an invasion of the eastern provinces of the Empire. His son Gallienus, who had shared his father's reign since 253, became sole Augustus in 260 or 261. According to Eusebius, Gallienus "conducted the government with more prudence, and immediately by means of edicts put an end to the persecution against us" (7.13.1). The edict of Gallienus was an important event since, by terminating the persecution, it opened the outer and institutional public spheres to the influence of the Christians. They were free once again to assemble; they received back their churches and were permitted to convene in cemeteries (7.13). Eusebius was conscious of the publicity value of ordinances issued by the authorities concerning Christians (Books 9–10). Already in Books 1–7 he is aware of this kind of channel, quoting Gallienus's rescript: "I have given my order that the benefit of my bounty should be published throughout all the world" (7.13.1). Yet Eusebius, as a careful "media" reporter, finds one sensational exception during this quiet period, the martyrdom of Marinus in Caesarea. This story is interesting from our point of view.

Marinus was a Roman soldier who was about to be promoted to the rank of centurion, but a rival claimant to the post revealed "before the tribunal" that Marinus was a Christian. This shows, as in other instances (already in Lyons and Vienne), that Christians could not be singled out easily when they served in institutions of the public sphere. At all events, he was given three hours by the judge to decide whether he wished to confess or be promoted. The bishop of Caesarea, where this drama took place, showed him a sword that he hid under his cloak as well as "a book of the divine Gospels" (7.15.4). Marinus, of course, opted for the book, confessed before the judge, and was summarily martyred. The aftermath is notable as well: "In that place Astyrius also is commemorated for the boldness which is dear to God. He was a member of the Roman Senate, a favourite of emperors, and well known to all both for birth and wealth. He was present with the martyr when he was being perfected, and raising the corpse upon his shoulder he placed it upon a splendid and costly robe, and laying it out with great magnificence gave it a fitting burial" (7.16.1). To this Eusebius adds: "A great many other facts are mentioned about this man by his friends, who have survived to our day." (7.16.1)

What then made Eusebius select this story out of so many others (another tale connected to Astyrius appears in the following chapter)? To begin with, the story was a "scoop" with strong media value, since the event happened during a time when no persecution of Christians was going on. Second, the story was originally taken from a source written by Marinus's friends, who "constructed" it very carefully. The most striking parallel is the rich man of Arimathea who buried Jesus (Matt. 27:57-60). Eusebius uses the story uncritically. Third, the story presents something completely new over against the martyrdoms so far described in the *Ecclesiastical History,* specifically, the "formal" elimination of a Christian from an institution, the army, which was a significant part of the institutional public sphere. This anticipates what would happen later during the time of Diocletian. Eusebius has the awareness of presenting news in the modern sense; he wishes to relate new information according to a hierarchy of priorities. Finally, the relevance of a story about the choice between holy book and sword leading to martyrdom brings us nearer to Eusebius's own period and is therefore a significant news item.

The Diocletian Persecution (Book 8)

At the end of Aurelian's rule, Eusebius tells us, another persecution almost occurred, but Aurelian died just before he put his signature to "decrees against us . . . thus it was clearly shown for all to see that the rulers of this world would never find it easy to proceed against the churches of Christ, unless the hand which champions us were to permit this to be done, as a divine and heavenly judgement to chasten and turn us, at whatever times it should approve" (7.30.21). These times had come again in Eusebius's own day, with the great persecution of Diocletian. Most of Book 8 is devoted to the account of the martyrs of those stormy days.

Eusebius reports a development that had apparently accelerated during the period from Aurelian (270-275) to 304, of Christians seizing the outer public sphere, this time in a completely different manner. Until Aurelian, and this is the "media reality" we get from reading the *Ecclesiastical History,* the manifestations of Christianity within the public sphere were in many instances a cause of antagonism and conflict. Christians were trying with all their might to get a foothold in the public sphere by using shocking deeds in the public baths, the market, the arena, and even in the prisons. In the army, too, we find some "loud" Christians. They were the "few" seen by the "many," to use Foucault's formulation. The "many" were impressed. Not only through martyrdom but also through other striking methods, the Christians successfully remained in the public eye. Dionysius's account (to be discussed in Chapter 6) about their behavior during the plague shows how they could shock their heathen neighbors. According to the *Ecclesiastical History* they also managed to show their presence within the outer public sphere by convening their assemblies and synods. Their churches and cemeteries, at that time to be seen in many cities, gradually became prominent symbols of their independent place within the outer public sphere. In many parts of the eastern Empire, their inner public sphere was gradually incorporated within the outer public sphere.[62] Eusebius comments,

> With what favour one might note that the rulers in every church were honoured by all procurators and governors! And how could one fully describe those assemblies thronged with countless men, and the multitudes that gathered together in every city, and the famed concourses in the places of prayer; by reason of which they were no longer satisfied with the buildings of olden time, and would erect from the foundations churches of spacious dimension throughout all the cities? (8.1.5-6)

Even if Eusebius is exaggerating, this is still important corroboration for what we have noted above.

But on the eve of Diocletian's persecution, we hear of an additional revolution that apparently accelerated during the last quarter of the third century. The Christians managed to seize some additional space within the public sphere, the institutional one. They became part of the institutional manifestation of power. Gradually they penetrated the army (hints of which we have already received) and became councilors and important officials in the Roman administration, as well as members of city senates. There were many people of wealth among them. In other words, at the beginning of the fourth century Christians filled many key positions all over the Roman East, a fact corroborated by other evidence.[63] In terms of mis-

---

62. A different phenomenon is the penetration of Christians into the outer and institutional public sphere as "regular" citizens.

63. See Peter Brown, *Power and Persuasion in Late Antiquity: Towards a Christian Empire* (Madison: University of Wisconsin Press, 1992).

sion and media performance, this development was crucial, and the success of the Christians was arguably what brought Constantine to adopt such a positive stance towards them. But first Diocletian's reaction.[64]

Diocletian realized that this unprecedented, successful invasion of the public sphere by Christianity from the market through formal institutions (the three dimensions of the public sphere) constituted a dangerous development. Eusebius in *Hist. Eccl.* 8.1 and elsewhere hints at such an anxiety on the part of the emperor. This is the main reason, to judge from Eusebius's account, that Diocletian embarked on his persecution; otherwise, it is hard to explain why such a moderate emperor (8.12.9) launched such a harsh policy. His successors shared his views concerning the Christians, and according to Lactantius it was Galerius who incited Diocletian in this matter.[65]

As a consequence of the changing circumstances during the first decade of the fourth century, Eusebius employs a different manner of presentation. Books 8–10 have a decidedly different character than the preceding books of the *Ecclesiastical History.* Indeed, Eusebius decided to add these books during the years of persecution, neglecting all the other familiar themes found in the earlier books. The persecution becomes the only significant historical development related in Book 8. "Significance" is a key term we will discuss later. Here it will suffice to say that only if we do not judge Eusebius against the background of the rationalistic historiography of Thucydides, Polybius, Poseidonius, and Josephus, but examine his writing as a completely new genre, can we appreciate how ingenious he really was. Let us look briefly at what he does in Book 8 concerning martyrdom.

The Framework of Eusebius's "News Reporting"

For the first time in the *Ecclesiastical History,* Eusebius clearly blames the persecution on the behavior of the Christians themselves:

> But when, as a result of greater freedom, a change to pride and sloth came over our affairs, we fell to envy and fierce railing against one another, warring upon ourselves . . . until the divine judgement with a

64. For Diocletian's policies in general, see Timothy D. Barnes, *The New Empire of Diocletian and Constantine* (Cambridge, Mass.: Harvard University Press, 1982); and Millar, *Emperor in the Roman World,* passim.
65. Lactantius, *De Mortibus Persecutorum* 10ff.

sparing hand, as is its wont . . . quietly and moderately began to exercise
its oversight, the persecution commencing with the brethren in the
army . . . then indeed, then according to the word spoken by Jeremiah,
the Lord hath darkened the daughter of Zion in his anger. . . . All things
in truth were fulfilled in our day, when we saw with our very eyes the
houses of prayer cast down to their foundations from top to bottom.
(8.1.7–2.2)

This theological statement constrains Eusebius from the outset to compose his account of the persecution within a narrow framework, in contrast to the broader one typical of the earlier books. (This procedure is
typical of media performance today, when a particular ideology would
hamper the presentation of certain issues.) Thus we can explain his extensive account of Galerius's divine punishment in Book 8.[66]

News in Times of Emergency

Whereas Eusebius was dependent on written accounts and a few eyewitness reports for the history recounted in Books 1–7, he was himself an eyewitness to the events of Diocletian's reign recounted in Book 8. He has become a field reporter for some of the incidents, in particular those that
occurred in his own town of Caesarea. This is the substance of the change
we see in the later books. In contrast to his aim in the earlier books, he tries
in Book 8 to be comprehensive in the geography of his history, citing accounts about persecution from many places in the Roman East.[67] But, like
a responsible reporter, he is aware that he cannot cover everything everywhere: "how could one here number the multitude of the martyrs in each
province, and especially of those in Africa and Mauretania, and in Thebais
and Egypt?" (8.6.10). As in previous books, he relates events of the same
sort but always adds new information, employing a principle that we know
from our modern news media. A fine example is the remarkable listing of
tortures that he rehearses in great detail in the various martyrdoms (for
instance, in the letter sent by Phileas of Thmuites to his community,

---

66. This fits Eusebius's theological framework; a similar motivation is at work in
2 Maccabees 9. See Doron Mendels, *Identity, Religion and Historiography: Studies in
Hellenistic History* (Sheffield: Sheffield Academic Press, 1998), Chap. 20.

67. Timothy D. Barnes, *Constantine and Eusebius* (Cambridge, Mass.: Harvard
University Press, 1981), 149ff.

8.10.2-10). We have already seen that there is hardly any repetition in the nature of the torture from one martyr to another. His audience probably loved these descriptions; hence, although he himself says that one example of martyrdom would suffice, he proceeds to offer many examples. Referring to the public martyrdom of a man named Peter, he says, "We shall mention the kind of death that one of them met, and leave our readers to gather from that instance what happened to the others" (8.6.1). In what follows, he describes the "spectacle" *(thea)* of various kinds of martyrs and the different methods of torture they endured in public for long periods of time.

But above all Eusebius knew that relevance and stimulation were necessary to gain and keep the attention of an audience. Otherwise, he could have given a detailed description of the martyrdoms in line with his *Acta.* More than classical and Hellenistic historians, he was aware of his recipients since he was imbued with the concept of mission. He assumed the role not of an objective historian but of a communicator who opts "to serve a particular audience, or some goal of the organization according to personal preference."[68] It bears emphasizing that people in the ancient world read aloud; thus, drama and fresh information were important factors in promoting a written document of any kind.

Eusebius mentions some of his methods in Book 8 when he explains why he is not striving for completeness.[69] Speaking of Diocletian's acts of persecution, he says,

> But as to these, it is not our part to describe their melancholy misfortunes in the issue, even as we do not think it proper to hand down to memory their dissensions and unnatural conduct to one another before the persecution. Therefore we resolved to place on record nothing more about them than what would justify the divine judgement. Accordingly, we determined not even to mention those who have been tried by the persecution, or have made utter shipwreck of their salvation, and of their own free will were plunged in the depth of the billows; but we shall

---

68. McQuail, *Media Performance,* 86.
69. I disagree with Barnes, who maintains, "The eighth book of the *Ecclesiastical History* represents Eusebius' attempt to transform the rewritten *Martyrs of Palestine* into a general account of the persecution. The process of adaptation has produced vagueness, confusion, even outright error" (*Constantine and Eusebius,* 156). These features of Book 8 are intentional; the genre Eusebius adopts requires such chaotic narratives, which caused occasional errors.

add to the general history only such things as may be profitable, first to ourselves, and then to those that come after us. Let us proceed, therefore, from this point to give a summary description of the sacred conflicts of the martyrs of the divine Word. (8.2.2-3; cf. 8.12.11, 8.13.7)

No historian in antiquity declares so frequently as Eusebius what he has chosen not to include. This is another respect in which he operates much like a modern editor, establishing his general framework and purposefully making his selections within that framework. Eusebius's relation to his sources is analogous to that of the "gatekeeper" in modern mass media; he is "continually faced with a set of essentially normative dilemmas"[70] and usually decides in a subjective manner what is relevant and significant for a particular audience rather than for a general one, unfairly suppressing (usually by omission or a negative attitude) other relevant sources that impede his goals. Hence completeness was not Eusebius's concern at all, and a general reader in his time received knowledge of the history of the Church in a partial and unbalanced manner, a "media reality" rather than an actual reality. Modern historians of antiquity cannot learn from Book 8 what the terrible dissensions were that brought about God's wrath on the eve of persecution. Nor are they any better informed about what happened outside the narrow world of persecution (even the familiar themes tackled in Books 1–7 are eliminated, although they did not cease to exist as issues in the Church). The communication of general knowledge, which many modern media people care about, is lacking in this book. Book 8 cannot be considered a coherent historical narrative of the Church in Eusebius's period. It is a selection of episodes in the history of the Church that were significant to the author and his audience.

Was Eusebius really that sloppy (as Timothy D. Barnes says concerning Book 8)?[71] The answer is no. Eusebius's account is comparable to news reports in wartime. Take the American news during Vietnam.[72] In such instances, all other news disappears or becomes marginal. Book 8 thus looks more like a modern media channel during a time of war. In line with Eusebius's brilliant devices in presentation, we can consider Book 8 as part

70. McQuail, *Media Performance*, 83-84. For the history of the term "gatekeeper," see M. Schudson, "The Sociology of News Production Revisited," in *Mass Media and Society*, ed. James Curran and Michael Gurevitch (London: Arnold, 1991), 142-43.

71. Barnes, *Constantine and Eusbeius*, 156-57.

72. See in general Clarence R. Wyatt, *Paper Soldiers: The American Press and the Vietnam War* (New York: Norton, 1993).

and parcel of the new genre he is employing. Book 8 is not a sloppy concoction; it is an intentional presentation for a large audience that was not interested in a long and complicated history like the long one in Eusebius's *Martyrs of Palestine*. The audience was more interested in a lively presentation, not necessarily tediously connected by a monotonous chronological framework.

That the Church was involved in a terrible conflict for a long period explains why Eusebius deliberately eliminated all other news and ignored the concept of time. All other news became irrelevant and unprofitable, for his own day and for the generations to come. In line with V. Held's typology, we may say that other news items did not fit into Eusebius's perception of the "public interest" to which he was extremely sensitive, judging from his polemical writings.[73] Held defines one category of "public interest" (citing Plato, Aristotle, and many others) as "what is most in accordance with the single ordered and consistent scheme of values under which what is valid for one is valid for all." This entails "the assertion of some absolute normative principle, usually deriving from some larger social theory or ideology." Eusebius is guided by an exceptional "preference schedule";[74] he acts in accordance with "certain preferred kinds of information or cultural provision, or condition of access or free operation, etc."[75] He works in the same way in other books as well, but in Book 8 he is even more extreme for the above mentioned reasons. Polybius never worked in such a manner; he understood that for his history to be "profitable," it had to be balanced, complete, and objective. He did not achieve these goals, of course, but he made an incredible effort to do so. Polybius and other historians of his stature took the notion of relevance with a grain of salt. Josephus tells of a situation similar to the pre-Diocletian one on the eve of the Great War (*Ant.* 20.166, 180-181). He declares that God punished the Jewish religious leadership for its internal dissension and hatred, and he writes elaborately about this even though the account was very unpleasant to Jewish ears. He did the same when he recounted events in Jerusalem during the Roman siege in 68-70 C.E. Although Eusebius hints at dissensions in the Church, in contrast to Josephus he does not go

73. McQuail, *Media Performance*, 22-33, citing Virginia Held, *The Public Interest and Individual Interests* (New York: Basic Books, 1970).

74. McQuail, *Media Performance*, 27, 29, citing Barry M. Mitnick, *The Political Economy of Regulation: Creating, Designing, and Removing Regulatory Forms* (New York: Columbia University Press, 1980).

75. McQuail, *Media Performance*, 29.

into the details since they were marginal to his main purpose, that of narrating martyrdom in a fluent and interesting manner.

Perseverance in the Public Sphere

Two kinds of accounts can be discerned in Eusebius's long account of ten years of martyrdom in Book 8. The first appears in his general statements concerning many anonymous martyrs, such as in 8.3.1, where he says that "very many rulers of the churches contended with a stout heart under terrible torments, and displayed spectacles of mighty conflicts" (see also 8.6.9; 8.8; 8.10.12). The second is the description of those martyrs whose names are given. Here we find the more specific stories of distinguished people, some of whom had important positions in public institutions, and other prominent people in the hierarchy of the Church (which had by now become part of the outer public sphere).

Eusebius presents the martyrs of Diocletian, his corulers, and his successors as people who fought to maintain their established place in the outer and institutional public spheres. This is a different presentation from the one adopted in the earlier books. According to the media reality Eusebius presents, the martyrs of Book 8 neither made an attempt to attract public attention (like those in the second century) nor had to fight for a place within the outer and institutional public spheres. They were martyred because they had already established themselves (in some instances very strongly) within the public sphere. In other words, for the martyrs of, say, the second century, the arena was the focal point for the manifestation of their presence in the public sphere. Yet for many of the martyrs of Diocletian's day, the pyre or arena became a battlefield for the preservation of their acquired positions within the institutions of the outer and institutional public spheres. Here it will suffice to note that Diocletian's edicts are presented by Eusebius as an attempt to terminate the hold of Christians within the public sphere (8.2.4-5).[76]

When the elimination of Christians from the army started (apparently before the edict), "a great many soldiers of Christ's kingdom, without hesitation, unquestionably preferred to confess Him than retain the seeming glory and prosperity that they possessed. And already in rare cases one

---

76. Note in particular the proclamation "that those who held high positions would lose all civil rights."

or two of these were receiving not only loss of honour but even death in exchange for their godly steadfastness" (8.4.3-4). At that time there was still a "certain moderation" on behalf of the authorities in purging the army, since it was feared that the multitude of believers was too many and too strong (8.4.4).[77] This means that on the eve of the great persecution there was an awareness, perhaps unjustified, of the place Christians occupied in the various quarters of the public sphere. Perhaps some pagans took the Christian concept of the Logos (that it is everywhere) very seriously. Later, when the supreme commander *(stratopedarchēs)* "prepared himself still further for battle, it is quite impossible to recount the number or the splendour of God's martyrs" (8.4.4, 8.12.1, and elsewhere).

In another section of the public sphere,

> the moment the decree against the churches was published at Nicomedia, a certain person by no means obscure, but most highly honoured as the world counts pre-eminence, moved by zeal toward God and carried away by his burning faith, seized and tore it to pieces, when posted up in an open and public place, as an unholy and profane thing; [and this he did] while two emperors were present in the same city, the senior of them all, and he who held the fourth place in the government after him. But this man was the first of those at that time who thus distinguished himself; and, at the same time, in his endurance of such results as naturally followed a daring act of this kind, he maintained an untroubled and undisturbed demeanour to his very last breath. (8.5.1)

This distinguished hero demonstrated in a symbolic manner that the Christians had become a *fait accompli* within the public sphere (cf. also 8.9.6-7, on Philoromus, "who had been entrusted with an office of no small importance in the imperial administration at Alexandria"; and 8.11.2, on the finance "minister" Adauctus).

Yet another part of the outer public sphere came to the fore when Diocletian became determined to eliminate Christian institutions altogether: "an imperial command went forth that the presidents of the churches everywhere should be thrown into prison and bonds" (8.6.8), that is, should be eliminated without getting a public hearing. Eusebius re-

---

77. On Christians in the imperial army, see J. Helgeland, "Christians and the Roman Army from Marcus Aurelius to Constantine," in *Aufstieg und Niedergang der Römischen Welt,* vol. II.2.23, ed. Hildegard Temporini (Berlin: de Gruyter, 1979), 724-834.

ports that "the spectacle *(hē thea)* of what followed surpasses all descriptions; for in every place a countless number were shut up, and everywhere the prisons, that long ago had been prepared for murderers and graverobbers, were then filled with bishops and presbyters and deacons, readers and exorcists, so that there was no longer room left there for those condemned for wrongdoing" (8.6.9).[78] Other orders followed, to the effect that "those in prison should be allowed to go in liberty if they sacrificed, but if they refused, should be mutilated by countless tortures" (8.6.10). The public sphere was completely cleansed of Christian high officials and magistrates (cf. also other examples, such as Phileas, bishop of the church of the Thmuites in Egypt, who "was a man distinguished for the services he rendered to his country in public positions," 8.9.7; and the summary of the distinguished church people martyred, 8.13). In one instance a whole city was destroyed since all its inhabitants "to a man, the curator himself and the duumvirs with all the officials and the whole assembly, confessed themselves Christians" (8.11.1).

According to Eusebius, when the authorities realized that Christians remained in the public sphere in spite of persecution, they changed their policies; they ceased the mass killings of martyrs, since they probably understood that this method worked against them. Christians did not disappear and in many instances even gained a great deal of publicity through the endurance of the martyrs. Thus, Eusebius says ironically, the rulers became "humane" and "orders were given that their eyes should be gouged out and one of their legs maimed. For this was in their opinion humanity and the highest of punishments inflicted upon us" (8.12.10). In other words, as with the yellow star imposed by the Nazis on Jews, the worst punishment at this juncture was that some Christians were singled out within the public sphere (in which they wanted to participate) and were even sent away to the copper mines, which had the effect of dark cells, far from the public eye (8.12.10).[79]

78. Whenever one, two, or even a dozen Christians were imprisoned, this was still a "hidden" martyrdom, whereas when many were confined (as in Diocletian's persecution), it became a "spectacle" *(hē thea)*.

79. See further my Epilogue below.

Eusebius's Use of Space and Time

In contrast to his former books, Eusebius makes a more serious attempt in Book 8 to give a comprehensive account of the geography of martyrdom. He does not jump from one place to another or omit many places altogether, as he did in Books 1–7, but describes many regions that underwent martyrdom. However, his account still lacks completeness as to the regions and people involved in persecution. Here we should also mention the horizontal criterion of the unbalanced report covering long periods of time. One gets the impression from Eusebius that martyrdom in the fourth century was much more frequent and widespread than in all the former periods of the Church's history. This is of course more of a perceived or media picture of reality than a factual picture, since we know that Eusebius did not include in the *Ecclesiastical History* accounts of martyrs from many regions of the empire in the second and third centuries.

Moreover, although Eusebius knew very well what chronology was about (he himself, as we already mentioned, wrote a *Chronicon*), he here performs very poorly in this respect. In Book 8 he is even more chaotic in terms of chronology than he was in Books 1–7.[80] Moreover, the reader is lost since he is not able to find out (except for the general chronological framework) what happened when, and what periods of time elapsed between one event and another. The reader does not even learn how long a certain event took. For instance, when Eusebius describes terrible methods of torture he says: "and indeed all these things were done, not for a few days or some brief space, but for a long period extending over whole years — sometimes more than ten, at other times above twenty persons being put to death; and at others not less than thirty, now nearer sixty, and again at other times a hundred men would be slain in a single day" (8.9.3). Usually he does not even trouble to make such comments on time. In this respect, Eusebius anticipated the treatment of time in our mass media, where the exact duration of events is rarely conveyed in a complete manner. Taking into account the limited span the media have for their main news, it is obviously impossible to present events in the real time they occurred. There are events that take hours, days, and months, which the media have to deal with in a few minutes, and not necessarily in their linear order of occurrence. Hence in this respect, as in many others, Eusebius ingeniously acts against the annalistic tradition and

---

80. See Barnes, *Constantine and Eusebius,* esp. 149ff.; Richard Laqueur, *Eusebius als Historiker seiner Zeit* (Berlin and Leipzig: de Gruyter, 1929), Chap. 2.

the classical and Hellenistic Greek historians who handled the framework of time somewhat more carefully. Eusebius's method of presentation becomes even clearer when compared with Lactantius's account of the circumstances that brought about the persecution under Diocletian.[81]

Conclusion

Eusebius is not a historian in the tradition of Thucydides and Polybius. The *Ecclesiastical History* was written by Eusebius as it stands now intentionally, since he had enough sources (which he already used in the *Martyrs of Palestine*) and had many opportunities to edit his work if he really wished to do so. He created his own genre in the role of editor and reporter. As an editor, he deemed it necessary to report the significant and relevant, rather than to write an exact and comprehensive history of the specific theme he chose to relate. He excluded from his account much more material than was commonly done among historians in antiquity. This new genre, so different from the historical writing of Ephorus, Polybius, Josephus, and Plutarch,[82] also dictated different criteria of composition. We have seen that Eusebius offers only a limited diversity; his accounts do not yield a true and complete picture of the society in which the events happened. For instance, one gets a glimpse of the populace and aristocracy as well as the position of the authorities on certain issues at certain junctures, but all this is rather poorly presented in other periods. His accounts of martyrs lack proportionality and fail to give a diversified picture even of the Christian society (for instance, he refuses to deal with heretical martyrs.)[83] We have also seen that geographical diversity can hardly be found in the *Ecclesiastical History,* and geography is thus presented in an unbalanced manner. By and large, Eusebius lacks diversity in the sense of writing a "national" comprehensive report of the rise of Christianity.[84]

81. Lactantius, *De Mortibus Persecutorum* 7-13.

82. And also from Eusebius's own *Demonstratio Evangelica* and *Vita Constantini.* On the latter, see Averil Cameron, "Eusebius' *Vita Constantini* and the Construction of Constantine," in *Portraits: Biographical Representations in the Greek and Latin Literature of the Roman Empire,* ed. M. J. Edwards and Simon Swain (Oxford: Clarendon: 1997), 145-75.

83. On the *Ecclesiastical History* as a history of Christian orthodoxy, see Glenn F. Chesnut, *The First Christian Histories: Eusebius, Socrates, Sozomen, Theodoret, and Evagrius,* 2d ed. (Macon, Ga.: Mercer University Press, 1986), 127ff.

84. In line with McQuail, *Media Performance,* 151-52.

In Eusebius's history, the world as he reflects it is distorted, but less so in particular themes such as martyrdom and heresy. In line with the conclusions reached by McQuail,[85] we can say that Book 8, much more than Books 1–7, gives the impression that the whole world was full of martyrs and persecutions. Eusebius himself alludes to the fact that this is a distorted picture (cf. 8.12.9, where he admits that under Diocletian the "government was well-disposed and mild towards all"). Here we may adapt one of McQuail's conclusions and apply it to Eusebius's historiography. He says that "the media world-map places the rich industrialized nations disproportionately at the centre of attention and bears little relation to relative population size or land area."[86] In his map of early Christianity, Eusebius similarly places Christian martyrdom disproportionately at the center.

We have also seen that Eusebius does not care for the concept of time; he indicates duration only by external events such as the reigns of emperors or bishops. He is selective both in the nature of the sources he uses and in the information he decides to choose from his many available sources. Moreover, he is extremely selective in the events he chooses to relate. Eusebius's account lacks balance in the presentation of history; he establishes his priorities of "news" selection very carefully. He omits material freely, which results in enormous gaps in his presentation of the history of the Church itself. His language is not neutral. He works within wide frames of reference (8.1-2; 8.7.2, sin-punishment-repentance scheme), but when it suits his purposes, he employs narrow ones. Eusebius's narratives are skewed by his dramas and constructed stories. His history of martyrdom is replete with all kinds of biases, both hidden and revealed. Factualness, accuracy, and completeness are not his strongest points as editor and reporter, although a good "media reality" emerges from his accounts. Relevance, on the other hand, plays an extremely important role in his judgement. For readability, he deserves a high score. He is extremely sensational; social order and control of society are among his great concerns, especially when applicable to the Christian communities.

Eusebius's attitude toward pagan society is reminiscent of the posture of the typical, critical modern journalist toward the society at large. Indeed, he promotes "innovation and change" and wishes to reflect the shifts of social norms and values of Christianity within the general society.

85. Ibid., 167.
86. Ibid.

He also acts as a "free" media man,[87] adopting a critical attitude toward the authorities. He likes to write about famous people and outstanding events. He does not seem to have a great respect for objectivity, being more than happy to relate a story with great moralistic value instead of collecting accurate historical data (cf., e.g., 8.7.4-6; 8.9.5-7).

When all of this is taken into consideration, martyrdom as presented in Eusebius's *Ecclesiastical History* turns out to be a concoction of factual reality and perceived (media) reality within a theological framework. Eusebius wrote a "media history," which is to say that he had a keen awareness that his presentation was itself a media channel. He depicts martyrdom as playing a crucial role in the media revolution of early Christianity. Both Eusebius and the Catholic Church were great believers in the spectacle of martyrdom as an effective source of information to audiences of various strata of society. And martyrdom itself had a cumulative effect as a message transmitted over a long period of time. It is unfortunate that we cannot measure its effects on the attitudes of audiences towards Christianity.

87. Ibid., 240.

CHAPTER 4

Orthodoxy and Heresy: Competing Media Channels

I n Books 1–6 of the *Ecclesiatical History,* Eusebius treats a variety of "heresies" as media channels useful for promoting Christian "orthodoxy" in the outer public sphere. In a situation in which many religions were competing in the marketplace, and individuals could make a choice,[1] Christian media channels became necessary and effective devices for transmitting the Christian message. Eusebius viewed the orthodox opposition to heresy as a battle for the inner and outer public spheres.[2] His anger against heretics is

1. See Peter L. Berger, *The Social Reality of Religion* (London: Faber, 1969); J. North, "The Development of Religious Pluralism," in *The Jews among Pagans and Christians in the Roman Empire,* ed. Judith Lieu, John North, and Tessa Rajak (London: Routledge, 1992), 174-93.

2. *Orthodox* ("right") in Eusebius has a basic meaning, usefully defined by Bart D. Ehrman, *The Orthodox Corruption of Scripture: The Effect of Early Christological Controversies on the Text of the New Testament* (New York: Oxford University Press, 1993), 5: "it is that kind of belief preached by the apostles and their followers from the beginning, as opposed to major deviations that came subsequent to it, deviations that deny such indispensable Christian doctrines as the goodness of the creation, or the deity of Christ, or the unity of the Godhead. Heresies, then, are secondary incursions into the community of true believers, inspired — as is all evil for Eusebius — by the devil and his wicked demons, who move willful persons to corrupt the faith proclaimed by the apostles of Jesus." See also H. E. W. Turner, *The Pattern of Christian Truth: A Study in the Relations between Orthodoxy and Heresy in the Early Church* (London: Mowbray, 1954), 3-35; and Alain Le Boulluec, *La notion d'hérésie dans la littérature grecque IIe-IIIe Siècle,* vol. 1 (Paris: Études augustiniennes, 1985), 36-91.

not to be explained only on grounds of theological deviation (which gets little attention in the *Ecclesiastical History*). Rather, it was the considerable success of some heresies in penetrating the inner and outer public spheres, and their perseverance for decades and even centuries, that aroused his fulminations. In some quarters, heresies managed to reach many more segments of the population than orthodoxy could, or ever did, at any time.[3] Since heresies created new ideas and rhetoric in order to "market" their views better, and since Eusebius was convinced that everyone in the outer public sphere was potentially receptive to the Christian mission, his methods of presentation were designed to show that aggressive opposition to heretics could be employed as a media asset by the orthodox Church itself. Taken together with the other media channels discussed in this book, there is no doubt that the dynamic encounter between orthodoxy and heresy became part of a "media campaign" that in Eusebius's view had an impact in the public spheres. We may assume that much of what he expresses concerning heretics reflects a media competition that occurred in reality.

Heresy as a Media Asset

Already in his introduction, in Book 1, Eusebius uses a device found in our modern media, namely, making an opening negative statement about an opponent. He declares that among his other themes he will relate

> the number of those who were distinguished in her government [of the Church] and leadership in the provinces of greatest fame; the number of those who in each generation were the ambassadors of the word of God

---

3. There is a vast literature on heresy in early Christianity, and I will mention only some necessary works. A good discussion can be found in the two volumes of Alain Le Boulluec, *La notion d'hérésie* (with older bibliography). The classic study of Walter Bauer, *Rechtgläubigkeit und Ketzerei im ältesten Christentum* (Tübingen: Mohr Siebeck, 1934), is available in an English edition: *Orthodxy and Heresy in Earliest Christianity*, ed. Robert Kraft and Gerhard Krodel (Philadelphia: Fortress, 1971). See also Gérard Vallée, *A Study in Anti-Gnostic Polemics: Irenaeus, Hippolytus, and Epiphanius* (Waterloo, Ont.: Wilfrid Laurier University Press, 1981); Gerd Lüdemann, *Heretics: The Other Side of Early Christianity*, trans. John Bowden (Louisville: Westminster John Knox, 1996); Ehrman, *Orthodox Corruption of Scripture;* Birger A. Pearson, "Eusebius and Gnosticism," in *Eusebius, Christianity and Judaism,* ed. Harold W. Attridge and Gohei Hata (Detroit: Wayne State University Press, 1992), 291-310; and Robert M. Grant, *Eusebius as Church Historian* (Oxford: Clarendon, 1980), Chap. 8.

either by speech or pen; the names, the number and the age of those who, driven by the desire of innovation *(neōteropoiias)* to an extremity of error, have heralded themselves as the introducers of knowledge, falsely so-called, ravaging the flock of Christ unsparingly, like grim wolves. (1.1.1)

These are harsh words. But, as we will see, this sort of language actually transforms the opponent into a propagandistic asset. In our own mass media, many opponents, either minorities or dissenting factions within the same group, get labeled "terrorists," "bandits," "savages," or "murderers." For more than twenty years the PLO was considered by Israel and many countries in the West a terrorist organization, an attitude expressed in harsh verbal terms. However, since the Oslo Peace Accord most of the pejorative words have disappeared, and various positive ones are used instead, both within and without Israel.[4] The same can be said about the rhetoric used by West Germans to denote Easterners before unification. After the collapse of the Berlin Wall, the pejorative vocabulary went out of fashion, and the language used on both sides became more favorable.[5] Negative terms are selected from a well-designed arsenal, and the rhetoric is shaped in accordance with the social and moral values of the user.[6] It has been shown by modern media scholars that terminology is selected by the mass media in line with what the dominant institution and its audience perceive as the correct social order.[7] Hence every minority that differs even slightly from the majority group (or that seems to) is perceived as a threat to the correct social order. It should be remembered that orthodox Catholicism regarded heretics as outcast minorities, even though in certain regions heretics were in reality the majority.[8]

Eusebius chose to present his highly selective material concerning heresy within a communication framework *(schēma)*. He, and some of

4. On the Oslo peace accord, see *Newsweek*, International Edition, 13 September 1993, 7-15; 20 September 1993, 7-15; 27 September 1993, 9-17.

5. Ernst Schürer, Manfred Keune, and Philip Jenkins, eds., *The Berlin Wall: Representations and Perspectives* (New York: Lang, 1996).

6. On epideictic rhetoric, see D. L. Sullivan, "Establishing Orthodoxy: The Letters of Ignatius of Antioch as Epideictic Rhetoric," *The Journal of Communication and Religion* 15, no. 2 (1992): 71-86.

7. Denis McQuail, *Media Performance: Mass Communication and the Public Interest* (London: Sage Publications, 1992), 66-80.

8. This is one of the main theses of Bauer, *Orthodoxy and Heresy.*

his predecessors, designed this schema in order to express the "right values" of institutional orthodoxy, and to transmit them in clear terms to their audiences. This framework of communication used a great number of terms that referred to the "right" values in Greek political language at that period, such as *eirēnē* ("peace"), *koinōnia* ("fellowship"), *doxa* ("honor, glory"), and *alētheia* ("truth"). It was not accidental that universal terms denoting the values of pagan society were used rather than distinctly Christian ones. An antithetical vocabulary was also created in order to denote the bad guys, the opponents, such as *neōterizontes* ("innovators, revolutionaries"), *polemioi* ("warmongers"), and so forth. Media agents in antiquity used such methods before Eusebius.[9] But here we have a clear case of a historian who represents the views of a strong, effective, and worldwide organization that works with a charter. In other words, it is highly probable that what Eusebius says about heretics represents the kind of terminology communicated by the orthodox Catholic Church and transmitted to a body of "users" through a strong and well-articulated network.[10]

How would Eusebius's invective against heretics have struck an ancient audience? Let us go back to the introductory paragraph quoted above. Eusebius presents (or rather misrepresents) the orthodox Church's opponents as revolutionaries who are error incarnate and who spread false knowledge that ravages the flock like grim wolves. This, of course, is antithetical to the "ambassadors" of God, who are all positive. But how can such language promote orthodoxy? The answer is complex. For now I will note only that Eusebius depicts heresy not merely as trouble from within (like a Greek *stasis*, "revolution") but also as opposition from *outside* the legitimate order. Of course, media performance itself involves the spread of knowledge, and Eusebius acknowledges that the heretics spread knowledge in ways similar to those of the orthodox Church, by "speech or pen."

When pejorative terminology is repeated over and over again, and

9. Polybius and the Aetolians would be examples; see Doron Mendels, *Identity, Religion and Historiography: Studies in Hellenistic History* (Sheffield: Sheffield Academic Press, 1998), Chap. 3. Pejorative language abounds in the Qumran literature (e.g., in the *Damascus Covenant*), where at times the rhetoric aimed at rival Jewish groups is harsher than the anti-Jewish polemics of the New Testament.

10. When a modern ultra-Orthodox rabbi uses derogatory language against Reform or Conservative Jews, it is quite likely that the same language is used by his community.

the opponent is excluded by rhetorical means from the "right" *(orthos)* way, the latter's image is strengthened and its identity enhanced.[11] The heretic, if his group perseveres, can similarly define himself better by using the same media methods (like the Orthodox, Reform and Conservative movements in modern Judaism).[12] The emphasis on the opponent makes orthodoxy stronger by definition, because it helps to reshape the opinions of the reader or listener about what the right order should be: the Aetolians are "ungodly" *(asebeis),* so the Achaeans are automatically "godly" *(eusebeis);* ultra-Orthodox Jews are "parasites," so their opponents among secular Jews are "good citizens." By employing such methods, Eusebius excludes heretics altogether from the right and just way and thereby illuminates the right order of things.

Other devices reflect the "media revolution" of Eusebius himself. For instance, he never goes into detail when he has to relate the nature of a heresy.[13] This is not a problem of availability of sources, or of any inability on his part to describe those details. On the contrary, it is a strategy designed to communicate only the necessary information concerning heretics. Eusebius selects only issues that are sensational, interesting, and amazing, or those that might be of special interest to his pagan audience in terms of their social codes. Like a modern reporter, Eusebius is concise, brief, and abrupt in his entries concerning heresies, so that the modern historian receives but superficial and scanty information about them. But this method served his "media performance" purposes. In short, Eusebius's presentation of heresy represents a media strategy in which the heretics grant orthodoxy its legitimacy to survive and fight the unlawful, the other, the stranger.

These assumptions are supported by research on racism and the press conducted in the Netherlands by Teun van Dijk.[14] Since his conclusions are helpful for our research, I will present them at some length in his

---

11. This has been shown by sociologists dealing with modern history. See in general L. R. Kurtz, "The Politics of Heresy," *American Journal of Sociology* 88 (1983): 1085-1115.

12. Note, for example, the struggle for identity in the reform synagogue; see Frida Kerner Furman, *Beyond Yiddishkeit: The Struggle for Jewish Identity in a Reform Synagogue* (Albany: State University of New York Press, 1987).

13. On Eusebius's treatment of heresy and heretics, see Grant, *Eusebius as Church Historian,* Chap. 8.

14. Teun A. van Dijk, *News Analysis: Case Studies of International and National News in the Press* (Hillsdale, N.J. and London: Erlbaum, 1988), 135-213.

own words.[15] His study of minority groups in Holland (compared with other European countries) shows that:

> The attention for ethnic groups in the media is very limited, unless minority groups are associated with violence, illegality, crime, or strange cultural behavior, that is, with deviance of many kinds. . . . The causes or the context of such problems are seldom analysed in the press and hardly ever explained in terms of white racism.
>
> News values (e.g., negativity) and ethnic prejudices of editors and reporters provide a framework in which ethnic groups and the whole ethnic situation are perceived and represented in a biased way . . . as a permanent threat — as a conflict between us and them, between those who want to get in and do not belong here and those of us who belong here . . . such prejudices, which are also shared by large segments of the media public, favor attention for, and memory and selection of, those stories that are consistent with such opinions . . . the authorities and especially the national or local government . . . do have preferential access to the media because of their elite status, power, high credibility. . . . Thus their versions of the facts will get routine attention, and they are represented as neutral or positive actors, so that, by contrast, more negative images about minorities will result.
>
> Journalists contribute to the autonomous production of racism at least as much as they participate in its reproduction. Their news values, as well as their goal of ensuring or boosting sales, require dramatization and hence negative portrayel of nonelite, ethnically different outgroups in terms of conflicts and deviance . . . the *way* the authorities or other elites are represented and evaluated, e.g., as active, firm, arbitrating, and neutral (or positive), is not part of the social facts but rather part of the media production of a consensual definition of societal structure. The same is true of ignoring or denying the many other dimensions of the ethnic situation.
>
> Analysis of much everyday talk indicates that many people are not only increasingly afraid of crime and violence but explicitly associate this with minority-group members. . . . The media not only play an active role in the production of negative ethnic attitudes, but in our present society this role is vital. They autonomously and persuasively reproduce the ethnic attitudes of a power elite and produce the discursive and communicative conditions and, hence, the cognitive and societal condi-

15. Ibid., 208-23.

tions of the reproduction of racism . . . racism [is] a structural, societal framework that enables and reproduces dominant group power.

Now we may ask whether we can apply these results to our study of Eusebius and heresy. First, we should recall that van Dijk's conclusions were published in 1988 and refer to the seventies and eighties. But this should not deter us from using them, since his study describes a situation reflecting a reality taken from our recent history. Second, we need not apply all that van Dijk and others say to the phenomenon of ancient heresy, but only what is helpful in our case. I should also point out that when I use the term "minority" for a heresy, I use it in Eusebius's sense, and not as an objective term (Walter Bauer has argued that in certain instances the heretical minority was in reality the majority).[16]

Minorities and heresies are comparable in many respects: (1) In both cases we have a group that plays the role of an elite majority (social elite, orthodoxy) with the means and power to "design" and "construct" its minorities. (2) In both instances the group that represents the "right order" uses negativity to denote the minority; hence, it selects whatever sources, stories, and language it wishes to describe and "construct" the minority group. (3) The minority group is presented in such a way as to show how right, positive, and moral the holder of power really is. (4) In both cases the dominant group holds the communication mechanisms with which it creates the distorted picture of other minority groups. A network that can manifest without interruption the powerful side can be found in both cases. (5) The struggle of the elite group against the minority is pursued in order to legitimize its identity within the public sphere.

Although Eusebius presents heresies and heretics in line with attitudes formulated already by Catholic Christianity,[17] I would like to focus on the medium rather than the reality. Eusebius shaped the picture of orthodoxy in its values and societal organization by "constructing" the image of the heresies in a certain manner. Let us look at some examples.

---

16. Bauer, *Orthodoxy and Heresy;* and see Ehrman, *Orthodox Corruption of Scripture,* 7-9, for Bauer and his critics. On p. 7 Ehrman notes correctly that "Bauer does not assume that orthodoxy refers to 'right beliefs' and heresy to 'willful misbelief.' He uses the terms descriptively to refer to social groups, namely, the party that eventually established dominance over the rest of Christendom (orthodoxy) and the individuals and groups that expressed alternative theological views (heresies)."

17. Ehrman, *Orthodox Corruption of Scripture,* 5-7.

Simon Magus

First, the case of Simon Magus (2.13.1–2.15.1).[18] Eusebius says that "seeing that the faith in our Saviour and Lord Jesus Christ was already being given to all men, the enemy of men's salvation planned to capture the capital in advance, and sent there Simon . . . and by aiding the fellow's tricky sorcery won over to error many of the inhabitants of Rome" (2.13.1). Then he adduces a source (Justin's *Apology* to the emperor Antoninus) to confirm his statement but selects from it only a small piece of derogatory rhetoric.[19] Simon, in line with John 4, is depicted by Justin as a Samaritan who "worked miracles by magic through the art of the demons possessing him; he was reckoned as a god in Rome, your capital city, and honoured as a god among you. . . . Irenaeus agrees with him [Justin] in the first book against heresies where he collects the stories about Simon and his unholy foul teaching" (2.13.3-5). Eusebius adds that he will not relate more of the "false doctrinal principles" of Simon since they can be found in Irenaeus. He works here like a reporter who quotes his sources but does not want to cite them in full because his audience will become impatient and perhaps learn some "positive" lessons about the heresy, a prospect that he wishes to prevent. Moreover, some of the stories that Eusebius so carefully selects were no doubt already circulating within the communities:

> We have received the tradition that Simon was the first author of all heresy. From him, and down to the present time, those who have followed, feigning the Christian philosophy, with its sobriety and universal fame for purity of life, have in no way improved on the idolatrous superstition from which they thought to be set free, for they prostrate themselves before the pictures and images of Simon himself and Helena . . . and undertake to worship them with incense and sacrifices and libations. (2.13.5-6)

Three points should be made. First, Eusebius mentions stories and a tradition concerning the heresy, and the "universal fame" of Christian philosophy, that these heretics feigned to adopt. He actually formulates a well-

---

18. Stories relating to Simon are also found in the Pseudo-Clementines, especially in the Clement Romance, for which see Wilhelm Schneemelcher, ed., *New Testament Apocrypha*, vol. 2, *Writings Relating to the Apostles, Apocalypses, and Related Subjects*, English trans. ed. R. McL. Wilson (Louisville: Westminster John Knox, 1992), 504-30. For Simon Magus in general, see Irenaeus, *Adversus Haereses* 1.23.

19. For Justin and Simon, see Le Boulluec, *La notion d'hérésie*, 1:79ff.

known image of Simon Magus that was prevalent among orthodox Christians. Second, Eusebius uses negative language of the most dreadful kind to describe Simon and his heresy:

> Their more secret rites, at which they say that he who first hears them will be astonished, and according to a scripture current among them will be 'thrown into marvel,' truly are full of marvel and frenzy and madness; for they are of such a kind that they not merely cannot be related in writing, but are so full of baseness and unspeakable conduct that they cannot even be mentioned by the lips of decent men. For whatever foulness might be conceived beyond all that is base, it is surpassed by the utter foulness of the heresy of these men. (2.13.6-7)

He finishes by saying that "of such evil was Simon the father and fabricator, and the Evil Power, which hates that which is good and plots against the salvation of men, raised him up at that time as a great antagonist for the great and inspired Apostles of our Savior" (2.14.1). Third, Eusebius believes that Simon took over segments of the outer public space (at the expense of orthodoxy): "Simon captured the capital in advance"; he "won over to error many of the inhabitants of Rome" and was "honoured as God in Rome"; his adherents "prostrate themselves before pictures and images of Simon himself and Helena."

From this description it is almost impossible to get any "objective" impression of Simon and his ideas. It is distorted in every conceivable way and resembles an article in a tabloid newspaper rather than the account of a serious historian. Polybius, by contrast, though he denigrates the Aetolians, tells their history in a more or less accurate manner.[20] But Eusebius is not interested in history as Polybius and Thucydides were; he is rather interested in showing the purity and correctness of the orthodox Church, and the wrongness of its opponents. Hence his onesidedness is intentional. He works within a "schema," to use van Dijk's word. First, he chooses the most negative language available to denote social disorder and base morality. Second, he makes a selection of themes, some of which he apparently found in his sources (traditions, stories, the writings of heretics), and some of which he may have invented himself in order to portray

---

20. See Mendels, *Identity, Religion and Historiography,* Chap. 3. For an enormous bibliography on the methods used by tabloid newspapers, see Gerald S. Greenberg, *Tabloid Journalism: An Annotated Bibliography of English-Language Sources* (Westport, Conn.: Greenwood Press, 1996).

the heresy at its ugliest. In line with van Dijk's conclusions, we can say that Eusebius was motivated by negativity and thus painted a completely un-balanced picture of the heretics. Third, he supports his evidence by re-spectable written sources from the past (Justin and Irenaeus), which show how trustworthy he is, but selects from them only the passages most con-ducive to attacking his adversary and attracting his audience.[21] In the spirit of van Dijk's results, Eusebius works as a "racist" journalist. How-ever, a great difference between him and a modern reporter (or journalist) would be that Eusebius did not reach the masses very quickly, if at all. Still, his intentions remain crucial: he thought that every individual "out there" was a potential reader of his *Ecclesiastical History* and that his missionary efforts therefore had the prospect of being effective.

But how can this derogatory description be considered a media asset from Eusebius's point of view? A historian who looks for hard "facts" in the presentation of Simon Magus will find that it is skewed and worthless. The "truth" about many aspects of Simon's doings in Rome will hardly be re-vealed. We are probably dealing with a "media reality," a mixture of factual reality and perceived reality. Such a reality is extremely partial in its duration (timeliness), diversity, statistical accuracy, and comprehensiveness. In this respect Eusebius is far from "objective." By his methods of presentation, he is the one who helps to shape the "common opinion" about false, bad, evil, and base heretics as opposed to orthodox Christians, who act truthfully and are both good and right in their behavior. Here Eusebius still speaks in general terms, positive and negative, black and white, and relates many details that do not cohere to form a "history" of this particular heresy. The details he ad-duces are just bits of information put together as in a modern newpaper. But this picture of the heretic highlights and shapes opinion concerning the true orthodox religion without always mentioning it explicitly.

As a good reporter, Eusebius starts with a positive statement promot-ing orthodoxy: "Seeing that the faith in our Saviour and Lord Jesus Christ was already being given to all men, the enemy of men's salvation . . ." (using "enemy," *polemios,* which for many people makes sense in their daily life). At the end of his depiction of Simon, he says,

> Nevertheless the grace of God which is from heaven helped its ministers and quickly extinguished the flames of Evil. . . . Wherefore no conspir-

---

21. For this reason, I am not so sure that Eusebius never read "a single piece of Gnostic literature," as Pearson, "Eusebius and Gnosticism," 304 maintains.

acy, either of Simon, or of any other of those who arose at that time, succeeded in those Apostolic days; for the light of the truth and the divine Logos himself, which had shone from God upon men by growing up on the earth and dwelling among his own Apostles, was overcoming all things in the might of victory . . . the Apostle Peter . . . came to the city of the Romans . . . [bearing] the costly merchandise of the spiritual light from the east . . . preaching the Gospel of the light itself and the word which saves souls . . . Thus when the divine word made its home among them [in Rome] the power of Simon was extinguished and perished immediately, together with the fellow himself. (2.14.2–2.15.1)

In contrast to Simon, who escaped to the capital (Rome) before Peter and was error incarnate, Peter "conquers" it as a spiritual light and a saver of souls.[22] Eusebius masterfully pits the representative of the "right" values, Peter, against the advocate of the "wrong" ones, Simon. Although from the account it is clear that Simon achieved considerable success in Rome, Peter is depicted as the real winner. Eusebius uses imagery associated with divinity, army, commerce, and publicity, which together constitute the power bases of ancient society. Further, he does not specify what deeds Peter actually performed in Rome to spread the faith; he simply presents him in a favorable light as one who easily enters the outer public sphere. From a historian's point of view, this description is useless, but from a media standpoint it is ingenious. Eusebius leaves serious history to one side and labors to create an image of orthodoxy as a powerful and influential entity. He juxtaposes the bright light of orthodoxy with the dark side of heresy. His heretic is a peripheral entity.

What Eusebius adds concerning the "hearers" of Peter is also interesting. He says that they "were not satisfied with a single hearing or with the unwritten teaching of the divine proclamation"; thus they asked Mark to write down Peter's words in order "to leave them a written statement of the teaching given them verbally" (2.15.1). Although Eusebius declares that all people have already received the faith of Jesus (2.13.1), he understands that the promotion of Christianity can be achieved not only by oral preaching and teaching but by the massive publication of Christian works.

22. For the details of the text, see H. J. Lawlor and J. E. L. Oulton, *Eusebius, Bishop of Caesarea: The Ecclesiastical History and the Martyrs of Palestine*, 2 vols. (London: SPCK, 1927-28), *ad loc.*

Menander

In Book 3 Eusebius relates the following: "Let us now continue the narrative *(historia)*. Menander succeeded Simon Magus and showed himself as a weapon of the devil's power not inferior to his predecessor" (3.26.1).[23] Here we should note that the account of Menander is interwoven among other subjects that Eusebius has tackled after his report on Simon Magus. As in our modern media, where the news deals with many issues and abruptly switches from one subject to another, Eusebius abruptly turns again to heresy. This is not because he did not edit his history but is rather a result of his technique of reporting the "main" news. In this aspect, too, he differs from the rationalistic classical and Hellenistic historians. If one takes Thucydides, Xenophon, Polybius, and Cassius Dio as models of historiography in antiquity, it is clear that they wrote linear history and that their respective histories were comprehensive and coherent. Standing at the very beginning of historiography, Herodotus made many digressions but still presented a linear history. "Creative historiography" in the Hellenistic period was inventive and chaotic. Livy wrote an annalistic account and so did many others. Not so Eusebius; he jumps from one subject to another, subjects that he announced in the *prooemium* in Book 1 of his *Ecclesiastical History*. From the outset he employs a strategy of tackling his subjects independently of each other and then interweaving them. This is well planned but not always successfully executed. Eusebius was aware of the historiography of his predecessors but still chose to write differently. Hence his abrupt moves from one topic to another, as in modern journalism, are intentional. This is what has led modern scholarship to criticize him as being careless and sloppy.

In Menander's case we again encounter harsh negative language. We should examine what emotions this language evokes and how it is made an asset for strengthening orthodoxy. According to Eusebius, Menander was a Samaritan who "progressed to the highest point of sorcery not less than his master [Simon], and abounded in great wonders" (3.26.1). Eusebius emphasizes that Menander convinced his followers that they were "no longer mortal but . . . destined to everlasting and ageless immortality" (3.26.2). He convinced them by means of magic and sorcery. Like a modern journalist, and in contrast to the methods commonly employed by Greek historiography, Eusebius mentions his sources by name, Justin and

23. For Menander, see Le Boulluec, *La notion d'hérésie*, 1:80ff.

Irenaeus. He does not like Menander, but since this heretic was just an epigone of the originator of the heresy, Simon, Menander gets a somewhat better "press" than his teacher. However, in conclusion Eusebius says abruptly: "It was assuredly at the instigation of the devil that the name of Christians was adopted by such sorcerers to calumniate by magic the great mystery of religion and through them to destroy the teaching of the Church on the immortality of the soul and the resurrection of the dead" (3.26.4).

Before moving on, we should pay attention to another media device. Eusebius usually adduces only short entries on heretics and their heresy. Such a device would be the exception in Greek historiography. With Eusebius it became the cardinal mode of writing history. One may assume that the audience he had in mind dictated this kind of strategy. Eusebius was well aware that his audience was interested in the "main news"; they wanted only limited information, not comprehensive or complicated accounts, and they had little use for theological speculation. Thus we do not find in Books 1–7 the very elaborate accounts of historical processes that we find in Polybius (or in sections of Diodorus Siculus and Dionysius of Halicarnassus). Eusebius was quite capable of producing elaborate theological compositions, as we know from his *Demonstratio Evangelica* and *Praeparatio Evangelica;* he also wrote an excellent historical biography in the form of the *Vita Constantini* as well as a *Chronicle.* But in his *Ecclesiastical History* he deviates from strict historical writing and invents his own genre: relatively short entries interwoven within a broader *schēma.* The abrupt moves, the small pieces of information, and the dissociation from long and complicated theological accounts all seem to be aimed at an unsophisticated audience. Eusebius is one of the fathers of the journalistic genre.

The Ebionites

Another group of heretics that Eusebius mentions are the Ebionites. They believed that Jesus was an ordinary man "who had achieved righteousness merely by the progress of his character and had been born naturally from Mary and her husband" (3.27.2). Moreover, "they insisted on the complete observance of the Law, and did not think that they would be saved by faith in Christ alone and by a life in accordance with it." Yet another heresy, also called Ebionite, "escaped the absurd folly of the first mentioned, and did

123

not deny that the Lord was born of a Virgin and the Holy Spirit, but never-theless agreed with them in not confessing his pre-existence as God, being the Logos and Wisdom" (3.27.3).[24] Eusebius adds that this second group "shared in the impiety of the former class, especially in that they were equally zealous to insist on the literal observance of the Law." He also says that they rejected the writings of Paul, made use of the *Gospel according to the Hebrews*, "and made little account of the rest." Like the other Ebionites, they observed the Sabbath "and the rest of Jewish ceremonial, but on Sundays celebrated rites like ours in commemoration of the Sav-iour's resurrection." He adds that the name Ebionites denotes "the pov-erty of their intellignece" (3.27.5-6).

The Ebionites receive a somewhat better press than the sorcerers Si-mon and Menander. The reason is threefold. First, they were not seen by Eusebius as a "pagan" heresy; they were less syncretistic.[25] Secondly, Eusebius did not see them as a threatening competition in the outer public sphere, like Simon Magus and the Montanists. Third, their view of Jesus was perhaps close to the Christology that he himself held on the eve of the council of Nicaea.[26]

Cerinthus, Papias, and the Nicolaitans

This brings us to the colorful heretic, Cerinthus.[27] He believed that the kingdom of Christ would be on earth "and that humanity living in Jerusa-lem will again be the slave of lust and pleasure." He is depicted by Eusebius as an "enemy of the scriptures of God" with a "desire to deceive" (3.28.2). He adds that Cerinthus "wished to attach a name worthy of credit to his own invention . . . and being fond of his body and very carnal he dreamt of a future according to his own desires, given up to the indulgence of the flesh, that is, eating and drinking and marrying, and to those things which

---

24. For the "two classes" (rather than two sects) of Ebionites, see Lawlor and Oulton, *Eusebius*, 2:97-98; and A. F. J. Klijn and G. J. Reinink, *Patristic Evidence for Jew-ish-Christian Sects* (Leiden: Brill, 1973), 19-43.

25. For syncretism in heresies, see in general Le Boulluec, *La notion d'hérésie*.

26. In recent scholarship there is a debate whether he was close to Arianism; cf. J. Rebecca Lyman, *Christology and Cosmology: Models of Divine Activity in Origen, Eusebius, and Athanasius* (Oxford: Clarendon, 1993), 85-86.

27. For Cerinthus, see Klijn and Reinink, *Patristic Evidence for Jewish-Christian Sects*, 3-19.

seem a euphemism for these things, feasts and sacrifices and the slaughter of victims" (quoting from Dionysius of Alexandria, 3.28.4-5). Like a good media person, Eusebius proceeds to relate a story, apparently apocryphal, about Cerinthus and John the Apostle (Polybius used such stories very rarely and with caution).[28] John entered a bath where Cerinthus was bathing and fled when he discovered that "Cerinthus, the enemy of the truth is within" (3.28.6). This story is quoted by Eusebius from a very important source, Irenaeus's *Against Heresies*.

Later in Book 3, Eusebius discusses Papias, who "says that there will be a millennium after the resurrection of the dead, when the kingdom of Christ will be set up in material form on this earth" (3.39.12). Eusebius comments: "I suppose that he [Papias] got these notions by a perverse reading of the apostolic accounts, not realizing that they had spoken mystically and symbolically" (3.39.12). And now comes the personal denigration: "For he was a man of very little intelligence, as is clear from his books. But he is responsible for the fact that so many Christian authors after him held the same opinion, relying on his antiquity, for instance Irenaeus and whoever else appears to have held the same views" (3.39.13). Eusebius here refutes, or attempts to refute, another false idea that could harm the Christian mission among the pagans. But, as in his account of other heresies, Eusebius masterfully presents the "main news," selecting it in such a way as to better define orthodoxy by putting it against the background of all the "errors" that supposedly derived and deviated from pristine orthodoxy itself.

In the case of the Nicolaitans, Eusebius allows the founder of a heresy to be rehabilitated. Although he calls the doctrine a heresy, he does not specify what exactly it was. From other sources we learn that the Nicolaitans ate meat that had been offered to idols and that they practiced sexual immorality (fornication and adultery).[29] Eusebius's short section on Nicolas deals with only a single incident, the account of which is taken from Clement of Alexandria's *Stromateis*: "He [Nicolas] had, they say, a beautiful wife; but after the ascension of the Savior he was accused of jealousy by the apostles, and brought her forward and commanded her to be mated to anyone who wished" (3.29.2). Eusebius then

28. See Mendels, *Identity, Religion and Historiography*, Chap. 9.
29. For the Nicolaitans, see Revelation 2:6, 15; and Duane F. Watson, "Nicolaitans," in *The Anchor Bible Dictionary*, 6 vols., ed. David Noel Freedman (New York: Doubleday, 1992), 4:1106-7.

cites, evidently with approval, Clement's judgment that "the exposure of the wife of whom he was jealous . . . was the abandonment of passion . . . For I think that according to the command of the Saviour he did not wish to serve two masters — pleasure and the Lord" (3.29.3). In this case Eusebius uses the techniques we mentioned above, but for positive reasons.

After dealing with some evidence from Hegesippus not related directly to the subject of heresy, Eusebius abruptly states:

> Besides this the same writer, explaining the events of these times, adds that until then the church remained a pure and uncorrupted virgin, for those who attempted to corrupt the healthful rule of the Saviour's preaching, if they existed at all, lurked in obscure darkness. But when the sacred band of the Apostles and the generation of those to whom it had been vouchsafed to hear with their own ears the divine wisdom had reached the several ends of their lives, then the federation of godless error took its beginning through the deceit of false teachers who, seeing that none of the Apostles still remained, barefacedly tried against the preaching of the truth the counter-proclamation of "knowledge falsely so-called." (3.32.7-8)

With their (false) knowledge, the heretics competed with orthodoxy over the very same constituencies in the market place. After the apostles were gone, and with the canon of the New Testament still not crystallized, it was relatively easy to contradict orthodoxy with all kinds of arguments. However, it was the massive media counterattack launched by orthodoxy (which had a stronger worldwide organization than any heretical group) that assured its publicity victory over the heretics. Apart from this media offensive, it would be hard to explain how the Catholic Church — which in certain cases was itself a local minority — contrived to emerge as the only legitimate form of Christianity in 325 C.E. (even though confronted at that time with the Arian heresy).

Eusebius made a careful selection, and the little he relates about heresies is usually set out in simplistic terms (in contrast to the heresiology of Irenaeus, for example). Although he had a great deal of material available for most of the heresies he covers (some of which get full accounts in Irenaeus, and as ancient historians we still have the rare good fortune to examine the extant sources), he took from it only what suited his purpose of defining the right and moral order of Catholicism (some of it included under the theological term *dogma*).[30] If we examine some of the issues Eusebius does introduce concerning heresies, we learn that he presents their "new" teaching as disrupting the *dogmata* of the Church. As we have seen, though, Eusebius considered the greatest menace of the heresies to be their audacious penetration into the public sphere. Orthodoxy was expending a great deal of effort to conquer this sphere for itself.

The apocryphal story of Cerinthus and John in the public bath, noted briefly above, demonstrates the early stages of the fight between orthodoxy and the heresy over the outer public sphere. It shows that the presence of heretics within the public sphere was a factor to be reckoned with. The presence of heretics in the marketplace constituted an obstacle that orthodox Christianity could not tolerate but that it found hard to combat at the end of the first and the beginning of the second century. The powerful presence of Cerinthus within the public bath is seen by Eusebius as an act of impurity;[31] Cerinthus turns the bath into an impure place. It should be noted that the presence of pagans did not bother John, most likely because pagans were the potential audience for the Christian mission. Cerinthus hence made it impossible for John to stay in the baths. But John does not turn violent or try to expel Cerinthus from the building with harsh words. He just leaves. The Church was attempting to conquer the public sphere but was not always successful. In Eusebius's presentation, the public sphere is to be cleansed of heretics in order for orthodoxy to prevail. This view will change later in the *Ecclesiastical History.*

This is only one aspect of the presentation. The other is that Eusebius describes the heresies in such simple terms that he effectively depicts them as unsophisticated, banal, and stupid. This was, of course, not true in reality (or according to other presentations).[32] But this particular presentation serves his aims of media performance. Eusebius, as we know, could write sophisticated treatises, but in his simplified presentation of heresies he wished to communicate to a "simple" audience the clear-cut message that heresies are an unsophisticated phenomenon as opposed to sophisticated orthodox Christianity. In our day, the mass media of the seventies and eighties presented minorities in simple terms, as banal, uncultured, and

30. On Catholic dogma, see the still useful survey of Adolf von Harnack, *History of Dogma*, 3 vols., trans. from the 3d German edition by Neil Buchanan (Boston: Little, Brown, 1897-1910).

31. To adopt the terminology of Mary Douglas, *Natural Symbols: Explorations in Cosmology* (London: Barrie & Rockliff: Cresset, 1970).

32. Cf. for instance, Irenaeus, *Adversus Haereses.*

stupid (in comparison to the sophistication of the elite dominant group; Van Dijk has shown that this is sometimes only implied). The technique of presentation remains the same: short entries, verbatim quotation of sources to give the impression of reliability, abrupt turning points, little substantial information, a great deal of gossip putting the heretic in a bad personal light, negative language taken from the arsenal of moral values of pagan society at the time, and so on.

Saturninus and Basilides

As Eusebius proceeds with his history, the presentation of heresy and heretics becomes more harsh and derogatory. The more he talks about heretics, the more he returns to his famous refrain about the situation of the Church: "Like brilliant lamps the churches were now shining throughout the world, and faith in our Saviour and Lord Jesus Christ was flourishing among all mankind" (4.7.1). Variations of this statement recur often in the *Ecclesiastical History,* and the very repetition is noteworthy. It is quite clear that even when Eusebius makes these kinds of statements he is not reflecting reality. On the contrary, he inserts them in particular when one can get the impression from reading his account that the Church was weak or had reached a low point in its history. He uses them in the same manner that today's mass media use advertisements: short, simple, exaggerated, repetitive, and not necessarily true. We will analyze this in Chapter 6.

Eusebius says that Satan himself, "the devil who hates what is good, as the enemy of truth . . . turned all his devices against the Church" (4.7.1)[33] and adds that

> Formerly he [the Devil] had used persecutions from without as his weapon against her [the Church], but now that he was excluded from this he employed wicked men and sorcerers, like baleful weapons and ministers of destruction against the soul, and conducted his campaign by other measures, plotting by every means that sorcerers and deceivers might assume the same name as our religion and at one time lead to the depth of destruction those of the faithful whom they caught, and at others, by the deeds which they undertook, might turn away from the path to the saving word, those who were ignorant of the faith. (4.7.2)

33. See in general Elaine Pagels, *The Origin of Satan* (New York: Random House, 1995).

Eusebius is aware of the effects of the missionary efforts of the heretics themselves. He expresses the view that heresies were a dangerous course for orthodoxy since many Christians (as well as pagans) were attracted by their teaching. He also is aware of the publicity that heresies received, presumably because at times they presented themselves as selling more attractive "merchandise" than the orthodox Church ever did. He therefore denigrates them without explaining exactly and in depth what their message is: "Thus from Menander, whom we have already introduced as Simon's successor, there proceeded a certain snake-like power with two mouths and double head, and established the leaders of two heresies," Saturninus and Basilides (4.7.3).[34] Operating like a reporter who does not actually adduce material information, Eusebius relies on Irenaeus for the judgment that "Saturninus uttered for the most part the same falsehoods as Menander, but Basilides under the pretext of secret doctrine, stretched fancy infinitely far, fabricating monstrous myths for his impious heresy" (4.7.4).

Eusebius here brings forward his idea of what the media methods of Christianity were at that time. He mentions "struggle" against heresy, and writings that "provided methods of defence against the heresies" (4.7.5-6). He mentions Agrippa Castor, who wrote against Basilides and revealed "the cleverness of the man's deception." Here he gives a short description of Basilides' heresy, but picks up certain particular points (apparently from Castor's book): (1) He named his own prophets Bar Cabbas and Bar Coph and "set up some others from himself who had never existed" but "invented barbarous names for them to astonish those who were influenced by such things." (2) "He taught that there was no harm in eating things offered to idols" and (3) "light-heartedly denied the faith in times of persecution." (4) "Like Pythagoras he enjoined those who came to him to keep silence for five years." Eusebius adds that Castor "offers a magnificent refutation of the error of the heresy described" (4.7.7-8). We will analyze this refutation in a moment. But let us first connect this to the heresy of Carpocrates, about which we hear very little.

---

34. For Saturninus, see Aline Pourkier, *L'hérésiologie chez Épiphane de Salamine* (Paris: Beauchesne, 1992), 167-204. For Basilides, see ibid., 205-56; and Winrich Alfried Löhr, *Basilides und seine Schule: Eine Studie zur Theologie- und Kirchengeschichte des Zweiten Jahrhunderts* (Tübingen: Mohr Siebeck, 1996).

Carpocrates

Eusebius introduces Carpocrates as "the father of another heresy which was called that of the Gnostics. These did not, like Basilides, desire to transmit the magic of Simon secretly but openly *(phaneron)*, as though it was some great thing, speaking almost with awe of their magical ceremonies, of love charms, of the bringers of dreams and familiar spirits, and of other similar performances" (4.7.9).[35] They teach that "those whose purpose was coming to initiation in their mysteries, or rather in their obscenities, must perform all the shocking deeds because in no other way can they escape the 'rulers of the world,' as they would say, except by fulfilling to all of them what was necessary through their mysteries" (4.7.9).

Thus the Carpocratians shifted from the private realm of mystery to the open world of publicity. Eusebius perceives this kind of publicity as harmful to the reputation of orthodox Christianity; he accuses the Carpocratians of having

> brought much weight of discredit upon the divine word among the unbelieving Gentiles, because the report which started from them was scattered calumniously on the whole race of Christians. It was especially in this way that it came to pass that a blasphemous and wicked suspicion concerning us was spread among the heathen of those days, to the effect that we practised unspeakable incest with mothers and sisters and took part in wicked food. (4.7.10-11)

In other words, Eusebius acknowledges the strong effect that publicity can have on pagans and Christians alike, and he views pagans as a highly important factor in the marketplace. He therefore fights heresies in his writing with all the media devices at his disposal (and he believes that he is successful, 7.12-13). We can assume that this kind of presentation reflects both the discourse and the devices that were employed in reality by orthodoxy against heresy.

Be that as it may, Eusebius ends this particular section by saying that

> the brightness of the universal and only true church proceeded to increase in greatness, for it ever held to the same points in the same way, and radi-

---

35. For Carpocrates, see Pourkier, *L'hérésiologie chez Épiphane de Salamine*, 257-89; for the relevant texts, see Walther Völker, ed., *Quellen zur Geschichte der Christlichen Gnosis* (Tübingen: Mohr, 1932), 33-38.

ated forth to all the race of Greeks and barbarians, the reverent, sincere, and free nature, and sobriety and purity of the divine teaching as to conduct and thought. Thus with the lapse of time the calumnies against the whole teaching were extinguished, and our doctrine remained as the only one which had power among all and was admitted to excel in its godliness and sobriety and its divine and wise doctrines. (4.7.13-14)

This, of course, does not reflect the reality of the times that Eusebius depicts but it does reveal his belief in the manifestation of power in the public sphere ("among all").

Marcion

For the heresy of Marcion, Eusebius relies on the testimony of Justin Martyr, who "in the garb of philosopher served as ambassador of the word of God" and wrote "a treatise against Marcion" at a time when "the heretic was alive and notorious" (4.11.8).[36] He then cites Justin on Marcion (*Apology* 1.26):

> And there was a certain Marcion of Pontus who even now is still teaching those who believe him to think that there is another God greater than the creator. Throughout the whole race of men by the instigation of demons he has made many *(pollous)* to speak blasphemously and to deny that the Maker of this universe is the Father of Christ, and to confess that there is another greater than He. All those who begin from them, as we said, are called Christians just as the name of philosophy is common to philosophers though their doctines vary . . . and we have a treatise against all the heresies which have arisen which we will give to any who wish to study it. (4.11.9-10)

Eusebius is less harsh concerning Marcion than he was in some previous cases. Perhaps he re-edited this part during the time he was in sympathy with Arius, and Marcion's heresy was, as it were, less syncretistic.[37] As in

---

36. For Marcion's heresy, see Adolf von Harnack, *Marcion: The Gospel of the Alien God,* trans. John E. Steely and Lyle D. Bierma (Durham, N.C.: Labyrinth, 1990); R. Joseph Hoffmann, *Marcion: On the Restitution of Christianity: An Essay on the Development of Radical Paulinist Theology in the Second Century* (Chico, Calif.: Scholars Press, 1984); Barbara Aland, "Marcion: Versuch einer neuen Interpretation," *Zeitschrift für Theologie und Kirche* 70 (1973): 420-47; and Han J. W. Drijvers, "Marcionism in Syria: Principles, Problems, and Polemics," *The Second Century* 6, no. 3 (1987-88): 153-72.

37. However, see Drijvers, "Marcionism in Syria."

other cases, Eusebius shows here that he was well aware of the fierce competition among the various Christian groups. He is worried about the fact that a heretic like Marcion had "those who believe him" and that he "made many to speak" throughout the pagan and Christian worlds.[38] Again, in Eusebius's opinion this competition appears more troublesome than the substance of the heresy itself. In producing this information through Justin's mouth, Eusebius has the "cover" of a great Church authority. I have already mentioned this method, but here I should add that by using such a device Eusebius seizes the opportunity to communicate sayings and opinions of the Church Fathers, formulated in simple terms, to a broad audience that would not normally read their writings. This brings to mind what our mass media do daily. They abridge complicated material by quoting abstracts and small fragments from authoritative sources that in their entirety are thought to be too complex and elaborate for a wide audience to grasp. Our modern mass media rely on a "canon" of authority for regular reference, when they cite the views of certain institutions and personalities. Eusebius too forms his "canon" of authoritative voices to be consulted. The formation of an informal canon alongside the official biblical canon went hand in hand with the formation of the library in Caesarea of which we will speak in Chapter 6.

Market Competition

We should look more closely at Eusebius's audiences. While he was writing the *Ecclesiastical History,* Eusebius obviously kept the nature of his public in mind. "Audience" has become a complex concept in the twentieth century, but it can still be defined in antiquity.[39] Denis McQuail notes that

> several diverse studies suggest that media content can itself provide a
> significant basis for identification or provide support for subcultural
> identities. This may be especially true of various youth subcultures, es-

38. Eusebius's worries had some basis, since Marcionite communities were spreading through Asia Minor and Syria; see Peter Brown, *The Body and Society: Men, Women, and Sexual Renunciation in Early Christianity* (New York: Columbia University Press, 1988), 87-91.

39. Denis McQuail, *Mass Communication Theory: An Introduction* (London: Sage Publications, 1994), 284, 324.

pecially where other elements, such as class and ethnicity, are also involved. The media often provide stylistic markers for establishing group boundaries. The phenomenon is not confined to youth, since there are examples relating to social status and national identity.[40]

We cannot discuss this issue in detail here, but historians can use the methods of mass media scholars quoted by McQuail to analyze the content of ancient historiography in order to discern the audiences of antiquity. Because Eusebius sincerely thought that everyone in the outer public sphere was ready to receive the Christian message, he in fact was writing for people in that sphere. Hence he used rhetoric and descriptions of a low common denominator, that is, language and social codes that everyone in that sphere could understand and decode. But his audience also included his own "social group".[41] Eusebius understood his audience and knew how to attract it, just as the heretics knew how to attract their audiences. For instance, the "pagan oriented" heresies that appear in the *Ecclesiastical History* (such as those of Simon Magus and Valentinus)[42] can be seen as a "gratification set" according to McQuail's typology, since they reached out to people who could not accommodate themselves to "pure" Christianity but needed pagan symbols, codes of behavior, and modes of discourse in order to be gratified. This audience, which did not overlap with that of the inner public sphere (although it may have included a segment of the latter), was in fact created by the heresy itself and had a common religious taste that defined its boundaries.[43]

Another group of heresies in Eusebius are those that have hardly any

40. Ibid., 308.

41. This is McQuail's terminology (ibid., 290): "this will correspond with an existing social grouping [such as a community or membership of a political, religious or ethnic minority], and with shared social characteristics of place, social class, politics, culture, etc."

42. For the recrudescence of ancient myths in Valentinus and other Gnostics, see Gedaliahu A. G. Stroumsa, *Another Seed: Studies in Gnostic Mythology* (Leiden: Brill, 1984); and Michel Tardieu, *Trois Mythes Gnostiques: Adam, Eros et les animaux d'Egypte dans un écrit de Nag Hammadi (II,5)* (Paris: Études augustiniennes, 1974). For texts relating to Valentinus, see Völker, ed., *Quellen zur Geschichte der Christlichen Gnosis*, 57-141; see also Christoph Markschies, *Valentinus Gnosticus? Untersuchungen zur Valentinischen Gnosis mit einem Kommentar zu den Fragmenten Valentins* (Tübingen: Mohr Siebeck, 1992).

43. Their base for mediating the message was the *didaskaleion,* a small study group. For its operation in the case of Valentinus, see Brown, *Body and Society,* 104-21.

obvious pagan elements but that "deviate" from the orthodox Church in the areas of Christology and doctrine (for example, those of Marcion, Paul of Samosata, and Beryllus). Their audiences were composed mainly of Christians within the inner public sphere (most pagans could not grasp the intricacies of Christian theological disputes), and perhaps even Jews who were close to their ideas. Bearing in mind that this kind of heresy was formed within the inner public sphere, we can say that it created its audiences in line with what McQuail and others call "fan groups." In McQuail's formulation,

> this kind of audience will be formed on the basis of an interest in a particular author, director or type of content (or genre), or through attraction to a particular personality (or a particular cultural or intellectual taste). Otherwise, it lacks any clear social definition or categorization. . . . Occasionally such kinds of audience are encouraged by the media to form into social groups (as with fan clubs) or they spontaneously transform themselves into social groups, with characteristic patterns of dress, behaviour and speech. Fiske suggested that "fandom" demonstrates the productive power of audiences, creating new and deeper meaning from the materials made available.[44]

In this context we may situate Paul of Samosata and Marcion. In the case of Paul, the creation of a fan group is apparent (cf. Chapter 2).[45]

Eusebius's views on media and market competition in the outer public sphere also come to the fore in his description of the heresies of Valentinus and Marcion. He insists that they had "wrong opinions," and in connection with the martyr Polycarp he says that "he constantly taught those things which he had learnt from the apostles . . . and in the time of Anicetus he visited Rome and converted many" of the Valentinian and Marcionite heresies to the Church of God, "preaching that the one and only truth which he had received from the apostles was that which is the tradition of the church" (4.14.4-5). The battle over the markets was waged (in Eusebius's "media reality") by missionary preaching, writing pamphlets, denigrating the opposition more on the personal level than on substantial matters, and presenting the whole struggle as a battle for the "true"

---

44. McQuail, *Mass Communication*, 290-91.

45. The break of family bonds and the "unfamiliar" message (Brown, *Body and Society*, 89-90) transformed the family and household connection into "fandom" groups.

tradition of the Church.[46] Elsewhere Eusebius states this more or less clearly:

> Heretics were even then no less defiling the pure seed of apostolic teaching like tares, and shepherds of the churches in every place, as though driving off wild beasts from Christ's sheep, excluded them at one time by rebukes and exhortations to the brethren, at another by their more complete exposure, by unwritten and personal inquiry and conversation, and ultimately correcting their opinions by accurate arguments in written treatises. It is clear that Theophilus joined with the others in this campaign against them from a noble treatise which he made against Marcion. (4.24.1)

About the latter he adds: "Philip . . . also made a most excellent treatise against Marcion. Irenaeus, likewise, and Modestus, who excels beyond the rest in exposing to everyone the man's error, did the same, and there are many others, too, whose works are still preserved among many Christians" (4.25.1). This statement shows that media efforts regarding the heresies were carried out on various levels. Here Eusebius emphasizes the more intellectual level of written treatises. To judge from what we find in the *Adversus Haereses* of Irenaeus, the complex and lengthy theological arguments adduced were much too elevated for the broader public, and Eusebius was aware of this. Thus we find in the *Ecclesiastical History* the lower level of "anecdotal" polemics used in verbal discourse. This lower level is what Eusebius apparently reflects in his description of heresies. As we have seen so far, it is banal, short, abrupt, anecdotal, and simple. Given the impressive circulation of books at that time,[47] Eusebius knew what he was doing.

Othodoxy and heresy in early Christianity are comparable in many respects to rival media channels that compete for the public's attention by purveying more or less the same basic information. Here again we may adapt the findings of McQuail, who argues,

---

46. Eusebius was aware of the problem of the corruption of the text of Scripture as well (e.g., *Hist. Eccl.* 4.23.12); for the participation of Orthodox Christians in this phenomenon, see Ehrman, *Orthodox Corruption of Scripture*. Eusebius lingers on the problems of a correct text (Origen's *Hexapla*).

47. See Harry Y. Gamble, *Books and Readers in the Early Church: A History of Early Christian Texts* (New Haven and London: Yale University Press, 1995).

Politically relevant news, outside of election contexts, seems to have followed a similar pattern of inter-channel homogeneity, lending support
to the view that multiplication of channels does not do a great deal for
the multiplication of access opportunities (or for extending the range of
access).... Newspapers are more likely to offer more alternative versions
of events and to employ more sources, partly because of political choice
and other bases of differentiation . . . partly because they simply have
more space in which to be different . . . The more the channels concerned are competing for the same 'market' of people or region at the
same time, the more we should expect duplication of content and
sources. Competitive imitation will play some part in this.[48]

These observations provide a helpful comparative background for
our investigation, since the various early Christian heresies shared many
basic symbols, terms of reference, and modes of discourse with orthodoxy.
They shared common religious doctrines and even literature. On the other
hand, competition over the same markets brought about heretical novel-
ties and changes within orthodoxy, which in turn had to fight them and
adjust itself to the new situations. This means that a heresy that wanted to
be attractive had to present, in addition to the common knowledge and
symbols it shared with orthodoxy, something different — something
novel, mysterious, and sensational — and yet close in its codes to the world
of its "consumers."

What in fact makes us choose between one newspaper and another,
or prefer one TV program over another? Usually it is a matter of personal
taste, political and religious affiliation, intellectual interest, availability of
time, social class, mood, and in many cases just habit. (For instance, I have
read the same newspaper for many years because I can decode its message
easily.) In antiquity, Christians, pagans, and Jews were exposed to various
media channels designed by various creeds. In certain periods and loca-
tions, there were two or more options available. The media devices to
which people were exposed included letters (read aloud in public), public
disputes, sermons, synods, and martyrdom. When faced with these "media
channels," Christians and pagans decided what to choose according to
their religious beliefs, intellectual level, social class, age, relations with the
local bishop, and their degree of attraction to gimmicks employed by the
various competitors.

48. McQuail, *Media Performance*, 173-74.

Montanus

Let us now look at the heresy of Montanus as presented by Eusebius, keeping one major question in mind: Why did people wish to switch from the "main" channel (orthodoxy) and opt for this "other" channel? What were the special media methods of the Montanists that led to the relatively great success of their heresy in so many regions of the world?

Already at the end of Book 4, Eusebius mentions that Apolinarius wrote a treatise against Montanus; in Book 5 he proceeds to quote from it extensively.[49] Similar to our modern mass media, Eusebius announces to his readers in advance what he is going to tell them in the coming "items." He begins by referring to "the heresy of the Phrygians, which had begun its innovations not long before and was then, as it were, beginning to sprout, while Montanus with his false prophetesses was making the beginning of the error" (4.27.1). Later, when Eusebius describes the martyrdom at Lyons, he intertwines a section on Montanus:

> Just at that time the party of Montanus and Alcibiades and Theodotus in Phrygia began first to engender among many their views concerning prophecy (for the many other wonderful works of the grace of God which were still being wrought up to that time in divers churches produced the belief among many that they also were prophets), and when dissension arose about the persons mentioned, the brethren in Gaul again formulated their own judgement, pious and most orthodox, concerning them, subjoining various letters from the martyrs who had been consecrated among them, which letters while they were still in prison they had composed for the brethren in Asia and Phrygia, and also for Eleutherus, who was then bishop of the Romans, and so they were ambassadors for the sake of the peace of the churches. (5.3.4)

From this we can deduce that Montanus achieved some success in attracting the attention even of the martyrs in Gaul. But we still do not hear anything specific about the nature of the heresy. Somewhat later we get a great deal of invective against the heresy, in the familiar language that Eusebius uses against other heresies as well:

49. For Montanus in general, see Ronald E. Heine, ed., *The Montanist Oracles and Testimonies* (Macon, Ga.: Mercer University Press, 1989); F. Blanchetiere, "Le Montanisme originel," *Revue des sciences religieuses* 52 (1978): 118-34 and 53 (1979): 1-22.

The enemy of the Church of God, who hates good and loves deeply all that is wicked, left untried no kind of plot against men and again strove to raise up strange heresies against the church. Of these some like poisonous reptiles crawled over Asia and Phrygia, and boasted that Montanus was the Paraclete and that the women of his sect, Priscilla and Maximilla, were the prophetesses of Montanus. Others flourished in Rome of which Florinus was the leader. He had been turned out of the presbytery of the church and with him was Blastus who had suffered a similar fall. These drew away more of the church and brought them to their own opinion, each trying to introduce innovations *(neōterizein)* about the truth in his own way. (5.14-15)

Eusebius was well aware that the accessibility of such heresies was a threat to the already well-defined constituency of the orthodox Church. Therefore he presents them negatively but neglects, as he did before, the real theological disputes between orthodoxy and the Montanist heresy. However, we can learn from his report that there were aspects in Montanism that attracted people, such as the prophecy of Montanus and his female colleagues Priscilla and Maximilla. Prophecy was an extremely important channel of media performance in antiquity; it was a most popular device that could easily reach the masses.[50] Hence it was a serious menace to orthodoxy, which did not use contemporary prophecy. Another threat to the orthodox institution was Montanus's self-proclaimed status as the Paraclete, which competed with the authority of the bishop within the public sphere.[51]

In this particular case, we can observe again how Eusebius operates in a way similar to what van Dijk describes as the typical racist stance, in that he does not give "equal opportunity" to his adversary to state his competitive views. Eusebius was aware of his power as mediator in the form of the written word; he was also an ardent believer in the Christian mission who feared the enormous influence heretical views could have on the reading and hearing public. Thus he avoided accounts that could propagate their views. How does he compare in this respect to other historians in an-

50. See David E. Aune, *Prophecy in Early Christianity and the Ancient Mediterranean World* (Grand Rapids: Eerdmans, 1983); and Robin Lane Fox, *Pagans and Christians* (New York: Knopf, 1986), 375-418.

51. Montanism was successful, for instance, in Anatolia; see Stephen Mitchell, *Anatolia: Land, Men, and Gods in Asia Minor,* vol. 2, *The Rise of the Church* (Oxford: Clarendon, 1993).

tiquity? Polybius consulted both pro-Hannibal and anti-Hannibal sources. Livy cited the views of Nabis and T. Q. Flamininus, although he did not like the Spartan tyrant at all.[52] Another familiar trick of Eusebius is that he lets others talk about heretics and heresies. He in fact had abundant material at his disposal concerning Montanus's heresy, as we learn from this passage: "Apolinarius, who has already been mentioned in this work, and with him many others of the learned men of that time, from whom abundant material for history has been left to us" (5.16.1). Eusebius comments further,

> One of these at the beginning of his treatise against the Montanists indicates that he had also taken part in oral controversy against them. He writes a preface in this way: "For a long and protracted time, my dear Abercius Marcellus, I have been urged by you to compose a treatise against the sect of those called after Miltiades [apparently, a leader of the Montanists], but until now I was somewhat reluctant, not from any lack of ability to refute the lie and testify to the truth, but from timidity and scruples lest I might seem to some to be adding to the writings or injunctions of the word of the new covenant of the gospel, to which no one who has chosen to live according to the gospel itself can add and from which he cannot take away. But when I had just come to Ancyra in Galatia and perceived that the church in that place was torn in two by this new movement which is not, as they call it, prophecy but much rather, as will be shown, false prophecy, I disputed concerning these people themselves and their propositions so far as I could, with the Lord's help, for many days continuously in the church. Thus the church rejoiced and was strengthened in the truth, but our opponents were crushed for the moment and our adversaries distressed. Therefore the presbyters of the place asked me to leave some note of what had been said against the opponents of the word of the truth. . . . Though we did not do so, we promised to write from home if the Lord permitted, and to send it to them speedily. (5.16.2-5)

Only now does Eusebius give some details about the heresy itself. The anonymous writer whom he quotes behaves like a cautious reporter who does not want to be misunderstood; he is reluctant to write anything down in haste, because he does not want to be misquoted and called a heretic himself. When one commits doctrinal opinions to writing, there is always

52. See Mendels, *Identity, Religion and Historiography,* Chap. 12.

the risk of being accused of writing against the "right" *(orthos)* way (this shows how unclear the boundaries between orthodoxy and heresy were at certain points). The anonymous writer goes on to tell about his open discussions in the church, and now at last some of this information is "leaked out" by Eusebius: Montanus, "in the unbounded lust of his soul for leadership gave access to himself to the adversary, became obsessed, and suddenly fell into frenzy and convulsions. He began to be ecstatic and to speak and to talk strangely, prophesying contrary to the custom which belongs to the tradition and succession of the church from the beginning" (5.16.7).

From the continuation we learn that Montanus succeeded in gaining many followers. Although Eusebius presents him as a "minority" (in van Dijk's terms), we can detect between the lines that this heresy was attractive to many. We have already seen that Eusebius opposed people like Montanus, who were successful in gaining substantial publicity within the domains of the inner public sphere as well as the outer one. Prophecy (and ecstasy) is again mentioned, and Eusebius adds,

> But when the arrogant spirit taught to blaspheme the whole catholic church throughout the world, because the spirit of false prophecy received from it neither honour nor entrance, for the Christians of Asia after assembling for this purpose many times and in many parts of the province, tested the recent utterances, pronounced them profane, and rejected the heresy — then at last the Montanists were driven out of the church and excommunicated. (5.16.9-10)

Having read these "news items" concerning Montanus, we still do not know what this heresy was about.[53] However, we hear from the second book of Eusebius's anonymous writer that Montanus and the women were said to have committed suicide, although the author himself is not sure of this (5.16.11-15). Then comes a whole section about the false prophetess Maximilla and the martyrdom of the Montanists (5.16.20ff.). We may recall that during times of persecution the orthodox martyrs refused to

---

53. The same is often true today after one reads news accounts of religious groups that are treated by the media as cults. See Mark Silk, *Unsecular Media: Making News of Religion in America* (Urbana: University of Illinois Press, 1995), who notes (pp. 94-95) that "in looking at press accounts of such groups as the Unification Church, the Church of Scientology, Hare Krishna, and the Children of God, the study found that trials and criminal investigations far outranked all other subject matter. Indeed, two-and-a-half times as much attention was devoted to legal conflicts as to the actual beliefs of the groups."

communicate with the Montanist ones and wanted to die separately. This can be interpreted as an intentional lack of communication designed to create definite boundaries between orthodoxy and heresy. In other words, the dominant group finds it essential to abstain from communication with the minority so as to protect their constituency from contaminating influences.

The prophesying of the Montanists was, as we have noted, a media asset. Indeed, the dominant orthodox group found it hard to admit that a prophecy uttered by their competitors could come true. A true prophecy would be an excellent way to attract the common people and thus "eat up" a segment of the orthodox constituency of believers. Eusebius was therefore relieved when he could demonstrate that the prophecies of Maximilla were not fulfilled. He was well aware of the merits of prophecy as a media gimmick. A prophecy that comes true can be an enormous publicity asset for any religion. Hence it is not accidental that in his *Demonstratio Evangelica* Eusebius takes great pains to show that the prophecies of the Old Testament were proven true through the coming of Jesus Christ.

Prophecy in its various manifestations is still covered extensively by the media today. So is "false prophecy." Mark Silk has shown convincingly that it is one of the labels used in the modern media in their coverage of religious news. Any serious deviation from the well-established Christian denominations in the United States is considered false prophecy by the media (in line with Matt. 7:15-16).[54] In the world of antiquity, this same procedure was implemented by the media channel of the orthodox Church.

The information about false prophecy was adduced by Eusebius from (another) Miltiades "who had also himself written a treatise against the heresy mentioned" (5.17.1). Here again Eusebius quotes a negative source without counterbalancing it with sources favorably inclined toward the heretics. Only now, after we have read many fragmentary pieces of information about Montanism, does Eusebius come to the points in dispute between orthodoxy and this heresy. He selects this information from yet another writer, Apollonius. He calls Apollonius "a writer of the church" (5.18.1), that is, one of those "canonical" authorities mentioned above. In order to give the information authenticity, to show that it was transmitted by someone close to the scene, he adds that Apollonius wrote when "the

54. Silk, *Unsecular Media*, Chaps. 4, 8.

141

so-called Montanist heresy was still flourishing in Phrygia" (5.18.1). Then, like a modern journalist, he says:

> Listen to the actual words which he [Apollonius] uses about Montanus: "But the deeds and the teachings of this recent teacher show his character. It is he who taught the annulment of marriage, who enacted fasts, who gave the name of Jerusalem to Pepuza and Tymion, which are little towns in Phrygia, and wished to hold assemblies there from everywhere, who appointed collectors of money, who organized the receiving of gifts under the name of offerings, who provided salaries for those who preached his doctrine in order that its teaching might prevail through gluttony." (5.18.2)

It is quite clear that Eusebius was less worried about the theological aspects of Montanism than about the organizational competition that it posed. He was bothered by its capacity to operate an alternative communications network, with teachers going out to preach a simple and attractive message to believers. He was also troubled by the Montanists' attempt to recreate the center in the periphery by their designating two Phrygian villages "Jerusalem." In short, the foundation of a new communications network was in his eyes a greater threat to the orthodox Church than any theological speculation.

From the same author Eusebius also adduces a denigration of the prophetesses of Montanism (5.18.3), and he ends this section about Montanus with extracts from another author, Serapion, a bishop of Antioch, who in turn draws upon the writings of Apolinarius: "And in order that you may know this, that the working of the so-called new prophecy of this false order is abominated in the whole of Christendom throughout the world, I have sent you the writings of Claudius Apolinarius, the bishop of Hierapolis in Asia, of blessed memory" (5.19.2). This expression shows again how sensitive Eusebius was concerning the issue of communication. It also shows that the network of communications existing within the inner public sphere of orthodox Christianity was a factor to be reckoned with when the spread of the faith was discussed. Pagans worshiping the same deities did not have the luxury of belonging to a worldwide organization that competed with the institutionalized worship of the emperor. Only during 311-313 would Maximian make an attempt to imitate the Christian communication organization, by creating a competitive pagan counterpart to it.

Other Heresies

Before proceeding with other heresies, we should reflect for a moment on the comparison made above with the phenomenon of competing mass media channels. Christians, as well as pagans and Jews who were interested in Christianity, were exposed to many competitive channels. Whereas they all had a common framework, some heresies radiated interesting and attractive variants. The orthodox Church at last got the upper hand, to judge from Eusebius, because it had a better organized and more effective network operating within the outer public sphere. Eusebius reflects this situation in his own methods of media performance. He operates as the main channel of the dominant organization, adducing only scanty information about the competing channels, and that in an unbalanced and incomplete manner.

We are now poised to examine some of the other channels that Eusebius mentions and to enlarge upon yet another element of the "media asset" that heresy became for the orthodox cause. In Book 4, Eusebius treats the heresy of the Encratites, which "at that time was beginning to sprout and to introduce into life its strange and corrupting false doctrine" (4.28.1).[55] His quotation from Irenaeus (*Against Heresies* 1.28.1) describes the beliefs of these heretics and associates Tatian with them:

> "The so-called Encratites proceeding from Saturninus and Marcion preached against marriage, annulling the original creation of God, and tacitly condemning him who made male and female. They also introduced abstention from what they called 'animate' things in ingratitude to the God who has made all things, and they deny the salvation of the first created man. This innovation was recently made by them when a certain Tatian first introduced this blasphemy. He had been a hearer of Justin but so long as he was with him, he produced nothing of this kind, but after the martyrdom of Justin he left the church, being exalted by the idea of becoming a teacher and puffed up as superior to others. He established his own type of doctrine, telling stories of invisible Aeons, like the followers of Valentinus, and rejecting marriage as corruption and fornication similarly to Marcion and Saturninus. And as his own contribution he denied the salvation of Adam" (4.29.2-3).

55. The Encratites were indeed spread all over Asia Minor; see Brown, *Body and Society*, 203. For the Encratites, see Henry Chadwick, "Enkrateia," in *Reallexikon für Antike und Christentum* (Stuttgart: Hiersemann, 1950-78), 5:343-65.

Thus, just as our modern mass media treat deviations from mainstream Christianity as suspect,[56] Eusebius once again accuses the heretics of strange and unnatural practices that go against fundamental cultural values.[57]

Eusebius mentions very briefly a related group who "strengthened the above mentioned heresy"; they were followers of a man named Severus and so were known as the Severiani: "These indeed use the Law and the Prophets and the Gospels, though they interpret the facts of the sacred scriptures in their own way, but they blaspheme the Apostle Paul, and reject his epistles and do not receive the Acts of the Apostles"[58] (4.29.4-5). Of Bardesanes in Mesopotamia, Eusebius says that although he condemned the Valentinians "and refuted many of their fables, and himself thought that he had changed to orthodox opinion . . . in fact he did not completely clean off the filth of his ancient heresy" (4.30.3). Apropos of Symmachus, Eusebius refers again to the Ebionites as those who "affirm that the Christ was born of Joseph and Mary, and suppose Him to be a mere man, and strongly maintain that the law ought to be kept in a more strictly Jewish fashion, as also we saw somewhere from the foregoing history [3.27.2]. And memoirs too of Symmachus are still extant, in which, by his opposition to the Gospel according to Matthew, he seems to hold the above-mentioned heresy" (6.17.1).

Later in Book 6, Eusebius again has some news to communicate, this time within the context of his account on Origen:

> Once more in Arabia at the above-mentioned time other persons sprang up, introducing a doctrine foreign to the truth, and saying that the human soul dies for a while in this present time, along with our bodies, at their death, and with them turns to corruption; but that hereafter, at the time of the resurrection, it will come to life again along with them. Moreover, when a synod of no small dimensions was then assembled together, Origen was again invited, and there opened a discussion in public on the subject in question, with such power that he changed the opinion of those who had formerly been deluded. (6.37.1)

Eusebius proceeds in the very next section to inveigh against yet one more deviation from the dogma of the orthodox Church: "At that time

56. Silk, *Unsecular Media*, 94ff.
57. Brown, *Body and Society*, 89, calls this kind of message, "unfamiliar" (and a "bleak vision," 94).
58. For the Severiani, see Lawlor and Oulton, *Eusebius*, ad loc.

also another perverse opinion had its beginning, the heresy known as that of the Helkesaites, which no sooner began than it was quenched" (6.38.1). For his description of the Helkesaites, Eusebius relies on a public address given by Origen on the text of Psalm 82:

> "There has come just now a certain man who prides himself on being able to champion a godless and very impious opinion, of the Helkesaites, as it is called, which has lately come into opposition with the churches. I shall lay before you the mischievous teachings of that opinion, that you may not be carried away by it. It rejects some things from every Scripture; again, it has made use of texts from every part of the Old Testament and the Gospels; it rejects the Apostles entirely. And it says that to deny is a matter of indifference, and that the discreet man will on occasions of necessity deny with his mouth, but not in his heart. And they produce a certain book of which they say that it has fallen from heaven, and that he who has heard it and believes will receive forgiveness of his sins — a forgiveness other than that which Jesus Christ has bestowed." (6.38.1)

Eusebius's fierce reaction to the Helkesaites can be explained by his disapproval of their attitude toward Scripture. The Bible, both Old and New Testaments, constituted the common unifying "charter" of the orthodox organization. We will come back to this issue in Chapter 5.

The Rhetoric of Hysteria

Before we conclude this chapter, we should ponder Eusebius's derogatory language. He deploys a formidable arsenal of pejorative labels in his depiction of heretics and their heresy: "filth," "wicked men," "ministers of destruction," "false," "arrogant," "poisonous reptiles," "haters of good," "enemy," "error," "blasphemy," "corruption," "perverse opinion," "mischievous teaching," "innovation," "wrong opinions." Words denoting negative values express disruption of the social and moral order and of the very basic principles of existence within a society,[59] and these negative values are carefully selected by Eusebius.

In an article on "Hysterical Style in the Press," Roger Fowler has observed that the response to Salmonella poisoning (and listeriosis) during the winter of 1988-89 in England "was hysterical in terms of its high emo-

59. Silk, *Unsecular Media*, Chap. 8.

tive content, the massive scale of press reporting and its extraordinary generalization to 'the poisoning of our world.'"[60] Moreover,

> Hysteria is not simply behaviour which is in excess of the events which provoked it; it is also behaviour which attains autonomy, which sustains itself as an expressive performance, independent of its causes. People behaving hysterically 'go on and on' (sustain) and 'shout and scream' (excess, express). Hysteria requires an expressive system, a mode of discourse, and, established, exists within that mode of discourse independent of empirical reality . . . the great egg scare was not a medical phenomenon, not an epidemic, it was a construct of discourse, a formation and transformation of ideas in the public language of the newspapers and television.[61]

Fowler demonstrates that in the media the most hysterical reactions were created by quotations from great authorities (in the case of the Salmonella incident, this was Professor R. Lacey, a Leeds microbiologist). Fowler elaborates on the results of his research by noting that some of the materials he analyzed "highlight a vocabulary of 'hazard' and 'risk'" and of "large-scale growth: 'astronomical increase', 'increase.'" He also identifies "a typical narrative of secret dealings between government departments, and between government departments and industry." Other media channels "are unusual in attempting to lay the blame on an individual, yet another one speaks of 'public anxiety' and 'growing confusion.'"

Fowler goes on to show

> how a high level of intensity, an excess of negative feeling is expressed. The most obvious source of stridency in the discourse is its permeation by terms denoting emotive reactions, always negative, clustering around the concepts of fear and confusion. The most common one is 'scare' (at least 27 times), also 'confusion' (10 times), 'anxiety' (6 times) and a number of related terms. . . . another prominent vocabulary set stresses 'danger', 'risk', 'hazard'; it includes words which connote deliberateness of malevolence such as 'threat', 'menace'. There is, particularly in the 'serious' papers, a multiplicity of technical and medical terms, terms of a kind which people find difficult, unfamiliar, frightening . . . but the lan-

---

60. Roger Fowler, "Hysterical Style in the Press," in *Media Texts, Authors and Readers: A Reader,* ed. David Graddol and Oliver Boyd-Barrett (Clevedon and Philadelphia: Multilingual Matters and the Open University, 1994), 90-99, esp. 91.
61. Ibid., 91-92.

guage does not have to be particularly melodramatic or ominously met-
aphoric to suggest that we are threatened by a very powerful and viru-
lent enemy. . . . there is a group of recurrent predicates — verbs, or
nouns derived from verbs — designating changes in numbers . . . [such
as] 'increase, rise, grow, spread, mount, expand, jump, leap, multiply,
proliferation, escalation.'[62]

It is quite clear that Eusebius construed a discourse that was fright-
ening and placed heresy in a highly negative position vis-à-vis the "right"
social and moral order. His presentation, as in the case Fowler analyzed,
was a hysterical one. The constant use of terms like "filth," "enemy," "perverse opinion," and "poisonous reptiles" qualifies as hysterical discourse.
Of course, we cannot prove that Eusebius actually caused hysteria, but his
motives of presentation are what matter here. However, such rhetoric
heard repeatedly in public doubtless did have an effect. That Eusebius in-
dulges so often in this sort of denigratory discourse suggests that his deri-
sive language was probably effective as a media device. In the research of
Fowler, the hysteria caused by a sickness emerges as a fabulous publicity
opportunity for the healthcare system and its experts. The voice of the
medical services is suddenly heard at full volume. The case of orthodoxy
and heresy in early Christianity is comparable. The open clashes in the
public sphere, the great noise and commotion generated by them, the pronouncements of synods convened to renounce the heretics — all these media phenomena inscribed the Christian cause on the public agenda in the
crowded marketplace of religion.

Conclusions

In order to summarize this study of Eusebius's methods in dealing with
heresy and heretics, I would like to draw upon some observations made by
Hamid Mowlana on media and community.[63] He defines community as "a
network of information flow or communication grids that can exist within
and outside national boundaries. Even beyond this, a community must be
based on values or a belief system of a much higher level, and therefore it
can transcend national boundaries." He notes that in both ancient and

62. Ibid., 95-98.
63. The following quotations are from Hamid Mowlana, *Global Communication
in Transition* (London: Sage Publications, 1996), 90-94.

modern societies "community formation is paralleled by the growth of information of an increasingly technical nature. . . ." He adds that in "older societies, for example, the traditional means of communication have ritualistic functions. . . . Association with those ritual functions provides legitimacy, and for this reason, the ritualistic function of a medium ought to be taken into account above and beyond communication function." He goes on to argue that

> when asked which comes first — the media or the community — the response must be the community. The media will never be able to create a community, although they play an important role. A community is created when people get together and communicate, when they act together. The media contribute to this as organizers, mobilizers, crystallizers, and legitimizers. The media also perform as an educator, a source of information, and advocate for policy or ideology, and a forum in which to transmit culture. This, however, is not community building but rather helping the community come to some action, providing integration and identity, or transmitting values and facilitating communication among members. . . . The community media are not meant to be neutral but to represent community interests . . . the media can provide crucial fora for conflict resolution. . . . Increasingly today, control of the distribution process is the most important index of the way in which power and values are distributed in a communication system, which may be the global community, a country, or some smaller cultural unit.

Hence Mowlana calls for a "shift in emphasis in the analysis of communication systems, especially mass communication systems, from an exclusive concern with the source and content of the messages toward analysis of the message distribution system." In other words, not production and formulation, but distribution and reception are the key factors to be investigated.

These observations are helpful in coming to some preliminary conclusions about the media revolution of early Christianity as presented in Eusebius's *Ecclesiastical History*:

1. In the early Christian community, there was a dynamic flow of information through many communication and media systems embedded in a "flat," non-hierarchical organization. The very flow of information helped to create a universal community (the Catholic Church and its opponents) that entered into competition with the communications network of the Roman Empire.

2. The "mass media" agents of the Christian world (martyrs, bishops, synods, letters, and so on) transcended national boundaries. The flow of information within the Catholic Church was universal in both content and manner of distribution; it was transmitted easily and rapidly from province to province within the Roman Empire.

3. The ritualistic function of participation was an important factor in the communication methods used by early Christianity; a great deal of knowledge was spread through the inner public sphere of the churches and other gatherings within a "flat" media organization.

4. The distribution systems of both orthodoxy and heresy were developed within the first three centuries of Christianity. In the battle over the public spheres, orthodoxy at last got the upper hand because it had a more effective and stronger distribution system than its rivals.

5. Communication and media systems, however primitive, helped create orthodoxy and define its position vis-à-vis heresy. The very existence of heresies and the boundaries erected by orthodoxy to exclude heretics from the "right" order helped shape the identity of orthodoxy itself and thus made it more salable in the marketplace of religion.[64]

6. Modern mass media research has shown that TV channels communicate on a much lower level today than, say, forty years ago. The reason for this is that the channels are in the process of adjusting themselves to the lowest common denominator of their mass audiences.[65] Similarly, Eusebius's simple and at times even banal presentation of heretics and heresies suggests a wide and unsophisticated audience of pagans, Jews, and "simple" Christians (as compared, for example, to the learned audiences of Origen and Clement of Alexandria). The content of public communication as presented by Eusebius — which probably reflects the reality of media performance within the orthodox Church of his day — is far from being theological and remains focused on simple and universal social and political values.

7. Since language remains a main factor in daily communication, Eusebius's rhetoric remains an important factor to consider. There can be no doubt that pagans and "simple" Christians were more re-

---

64. As the phenomenon of the Berlin Wall showed, the creation of a barrier — a boundary within the same national entity — helped to define all the democratic symbols that the West stood for, and vice versa. See Schürer, et al., *The Berlin Wall*.

65. McQuail, *Mass Communication*, 205.

ceptive to the level of language he adopted in his *Ecclesiastical History* than to elevated theological discourse. Eusebius used simple rhetoric as a means to achieve an effective media performance. For the sake of comparison, we may note that, whereas Polybius too used strong negative language, he, unlike Eusebius, did not have a world organization to back him in his aggressive attacks (the Achaean league was not a powerful world organization).

An analysis of Eusebius's *Ecclesiastical History* shows that heresy and heretics as opposition groups helped define orthodoxy. Heresies functioned as competing channels of information within the inner public sphere. In certain instances — in particular, in the case of pagan oriented heresies — they had great influence in the outer public sphere as well. As a consequence of the constant battle that orthodoxy had to fight with heresy, the media and distribution network of the Catholic Church was strengthened. In face of opposition and competition, more efforts were invested in strengthening the orthodox communicative organization. This becomes apparent when one compares the organization around 100 C.E. with the one that developed towards 313 C.E. The result was a clearer definition of the content of orthodoxy versus the various heresies, and versus paganism. Competition made the various organizations clarify their boundaries in a more rigorous manner. One may assume that in the years leading up to the battle of the Milvian bridge, the orthodox organization was famous enough to impress the pro-Christian emperor Constantine. We will come back to these issues in the following chapters. On the whole, Eusebius's performance as a media channel can be judged to be unbalanced, incomplete, and biased. His picture of heresy in the *Ecclesiastical History* is a concoction of perceived reality, media reality, and very little factual or statistical reality.

CHAPTER 5

Bishops and Synods:
Penetrating the Public Sphere

Eusebius's Treatment of Synods

Near the end of Book 6 of his *Ecclesiastical History,* Eusebius turns his attention toward a schism in the Church that arose in the aftermath of the Decian persecution. The leader of the schism was a Roman presbyter named Novatian (or, as Eusebius and subsequent Greek writers call him, Novatus). After a brief identification of Novatian as a rigorist who denied any hope of salvation to Christians who had committed apostasy and other grave sins, Eusebius gives an equally brief notice of Novatian's excommunication:

> Whereupon a very large synod was assembled at Rome, of sixty bishops and a still greater number of presbyters and deacons, while in the rest of the provinces the pastors in their several regions individually considered the question as to what was to be done. It was unanimously decreed that Novatus, together with the partners of his arrogance, and those who decided to agree with the man's brother-hating and most inhuman opinion, should be considered as strangers to the Church, but that such of the brethren as had fallen into the misfortune should be treated and restored with the medicines of repentance. (6.43.2)

Later Eusebius informs us that the resolution of the synod, held in 251 c.e., was still available (6.43.4).[1]

1. For the Novatian schism, see Hermann Josef Vogt, *Coetus Sanctorum: Der*

Why did Eusebius choose not to reproduce the decisions made by this synod in any detail? Evidently, he was aware that lengthy quotations of synodical proceedings can be unattractive because of their tedious details. In our own day, decisions reached at peace summits and international conferences are usually abridged or summarized in the media.[2] What is interesting for our discussion here is how consistently Eusebius deals with synods in the *Ecclesiastical History*.

Unfortunately for historians, Eusebius does not reproduce the resolutions of any other synods. In contrast to his usual habit of quoting sources, he does not do so in the case of synods. He altogether ignores the first synod, which was held in Jerusalem in 50-52 C.E. (Acts 15). Concerning the Montanist heresy, he declares only that "the Christians of Asia after assembling for this purpose many times and in many parts of the province, tested the recent utterances, pronounced them profane, and rejected the heresy. Then at last the Montanists were driven out of the church and excommunicated" (5.16.10). The councils concerning Montanus were held between 160 and 180.[3] This, of course, is a partial presentation that lacks any details such as those we read in *Libellus Syndicus* (ninth century), namely, that twenty-six colleagues of the bishop of Hieropolis condemned Montanus and Maximilla and "a holy and particular synod, assembled under the very holy Bishop Sotas of Anchialus, and consisting of twelve other bishops, convicted of heresy the currier Theodotus, Montanus, and Maximilla and condemned them."[4] We read in the *Ecclesiastical History* about the Easter conferences only that "the bishops in Asia were led by Polycrates in persisting that it was

---

Kirchenbegriff des Novatian und die Geschichte seiner Sonderkirche (Bonn: Hanstein, 1968); Russell J. DeSimone, *The Treatise of Novatian the Roman Presbyter on the Trinity: A Study of the Text and the Doctrine* (Rome: Institutum Patristicum Augustinianum, 1970); Hennecke Gülzow, *Cyprian und Novatian: Der Briefwechsel zwischen den Gemeinden in Rom und Karthago zur Zeit der Verfolgung des Kaisers Decius* (Tübingen: Mohr Siebeck, 1975); Vincent Twomey, *Apostolikos Thronos: The Primacy of Rome as Reflected in the Church History of Eusebius and the Historico-apologetic Writings of Saint Athanasius the Great* (Münster: Aschendorff, 1982), 115-119. Cf. also J. A. Fischer, "Angebliche Synoden des 2. Jahrhunderts," *Annuarium Historiae Concilium* 9 (1977): 241-52; idem, "Die antimontanistischen Synoden des 2.-3. Jahrhunderts," *Annuarium Historiae Concilium* 6 (1974): 241-73.

2. The Oslo peace accords would offer a recent example.

3. Charles Joseph Hefele, *A History of the Christian Councils from the Original Documents to the Close of the Council of Nicaea, A. D. 325*, 2 vols., 2d ed., trans. and ed. William R. Clark (Edinburgh: Clark, 1883-96), 1:79-80.

4. Ibid., 78.

necessary to keep the custom which had been handed down to them of old. Polycrates himself in a document which he addressed to Victor and to the church of Rome, expounds the tradition" (5.24.1). From Jerome's *Chronicle* we hear of another synod concerning the Easter controversy (in 196 C.E.): "Pope Victor wrote to the most eminent bishops of all countries, recommending them to call synods in their provinces, and to celebrate in them the feast of Easter on the day chosen by the Church of the West."[5]

Earlier in Book 6, Eusebius reports on the heresy of Beryllus,

> Beryllus, who, as we mentioned a little above [6.20.2], was bishop of Bostra in Arabia, perverting the Church's standard (*kanona*), attempted to introduce things foreign to the faith, daring to say that our Saviour and Lord did not pre-exist in an individual existence of His own before His coming to reside among men, nor had He a divinity of his own, but only the Father's dwelling in him. Whereupon, after a large number of bishops had held questionings and discussions with the man, Origen, being invited along with others, entered in the first place into conversation with the man to discover what were his opinions, and when he knew what it was that he asserted, he corrected what was unorthodox, and persuading him by reasoning, established him in the truth of the doctrine, and restored him to his former sound opinion. And there are still extant to this very day records in writing both of Beryllus and of the synod that was held on his account, which contain at once the questions Origen put to him and the discussions that took place in his own community, and all that was done on that occasion. (6.33.1-3)

A little further on, Eusebius reports that

> Once more in Arabia at the above-mentioned time other persons sprang up, introducing a doctrine foreign to the truth, and saying that the hu-

5. For the problem of the Easter conference, see Hefele, *Christian Councils,* 1:80-83, and for other synods, 1:83-85. On the idea of synods, see Hermann Josef Sieben, *Die Konzilsidee der Alten Kirche* (Paderborn: Schöningh, 1979), 384-423. For the history of synods from their beginning, see Myron Wojtowytsch, *Papsttum und Konzile von den Anfängen bis zu Leo I (440-461): Studien zur Entstehung der Überordnung des Papstes über Konzile* (Stuttgart: Hiersemann, 1981), 19-89; see also Fischer, "Angebliche Synoden"; idem, "Die antimontanistischen Synoden." For the succession of bishops as given in Eusebius's *Ecclesiastical History,* see Erich Caspar, *Die älteste römische Bischofsliste: Kritische Studien zum Formproblem des eusebianischen Kanons sowie zur Geschichte der ältesten Bischofslisten und ihrer Entstehung aus apostolischen Sukzessionenreihen* (Hildesheim: Gerstenberg, 1975); and Twomey, *Apostolikos Thronos.*

man soul dies for a while in this present time, along with our bodies, at their death, and with them turns to corruption; but that hereafter, at the time of the resurrection, it will come to life again along with them. Moreover, when a synod of no small dimension was then assembled together, Origen was again invited, and there opened a discussion in public on the subject in question, with such power that he changed the opinions of those who had formerly been deluded. (6.37.1)

Then, a few pages later, comes the laconic sentence already cited concerning Novatian (6.43.2), and in Book 7 we hear about the synods concerning Paul of Samosata. We do not get a detailed account of the resolutions of the three synods that convened on Paul of Samosata, but we learn somewhat more elaborate details about his behavior in a private letter sent from the last synod in 269 (cf. Chapter 2 above).

We now have to choose among the following options: Eusebius was either not interested in synods, or he was interested in them but had no available sources, or the sparseness of his accounts reflects a deliberate rhetorical strategy. That he had some interest in synods we can learn from the simple fact that he mentions them, and he does not typically treat matters that he deems unimportant for his audience (6.43.4). Moreover, we know that in most cases he did have available sources; at times, he even mentions this fact explicitly (he of course knew Acts 15, but he still did not trouble to introduce the first synod). Hence, the brevity of Eusebius's treatment of synods is likely deliberate. Three factors can help us understand why he treats them as summarily as he does.

1. Since the *Ecclesiastical History* was written before the greatest synod of all, the council of Nicaea in 325, Eusebius still viewed synods as a secondary development in the Church — although, as we shall see, he was aware of their value as media channels.

2. Eusebius's terse references to synods are in line with the nature of his selection methods. A detailed account of synods containing much theological debate was not something he wanted to communicate to his audience. Only when he found sensational material surrounding the synods did he choose to go into more detail. This we have already seen in the presentation of Paul of Samosata and will see again in the case of Novatian.

3. Offering full accounts of synodical resolutions would automatically grant a great deal of publicity to heretics. We have already seen that Eusebius was reluctant to go into much detail concerning heretics and heresies.

This third point needs more elucidation. Modern media studies have shown that a serious "objective" presentation (rather than just denigration) can produce an effect opposed to the one desired, namely, a "mobilization of new participants."[6] Liesbet Van Zoonen has demonstrated that

> attention is focused solely on the positive or negative function that media can fulfill for movements: they either mobilize public opinion and new participants, or they alienate public support; they either strengthen bonds among participants, or they disrupt integral cohesion. . . . If the media transmit the message correctly and without distortion, the wider public may be mobilized as participants or as supporters. On the other hand, if the media distort the movements' message, the public will be alienated and participants frustrated. Thus, the mass media are conceptualized as transmission belts producing single positive or negative stimuli to which an equally single response of audiences will follow.[7]

Eusebius, of course, did not think in these elaborate, modern terms, but he did know that presenting a factual, or even partially neutral, resolution could be dangerous in terms of its reception. Therefore, he understood that a concise and derogatory description of a heresy (not in the words of the authoritative synod itself) would be more effective in alienating his audience from a false doctrine. Throughout the *Ecclesiastical History,* he consistently applies this same notion to many topics other than heresy.

However, Eusebius was aware of the importance of synods as a device for "media exposure," and this becomes evident even in his economical accounts: (1) The concise reports reveal that synods were attended by a large group of people and were therefore major communication events. (2) Synods were held as political assemblies, similar to the local assemblies of Greek cities. But there was one major difference. The synods were held not as a onetime city affair, but as a big regional event. The *synodoi* of the Church not only share the term *synodos* with assemblies of the Greek Federal States (in the Hellenistic period),[8] but also seem to be similar in other respects (in their being regional assemblies, in their accumulating local authorities into one massive sovereignty, in their engaging in public demo-

6. Liesbet Van Zoonen, "A Dance of Death: New Social Movements and Mass Media," in *Political Communication in Action: States, Institutions, Movements, Audiences,* ed. David Paletz (Cresskill, N.J.: Hampton, 1996), 204.

7. Ibid., 205.

8. See J. A. O. Larsen, *Greek Federal States: Their Institutions and History* (Oxford: Clarendon, 1968).

cratic debate, and in their moving the convention from one place to another in the region). (3) The synods filled the outer public sphere of the cities where they convened. In the city of Rome a colloquy of sixty bishops might not have been very impressive, but a large group of bishops in Bostra caused a great deal of noise and movement. A church was a building within the city, a static institution daily housing dynamic community activity, whereas a synod was a stormy event that dramatically affected a whole city. (4) A synod also filled the inner public sphere and gave the local community strong assurance of being part of a grand universal organization. (5) Whereas the city assemblies discussed local matters, which were relatively unimportant,[9] the debates held during synods (they were held in public as we hear from the Beryllus affair) discussed highly interesting matters that were elevated, mysterious, and political. Central terms with significant political overtones such as *eirēnē, pistis, doxa, homonoia* and *polemos,* were freely aired in the synods under the umbrella of an international religious gathering.

In reality the church synods can be seen as branches of a universal "management" organization. In his study of communication with organizations, Robert D. McPhee, drawing on the research of A. Giddens, observes that

> every human activity dually *produces* and *reproduces* the social system and its associated structure of rules and resources. . . . 'Production' implies that strategic human actions are mediated by or draw upon structural resources: to speak we draw on language, to give orders we draw on the power resources of an official position. 'Reproduction' means that social structure is nothing but the outcome of the web of human actions — there would be no language or position if no one drew on it any way, and its nature depends on its enactment.[10]

McPhee reaches the conclusion that structure is in its essence a communication process:

> There *were* some reasonable grounds for this discovery. First, commonsense examples of Structure always include organization charts, job de-

9. Still useful is A. H. M. Jones, *The Cities of the Eastern Roman Provinces,* 2d ed. (Oxford: Clarendon, 1971).

10. Robert D. McPhee, "Organizational Communication: A Structurational Exemplar," in *Rethinking Communication,* vol. 2, ed. Brenda Dervin et al. (Newbury Park, Calif.: Sage Publications, 1989), 200.

scriptions, and other similarly symbolic, documentary, in a word, *textual* items. Second, employees in interviews and social scientists in their operational definitions treat such texts as primary if not privileged repositories of information about Structure. . . . But the document is not the Structure — after all, employees who have never seen the documents have a place in the Structure . . . and the documents can be, on all (other) accounts, inaccurate.[11]

Other elements to be reckoned with are the hierarchy and the vertical communication within the organization, with the important aspect of internal authority. This model is helpful, although we need not use it as it stands. The Church was an organization in the process of constant communication, and thus it performed successful communicative actions. There was the bishopric, a local "management" with a hierarchy (mentioned by Eusebius in Novatian's case)[12] and a duality of structure involving both "production" and "reproduction."

The Network of Episcopal Authority

The bishops filled the inner and at times also the outer public sphere in their dioceses. Their remarkable authority was expressed through rhetoric and action, for instance, in their helping the poor and the sick when nobody dared to do so in times of plague; by such acts they displaced the pagan cults and their priests. The local Roman authorities did not always have the resources, manpower, or courage to help the needy and dying in times of crisis. From Eusebius himself we learn that at certain junctures it was only Christians who came forward to help the needy in the outer public sphere. In other words, the manifestation of power of the Roman authorities was in many aspects quite static, or rather hollow. Pagans viewed the Christian manifestation of power as real and positive since it was active and dynamic.[13] One can speculate that the comfortable ritualized symbols of the Roman Empire became profoundly disappointing when people suffered a plague that was disregarded by the Roman authorities, or when

11. Ibid., 202.

12. *Hist. Eccl.* 6.43.2: "sixty bishops and a still greater number of presbyters and deacons"; cf. 6.43.11. These lists probably reflect the situation in the third century.

13. See Rodney Stark, *The Rise of Christianity: A Sociologist Reconsiders History* (Princeton: Princeton University Press, 1996), 73-94.

harsh tax collectors appeared, or a legion raided some district, or when some wayward new emperor appeared during the civil wars of the third century, and of course when people were severely punished under the Roman criminal system. During these times in particular, the statues and other cultic manifestations seemed static and powerless. The bishop and his staff were therefore a refreshing innovation that constantly radiated from the inner public sphere into the outer one.

The case of the eccentric Paul of Samosata shows very clearly how a bishop could create attractive, new ritualized symbols. Many citizens of the Roman Empire (both before and after 212 c.e.) were well aware that they had a one-sided relationship with the emperor and the Roman authorities.[14] We have an abundance of sources that support Christian propaganda against the symbolic rituals performed in honor of the emperor. For example, according to Justin's *Apology* 1.29, quoted by Eusebius (4.8.3), we hear that "all were intimidated to worship [the emperor Antoninus] as a god, though they knew his nature and origin." Similar statements abound in the writings of the Church Fathers, and if they express even a partial reality, the communication of pagans with the emperor was distorted, or rather nonexistent, for large segments of the population. Such Christian pronouncements aimed at undermining the power base of the emperor himself.

At all events, bishops filled the inner public sphere with communicative acts that radiated into the outer one as well. The bishop was available; he could be addressed daily by his constituency, and it was believed that his authority was derived from God. He was seen, in line with Ignatius's theology, as the representative of God in the diocese.[15] Moreover, the communicative relationships he created with his congregation were imbued with strong mutuality, namely, give and take in daily life. Beginning with Ignatius, we hear about the Church hierarchy (bishop, presbyters, and deacons), and his well-established ideas about the status of the bishop were no

14. This is probably no less true than Price's assumption that pagans believed in the Emperor; see S. R. F. Price, *Rituals and Power: The Roman Imperial Cult in Asia Minor* (Cambridge: Cambridge University Press, 1984), 1-22.

15. Allen Brent, *Cultural Episcopacy and Ecumenism: Representative Ministry in Church History from the Age of Ignatius of Antioch to the Reformation, with Special Reference to Contemporary Ecumenism* (Leiden: Brill, 1992), 91, rightly says that "the collective representation of the nascent Christian society became highly personalized in terms of representative persons, rather than objects which stood for, and with, the sacred story expressing the central norms, values, and beliefs of the groups."

doubt welcome within the Church. In his epistles — which in themselves can be seen as important media channels — he often equates the bishop's leadership of the community with that of God and Jesus (*To the Magnesians* 3: "to the Father of Jesus Christ, the Bishop of all").[16] In *To the Ephesians* 4 he says

> Thus it is proper for you to act in harmony with the mind of the bishop, as you are in fact doing. For your presbytery, which is worthy of its name and worthy of God, is attuned to the bishop as strings to a lyre. Therefore in your unanimity and harmonious love Jesus Christ is sung. You must join the chorus, every one of you, so that by being harmonious in unanimity and taking your pitch from God you may sing in unison with one voice through Jesus Christ . . . It is, therefore, advantageous for you to be in perfect unity, in order that you may always have a share in God.

In *To the Ephesians* 5, Ignatius says that fellowship with the bishop is

> not merely human but spiritual . . . how much more do I congratulate you who are united with him, as the church is with Jesus Christ and as Jesus Christ is with the Father . . . Let no one be misled: if anyone is not within the sanctuary, he lacks the bread of God. . . . Let us, therefore, be careful not to oppose the bishop, in order that we may be obedient to God.

This he repeats with various nuances in other epistles. Hence already around 100 c.e. this concept of inclusion and exclusion from the community as a result of the bishop's authority had taken hold among the Church Fathers.[17] They were aware from the outset that the creation of congregations led by strong authorities within a vast empire — in which national, religious, and ethnic identities were fading — was a crucial necessity for an emerging world organization.

The bishops and the hierarchy of the local church thus became a challenge to the authority of the secular and pagan authorities. This challenge was one of the reasons for the persecutions initiated by the Romans

16. This and the following citations from the letters of Ignatius are taken from J. B. Lightfoot and J. R. Harmer, *Apostolic Fathers: Greek Texts and English Translations of Their Writings,* 2d ed., ed. and rev. Michael W. Holmes (Grand Rapids: Baker Book House, 1992).

17. Cf. also Peter Lampe, *Die Stadtrömischen Christen in den ersten beiden Jahrhunderten: Untersuchungen zur Sozialgeschichte* (Tübingen: Mohr Siebeck, 1989), 334ff.

against Christians. The battle over influence within the outer and institutional public spheres resulted in fierce clashes between Christians and pagans, but the religious motivations were only secondary.

The authority of the bishop functioned at both local and universal levels. People in different regions of the world could have a daily rapport with him and, through him, with Christ and the Father. The new Christian organization, which was gradually being transformed by the bishops into a universal network, worked toward the common identity of believers. According to Ignatius they were "God-bearers," "temple-bearers," and "Christ-bearers." Thus Ignatius emphasizes the union and the sense of belonging that the communities gave their members. Against this background the emergence of the Christian organization as presented in the *Ecclesiastical History* can be seen as a communications revolution within the Roman Empire.

The network of episcopal authority ensured that the organizational web of the Church was sensed daily. Yet during a synod the organization's power was even more manifest, since this managing organ was seen as large as life by the many who were the potential customers within the marketplace. Moreover, the community of bishops in the world can be considered a "flat" horizontal organization, a type that had some advantages (the organizational pattern of the Roman Empire, on the contrary, was basically hierarchical). When one section was hurt by, say, persecution, other sections remained intact. However, the local organization of the diocese was vertical and hence hierarchical. This network, with the synod as its managing organ, can be compared with a modern world organization in the sense that its communication system had an international reach (even if the Church's network was much slower and less complex than that of modern worldwide organizations). The lines of communication among the dioceses of Gaul, Rome, Carthage, Alexandria, and Antioch operated constantly; reactions to recent developments within the Church were swift and intensive.

The early Church's acts of communication were performed on the basis of a common "charter." Synods can be seen as a mechanism that redefined this charter from time to time. There was, as in modern international organizations, a written charter (the New Testament) and an oral one (the tradition of orthodox dogma). The literature of the Gnostics and other groups regarded as heretical, however, demonstrates that this common charter was not always generally accepted. Hence the orthodox Church had to "reproduce" where the "production" could not stay static.

160

From the *Ecclesiastical History* we learn that there was a constant process of media activity that redefined the common charter and safeguarded the organization from a break in authority in one of its many branches. The organization was alert to the fact that a single defection on the part of a bishop of great authority — with the ability to create a new charter — had the potential of becoming contagious and effecting the whole web. We will illustrate this through Eusebius's presentation of the Novatian affair, which shows clearly that Novatian's political games were a menace to the authority of bishops and, therefore, a threat to the whole organization.

Thus, synods emerge from the *Ecclesiastical History* as a dynamic manifestation of the penetration of Christianity into the inner and, in many instances, the outer public spheres. The gatherings of many local bishops advertised the increasing power of the worldwide authority of the orthodox Church. The synods were an effective mechanism of the information flow within this network. Eusebius gives the impression that Christianity became a closed organization within the Roman Empire that in many ways was more effective than the system operating the Empire itself. The Church's organization was able to compete with the organization of the Roman Empire especially during the third century, when the latter suffered destructive inner conflicts. Hence in spite of the short period of persecutions under Decius (249-250 c.e) and the longer one under Diocletian and his successors, the Christian web (or webs, if we take heretics into account) turned into a useful power base for Constantine. Moreover, the synods were an important mechanism of what Alberto Melucci calls a "collective identifying process":

> Individuals acting collectively *construct* their action by defining in cognitive terms their possibilities and limits, while at the same time interacting with others in order to "organize" (i.e. make sense of) their common behavior . . . collective identity should thus be thought of as a *process* of negotiation and conflict that is always subject to challenge and change and that may be better characterized by the term *collective identifying*.[18]

The synods were part of the process of constructing a collective identity of the orthodox Church through negotiation and conflict, whereby oppo-

18. Alberto Melucci, *Nomads of the Present: Social Movements and Individual Needs in Contemporary Society* (London: Hutchinson Radius, 1989), 26.

nents deemed heretical were gradually excluded from the organization. The latter naturally attempted to form a competing network.

The Novatian Schism

Novatian was a schismatic whose teaching aroused great interest.[19] In the mid-third century he presented the Catholic Church with a real challenge; he proposed to exclude from it all the *lapsi* who wished to be received back automatically. One can imagine that Novatian was considered a particularly harmful person, because he advocated the permanent exclusion of many former members from the orthodox Catholic Church. The Church, as we know from Eusebius himself, was extremely sensitive about the numbers of its "registered" members. As we have already seen, Eusebius does not give Novatian a fair chance to state his own case but shows him rather as a crook who made a dirty deal in order to become bishop of Rome.

Let us now analyze Eusebius's text with the help of some useful observations made by Norman Fairclough in a recent study of media discourse:

> The critical discourse analysis approach thinks of the discursive practices of a community — its normal ways of using language — in terms of networks which I shall call 'orders of discourse'. The order of discourse of a social institution or social domain is constituted by all the discursive types which are used there. The point of the concept of 'order of discourse' is to highlight the relationship between different types in such a set (e.g. in the case of a school, the discursive types of the classroom and the playground): whether, for instance, a rigid boundary is maintained between them, or whether they can easily be mixed together in particular texts. . . . Social and cultural changes very often manifest themselves discursively through a redrawing of boundaries within and between orders of discourse. . . . These boundaries are also sometimes a focus of social struggle and conflict.[20]

19. For Novatian, see Alois Grillmeier, *Christ in Christian Tradition from the Apostolic Age to Chalcedon (451)*, trans. J. S. Bowden (New York: Sheed and Ward, 1965), 157-59; Vogt, *Coetus Sanctorum*; and Gülzow, *Cyprian und Novatian*.

20. Norman Fairclough, *Media Discourse* (London: Arnold, 1995), 55-56.

Fairclough makes a distinction between genre and discourse:

> A discourse is the language used in representing a given social practice from a particular point of view. Discourses appertain broadly to knowledge and knowledge construction. For instance, the social practice of politics is differently signified in liberal, socialist and Marxist political discourses; or again, illness and health are differently represented in conventional . . . and homoeopathic medical discourse. A genre, by contrast, is a use of language associated with and constituting part of some particular social practice, such as interviewing people (interview genre) or advertising commodities (advertising genre). Genres can be described in terms of their organizational properties — an interview, for instance, is structured in a quite different way from an advertisement.[21]

In the media, according to Fairclough, the order of discourse is "structured in terms of configurations of genres and discourses, and shifts within the order of discourse and in its relationship to other socially adjacent orders of discourse."[22] The media is positioned between public and private orders of discourse. "This mediating position, and the *external* relations between the order of discourse of the media and socially adjacent public and private orders of discourse such as books and magazines, is the key to understanding the media order of discourse and the *internal* relations between its constituent genres and discourses."

Having made the distinction between "mediatized political discourse" and regular political discourse (which is not mediatized),[23] Fairclough says that we "need to specify the repertoire of voices, discourses and genres within the order of mediatized political discourse, the relationships of choice and alternation within each of these repertoires, and how particular voices, discourses and genres are articulated together in differ-

---

21. Ibid.

22. This and the following quote are from ibid., 62-63.

23. Analyzing political discourse in the media through an interview with British Prime Minister Margaret Thatcher, Fairclough argues that she created a new political discourse, and that "for a new political tendency like Thatcherism to achieve power, it has to carve out a political base, a sufficiently powerful constituency of supporters. Such a political base is partly 'talked into' existence — politicians construct and reconstruct the people, the political public, in their discourse, and a measure of their success is the degree to which people accept, and so make real, these (often wildly imaginary) constructions" (Ibid., 179).

ent types of media output."[24] He starts with voices and argues that "there are two important questions about voices. One is to specify in more detailed terms which voices figure in mediatized politics . . . the other is to show how the various categories of voice are structured in relation to each other in mediatized political discourse — who, for example, tends to have the last word?"[25]

On the subject of genres, Fairclough maintains,

> While much media output draws upon established genres in rather conventional ways, some is more creative, generating novel genres through innovative combinations of established ones. Livingstone and Lunt (1994) see audience discussion programmes as creative in this sense, evolving a genre which combines three established genres of debate, romance and therapy, with the debate element itself involving a configuration of different genres of dialogue — quarrel, debate proper, critical discussion, inquiry and negotiation.[26]

We may also note that "tensions . . . can arise between political discourse and media formats."[27]

One more remark concerning Fairclough's conclusions before we turn back to Eusebius. In his first chapter, he analyzes the relationship between the reporter and the audience by focusing on how the well-known BBC television program *Panorama* presented a story on a ship, the *Shikishimi*, that had transported a cargo of nuclear material. He notes, for instance, how the program made "declarative sentences . . . statements

24. Ibid., 185. Speaking of genre, Fairclough says that "politicians never articulate their various discourses in a pure form, their talk is always situated, always shaped by genres such as political speech making, parliamentary questions and answers, debate, or negotiation. The point is always significant, but becomes crucial when mediatized political discourse is in focus. The genres of the mass media do not at all neatly correspond to the genres of politics, and this lack of fit is a source of constant tension and difficulty for politicians" (Ibid., 184).

25. Ibid., 185. "Ordinary people have featured for a long time in news and documentary programmes as 'vox pop,' edited and circumscribed extracts from interviewers with ordinary people which incorporate an element of popular reaction into reports on political and social issues" (Ibid., 186).

26. Ibid., 189.

27. Ibid., 191. Fairclough mentions several different genres that are drawn upon: "interview, presenter narrative, political commentary and analysis, political speechifying, expert opinion, and ordinary conversation and conversational narrative" (Ibid., 192).

about what will happen in the future. Despite the fact that future events are contingent on many things and therefore uncertain, these are firm, categorical statements — that is the effect of using the auxiliary verb *will* — and there is no qualification or 'hedging' (no 'probably' or 'maybe')." These categorical statements serve to establish a relationship between the reporter and the audience (and between the social identities of reporter and audience). The reporter is projected as a figure of authority — someone who knows the "facts" and has the right to tell them. Yet, as Fairclough emphasizes, there is a constant tension in the objectives of the media today, between giving information and providing entertainment. In the *Panorama* program, "this is evident in certain rhetorical, attention grabbing features: the direct question at the end, the metaphor of a *floating Chernobyl* which links reprocessing to the nuclear *cause célèbre* of Chernobyl in a witty and memorable phrase. . . . In any representation, you have to decide what to include and what to exclude, and what to 'foreground' and what to 'background.'"[28]

I have presented Fairclough's observations at some length because they will prove useful in what follows for understanding Eusebius's methods. If we place the *Ecclesiastical History* against these descriptions of modern media performance, and distinguish its character from the rationalist historiography of Thucydides and other ancient writers, we may speak of Eusebius as having created a new genre of history writing. In the *Ecclesiastical History* he works less as a historian than as a *mediator* of knowledge.

---

28. Ibid., 3-4. "In this case, certain details which you might have expected to be background or excluded altogether — on the grounds that they are common knowledge which a *Panorama* audience might be expected to share — have been foregrounded: describing the cargo as *deadly* and the voyage as *dangerous,* mentioning that plutonium is *one of the world's most toxic substances* and the *raw material of nuclear weapons*. This detail generates a sense of alarm, underlined by the reporter's delivery which stresses the words *deadly, dangerous* and *toxic*. It is sensationalist" (Ibid., 4-5). In another case, Fairclough shows an inconsistency between the image and the words: "This extract takes one step further the tendency in the earlier one for reporter and audience identities and relations to be on the entertainer-consumer model. The genre is passed-event narrative, and the story is told through a combination of words and what the programme identifies as a filmed reconstruction of the incident" (Ibid., 6).

The Clash of Methods and Materials

A constant clash exists between Eusebius's mediatizing methods and the content of the material he adduces. For instance, in his introduction he tells about Novatian and interweaves his own commentary. However, he makes no effort to accommodate his main source — a letter from Cornelius, bishop of Rome, to Fabius, bishop of Antioch — to his own introduction. In his introduction, after a passage from a letter written by Dionysius of Alexandria about the *consistentes* (pentitents who were admitted to the eucharistic prayers but barred from the Eucharist itself), Eusebius says,

> since Novatus [Novatian], a presbyter of the church of the Romans, being lifted up by arrogance against these [those who had "proved weak in the time of persecution"], as if there was no longer any hope of salvation for them, not even if they were to perform everything that a genuine conversion and a pure confession demand, became the leader of a separate sect of those who, in their pride of mind, styled themselves Puritans *(katharoi)*. Whereupon a very large synod was assembled at Rome, of sixty bishops and a still greater number of presbyters and deacons, while in the rest of the provinces the pastors in their several regions individually considered the question as to what was to be done. It was unanimously decreed that Novatus, together with the partners of his arrogance, and those who decided to agree with the man's brother-hating and most inhuman opinion, should be considered as strangers to the Church, but that such of the brethren as had fallen into the misfortune should be treated and restored with the medicines of repentance. (6.43.1-2)

Up to this point Eusebius operates like a narrator, transmitting knowledge that is useful but one-sided. This would be comparable to the methods of the *Panorama* report on the *Shikishimi* incident, in the use of expressions that communicate a clearly negative message to the audience. For example, we may consider Eusebius's remark "as if there was no longer any hope of salvation for them, not even if they were to perform everything that a genuine conversion and a pure confession demand." Talking about future prospects is legitimate in theological works, but not in an "objective" historical account. Eusebius's message is that adherence to the views of such a heresy takes away all hope from human beings. Also, terms such as "pride of mind" function like commentary in modern media pre-

166

sentations. The negativity of terms helps create Eusebius's close relationship with his audience, since they supposedly share the same values, or are potential sharers of them.

At any rate, Eusebius does not go into detail but writes only a short introduction and commentary, and then adds some information about the variety of sources he is using (letters, but within the letters one can detect various genres such as narrative, commentary, conversation, fictional stories, and synod resolutions). Eusebius announces that he has chosen one letter, from Cornelius to Fabius. This letter — at least in the sections Eusebius has chosen to present — tells a very different story from Eusebius's own introduction. We would have expected details about the heresy, but instead we get some unconnected incidents concerning Novatian, mainly sensational "political" ones. Thus a clear tension or even a clash emerges between the presenter's mediatizing introduction and commentary, and the material he communicates to his audience in the letter. Not only in the so-called "order of discourse" do we find a tension, but also in the genres that Eusebius adopts.

Genres Adopted by Eusebius

From the material at his disposal, Eusebius chose only extracts from the letter of Cornelius to Fabius:

> "But that you may know that for a long time back this marvellous fellow [Novatian] has been seeking the office of a bishop, and has succeeded in concealing in his heart this violent desire, using as a veil for his insane folly the fact that he had the confessors with him from the beginning, I wish to speak. Maximus, one of our presbyters, and Urban, both of whom twice reaped the highest meed of renown by confession, and Sidonius, and Celerinus, a man who, by the mercy of God, bore with the utmost endurance all kinds of tortures, and by the strength of his faith strengthened the weakness of his body, and so has mightily overcome the adversary — these men marked him, and detecting the craftiness and duplicity that was in him, his perjuries and falsehoods, his unsociability and wolf-like friendship, returned to the holy Church. And all the knavish tricks and devices that he had long dissembled in his heart, they made known in the presence both of a number of bishops, and also of very many presbyters and laymen, bewailing and repenting of the fact that for a brief space they had left the Church under the persuasion of this treacherous and malicious wild beast." (6.43.5-6)

Then comes the story of the circumstances surrounding Novatian's bishopric, which we will analyze shortly. Here it will suffice to say that this latter story is just an episode, a closed tale, designed to show the right political way (political "order of discourse"). It is a narration with commentary and some fiction and drama. Yet the text just quoted (6.43.5-6) is a kind of "interview" with Cornelius; the extracts actually answer questions implicitly posed by Eusebius. He tells the story of a few distinguished people who were first convinced by Novatian and later returned to the Church. In this Eusebius acts like our media. As Fairclough has noted,

> It is a common observation that news stories are personalized: the category of individual personality is widely evoked in news stories, whereas the category of social (and especially class) subject is correspondingly suppressed . . . many oppositions which appear on the surface of a text — for instance, between government and unions, management and strikers, western allies and foreign dictators — can be assimilated to an underlying opposition between 'us' and 'them.'[29]

This is exactly how Eusebius operates in this case. He speaks of "we" in a positive vein and "them" in a negative manner without granting "them" an equal hearing. For example, he does not deem it necessary to mention the names of those distinguished people who remained in Novatian's camp and who no doubt could provide some interesting stories. Be that as it may, Eusebius works with a blend of genres — commentary, narrative, letter, story, and fiction.

Orders of Discourse

After citing Cornelius's description of Novatian as a "wild beast," Eusebius jumps to another part of Cornelius's letter ("then shortly afterwards he says") recounting Novatian's ordination as bishop:

> "How extraordinary a change and transformation, brother beloved, we have beheld to have taken place in him in a little while! For in sooth this highly distinguished person, who was in the habit of pledging himself by some terrible oaths in no wise to seek the office of bishop, of a sudden appears as a bishop as if he were cast into our midst by some contriv-

29. Ibid., 24.

ance. For in sooth this master of doctrine, this champion of the Church's discipline, when he was attempting to wrest and filch away the episcopate that was not given him from above, chose to himself two companions who had renounced their own salvation, that he might send them to a small and very insignificant part of Italy, and entice thence by some made-up device three bishops, rough and very simple men. He confidently maintained and affirmed the necessity of their coming quickly to Rome, on the pretext that any dissension whatsoever that had arisen might be ended by their activity as mediators, conjointly with other bishops. When they arrived, inasmuch as they were too simple, as we said before, for the unscrupulous devices of the wicked, they were shut up by certain disorderly men like himself, and at the tenth hour, when they were drunk, and sick with the after effects, he forcibly compelled them to give him a bishop's office by a counterfeit and vain laying on of the hands, an office that he assumed by crafty treachery since it did not fall to his lot. One of the bishops not long afterwards returned to the Church, bewailing and confessing his fault; with whom we had communion as a layman, all the laity present interceding for him. And as for the remaining bishops, to these we appointed successors, whom we sent into the places where they were. This vindicator, then, of the Gospel did not know that there should be one bishop in a catholic church, in which he was not ignorant (for how could he be?) that there are forty-six presbyters, seven deacons, seven sub-deacons, forty-two acolytes, fifty-two exorcists, readers, door-keepers, above fifteen hundred widows and persons in distress, all of whom are supported by the grace and loving-kindness of the Master." (6.43.7-11)

After this useful and important list, the letter goes on with related matters that do not provide information concerning the heresy itself. However, later we learn that Novatian would force an oath upon his supporters: "'Swear to me by the Blood and Body of our Lord Jesus Christ never to forsake me and turn to Cornelius.' And the miserable person does not taste until he first calls down a curse upon himself, and instead of saying the Amen as he receives that bread, he says, 'I will not return to Cornelius'" (6.43.18-19).

The core of Novatian's schism is revealed in the material just quoted, and if we omit from the story (excluding the commentary) a few terms such as "bishop" and "church" and replace them with common secular terms, the description could apply to any political quarrel within a city of the eastern Roman Empire. But even if we do not eliminate such terms, the description

169

does not deal with theology or the matters mentioned in Eusebius's introduction to Novatian's story. Thus if we compare this order of discourse to the one used by Eusebius for describing the martyrs, or the language used for theological matters, it is indeed very different. To judge from the order of discourse employed here, we are not dealing with a theological rift in the Church, but with a political "disorder" caused by Novatian. It is worth noting that elsewhere in Book 6, Eusebius relates the ordination of Origen by the laying on of hands of the bishops of Caesarea and Jerusalem. This was done against the custom of the Church, but in this latter case Eusebius is quite approving. Be that as it may, Eusebius, through Cornelius's letter, wishes to set out an exact definition of the authority of the Church and to define its organizational pattern (by, among other things, listing the various positions within the hierarchy). Another tension is produced by the fact that a famous religious figure (Cornelius) whom the reader would expect to communicate through a theological order of discourse, employs simple political terms. A political order of discourse as opposed to other orders (theological, historical, biblical) can be found from time to time in the *Ecclesiastical History*.[30] Moreover, a political order of discourse was an important channel to the outer public sphere since there the story of Novatian's ordination would be quite naturally accepted.

A Repertoire of Voices

As in our modern mass media, we can detect a repertoire of voices in Eusebius's treatment of Novatian. There is an interplay of speakers starting with Eusebius himself, who is the presenter and editor. Next we have the voice of Cornelius, whose letter is quoted verbatim. And then there are the voice of the former supporters of Novatian, named in 6.43.6, who have returned from the outer public sphere to the Church. Novatian's voice is not heard at all, even in the incident dealing with the laying on of hands. Eusebius does allow Novatian to speak, but only within the negative circumstances of the swearing in of his supporters. Novatian's voice is heard again when Cornelius wishes to demonstrate that he was a treacherous person from the outset (in a past event which is now used as evidence against him):

30. As in the case of Thatcherism mentioned above, this order of discourse actually helped to construct the "correct" political organizational framework of the Church.

"... he who through cowardice and love of life at the time of persecution denied that he was a presbyter. For when he was requested and exhorted by the deacons to leave the cell in which he shut himself, and bring all the help to the brethren that it is right and possible for a presbyter to bring to brethren who are in danger and in need of succour, so far was he from obeying the deacon's exhortations, that he even went away and departed in anger. For he said that he no longer wished to be a presbyter, since he was enamoured of a different philosophy." (6.43.16)

Novatian's voice is not given a hearing explicitly even at a crucial juncture in the account, when Cornelius says that "he forcibly compelled them to give him a bishop's office" (6.43.9). Eusebius might have been referring to physical force, and not verbal methods. Again, another bishop who returned to the Catholic Church is heard: "One of the bishops not long afterwards returned to the Church, bewailing and confessing his fault" (6.43.10). And we hear, of course, the voices of the people in prison.

In other words, the repertoire of voices in Eusebius's account suggests that he was subtler than first appears. Throughout the account he gives preference to the voices that represent the right (orthodox) order ("we"). He in fact creates a hierarchy of voices, some heard, some just mentioned as mute actors in the drama. This method can be encountered in other cases as well, where voices are arranged hierarchically within the accounts. For instance, in the martyrdom stories we get an interaction of voices (one should remember that these accounts were read aloud, hence the importance of voices). We have seen that when the martyrs talk in front of the crowd and the Roman authorities, the martyr always has the upper hand. But who are the "agents" in the case of Novatian? He himself, the bishops and other functionaries who left the Church and returned, Cornelius, and Eusebius himself. All of these are voices from the inner public sphere. The *vox populi* is also represented, as we shall see, through a story about a man named Serapion.

Images

Eusebius could not use films or documentaries, but he evoked vivid images that people could imagine while they read. Thus we find a picture of drunken bishops, a picture of Novatian in prison, and a story about a cer-

171

tain Serapion. This time Eusebius adduces a story to demonstrate how wrong Novatian actually was.

> But to this same Fabius, when he was inclining somewhat towards the schism, Dionysius also, he of Alexandria, wrote, making many other remarks with reference to repentance in his letter to him, and describing the conflicts of those lately martyred at Alexandria. In the course of his narrative he tells a certain astonishing tale, which must needs be handed down in this work. It is as follows: "But this one example that happened amongst us I shall set forth for thee. There was a certain Serapion amongst us, an old man and a believer, who lived blamelessly for a long time, but in the trial fell. This man oftentimes besought [absolution], and no one paid him heed. For indeed he had sacrificed. And, falling sick, he continued for three successive days speechless and unconscious; but on the fourth he rallied a little, and calling his grandson to him, he said: 'How long, my child, do ye hold me back? Haste ye, I pray, and grant me a speedy release; do thou summon me one of the presbyters.' And having said this he again became speechless. The boy ran for the presbyter. But it was night, and he was unwell and could not come. Yet since I had given an order that those who were departing this life, if they besought it, and especially if they had made supplication before, should be absolved, that they might depart in hope, he gave the little boy a small portion of the eucharist, bidding him soak it and let it fall in drops down into the old man's mouth. Back came the boy with it, and when he was near, before he entered, Serapion revived again and said, 'Hast thou come, child? The presbyter could not come, but do thou quickly what he bade thee, and let me depart.' The boy soaked it and at the same time poured it into his mouth, and when he had swallowed a little he straightway gave up the ghost. Was it not plain that he was preserved and remained until he obtained release, that, with his sin blotted out, he might be acknowledged for all the good deeds he had done?" (6.44.1-6)

Eusebius inserts this story between Cornelius's letter and a letter of Dionysius to Novatian himself exhorting him not to cause a schism in the Church (6.46). Thus the story of Serapion has the status of a film clip in our modern media. It is a picture that "moves" as one goes along reading the passage (aloud). But does this image really demonstrate what has been said about Novatian in the preceding letter by Cornelius? Here we can again adapt the research of Fairclough. He analyzes an edition of the ITV current affairs program *This Week* entitled "Vigilante!" (10 September 1992). He shows that this extract "takes one step further the tendency in the earlier one for reporter and audience identities and relations to be on the entertainer-consumer model. . . . The extract, and indeed the programme as a whole, is on the borderline between information and entertainment, and between fact and fiction. The visual narrative of the film, in which the crowd is played by actors, is dramatic fiction . . . there are also apparent inconsistencies between words and images."[31] In Eusebius's report on the Novatian affair, the linguistic account — the knowledge or information that we receive about the political misbehavior of Novatian — is one thing, but it is the image or the dramatic section brought forward for demonstration (and no doubt for entertainment as well) that actually tackles the theological problem. Here we find a remarkable consistency. The "pictures," like the narrative, accentuate the negative portrayal of "them," the heretics.

The Placement of the Novatian Episode

Finally, we should comment on the position of the Novatian episode within the macrostructure of the *Ecclesiastical History*. This story (6.43-45) occupies a position similar to that of most episodes in our media. It is loosely connected to what happens before and to what occurs afterwards. It is a "closed" episode within Book 6, and is not connected either generically or in terms of cause and effect to the theme of heresy within the *Ecclesiastical History*.

It will be useful to examine the episode against the background of Teun van Dijk's analysis of the macro- and microstructure of news, which has been conveniently summarized by Norman Fairclough:[32]

> The concept of 'macrostructure' is central to the analysis of thematic structure: the macrostructure of a text is its overall organization in terms of themes and topics. It is a hierarchical organization, in the sense that we can identify the theme of a whole text (and sum up a single proposition), which can typically be spelt out in terms of a few rather less general themes, which can each in turn be spelt out in terms of a particular type of text. . . . A news report typically has a headline, a lead, an "event" element that covers the main events of the story, and a comment element.

31. Fairclough, *Media Discourse*, 6-7.
32. Ibid., 28ff.

Van Dijk's "microstructure," on the other hand, refers to "semantic relations between propositions — coherence relations of causality, consequence and so forth."

Before elaborating on this, we should look at some observations from Allan Bell's study of the structure of news stories:[33] "A story consists of one or more episodes, which in turn consist of one or more events. Events must contain actors and action, usually express setting, and may have explicit attribution. The categories of attribution, actors and setting (time and place) need to be recognized as part of the structure of news stories."[34] He recognizes three additional elements that can contribute to an event:

> follow-up, commentary and background . . . follow-up covers any action subsequent to the main action of an event. It can include verbal reaction . . . or non-verbal consequences . . . commentary provides the journalist's or news actor's observations on the action. It may be represented by context . . . it may be explicit evaluation . . . it may express expectations held by the journalist or a news actor on how a situation could develop next. . . . the category of background covers any events prior to the current action. These are classed as 'previous episodes' if they are comparatively recent. They probably figure as news stories in their own right at an earlier stage of the situation. If the background goes beyond the near past, it is classed as 'history.' . . . Follow-up and background can have the character of episodes in their own right. That is, episode is a recursive category and can be embedded under consequences, reaction, history and background.[35]

If we now consider those observations as a background for our analysis, we can position the Novatian affair within the *Ecclesiastical History*. The macrostructure of Eusebius's account is the theme of heresy, which is interwoven as a separate theme. The heresies are not linked to each other, and the text cannot be considered as comprising a comprehensive historical monograph on heresy. Heresies, as we have seen in Chapter 4, have some common features in Eusebius's presentation, but he does not see them as a logical historical sequence whose components are connected by

33. A. Bell, "Telling Stories," in *Media Texts, Authors and Readers: A Reader*, ed. David Graddol and Oliver Boyd-Barrett (Clevedon, England and Philadelphia: Multilingual Matters and the Open University, 1994), 112-13.
34. Ibid., 112-113.
35. Ibid., 113-115.

cause and effect. Thus the theory of separate historical monographs within the *Ecclesiastical History* (history of martyrdom, heresy, Jews, and so on) cannot stand. If we consider Book 6 as a whole, the disconnectedness of the Novatian affair within the book is even more conspicuous.

In terms of microstructure, we have already seen that the linkage between events within the Novatian case is not very tight, and that Eusebius assembles and then edits some disconnected events. However, in this episode, as well as in others, we have found elements of background, commentary, and sometimes even follow-up. Thus if the Novatian affair is representative of much of what Eusebius does in his *Ecclesiastical History*, and I believe that it is, we can say that this work is a collection of loosely connected episodes and events. Some of these were clearly connected in reality, but Eusebius fails to show a coherent and linear historical process.[36]

Eusebius's methods of presentation here are reminiscent of the ones employed by our modern newspapers. There is no real connection between the different items and episodes. Yet, as in a yearly run of a modern newspaper, there is a broad common denominator in the *Ecclesiastical History*. Unlike the histories of Thucydides, Polybius, and Cassius Dio, the *Ecclesiastical History* is not a coherent historical account, but much more like what we have in our mass media: a patchwork of episodes, events, drama, and fiction. There is no exact chronology within the episodes or the events described, and the concept of time is loosely applied; for example, there is no clue whether a certain event happened over the course of a day, weeks, or months; neither is there an exact indication of when an event transpired; nor is there an annalistic linear concept connecting the whole work, except for the very general one that the events described occurred during the four first centuries of the common era and are recounted within the framework of the reigns of Roman emperors. The chronology of the *Ecclesiastical History* is comparable to newspapers in the twentieth century that appear in a sequential order day after day but do not reflect a real inner chronology.

36. This is not the case with Polybius, who considered his history to be a presentation of a chain of events connected by cause and effect and to form a *symplokē* ("interweaving"); cf. his Book 12; and G. Schepens, "Polemic and Methodology in Polybius' Book XII," in *Purposes of History: Studies in Greek Historiography from the 4th to the 2nd Centuries B.C.*, ed. H. Verdin, G. Schepens, and E. de Keyser (Louvain: University of Leuven Press, 1990), 39-61.

Conclusion

What, then, was Eusebius's motivation in writing more elaborately about Novatian than about some other important heretics (such as Beryllus and Marcion)? Not the availability of sources. Eusebius worked like a modern journalist, whose job requires knowing "what is generally thought of as ordinary and normal in order to be able to recognize *difference* and *deviance* and to produce news stories at all." Eusebius had a "nose for news." And his reliance on a "socially shared set of ideas, norms, and values" marks him as part of a "'deviance defining elite' that continually reproduce dominant ideas about 'normal behaviour.'"[37] Thus, Eusebius is not a cheap gossip or a storymonger (like Suetonius, for instance). He selects the most deviant episodes, passing over the hard narrative history of synods and their decisions. He selects events and information that are different, special, and easily transmitted. (Thucydides, by contrast, puts in everything necessary for a comprehensive history of the Peloponnesian War.)

The case of Novatian — which is just one example among many, but a typical one at that — shows again that Eusebius's *Ecclesiastical History* may fruitfully be examined in light of the modern media. This work resembles newspapers and magazines more than it does the works of classical and Hellenistic historiography. Eusebius does not operate like a Greek or Roman historian. Nor does he simply offer a collection of *exempla,* as some later Byzantine historians did. With the *Ecclesiastical History,* he created a new genre of history writing. Adapting the results of media performance studies enables us to discern the genre of this work more clearly. The similarities of method and content between certain media performances and Eusebius's *Ecclesiastical History* are too obvious to be ignored. This approach to the field of ancient historiography frees us from dependence on the scheme of Greek and Hellenistic history writing that modern scholars have favored.

What also emerges from this study is that Eusebius did not just write a defense of the orthodox Catholic Church. Rather, he indicated the linkage between organized authority and its effect on communications and media performance within the inner, outer, and institutional public spheres. This linkage contributed to the rise of Christendom. By presenting the political fiasco of Novatian as he did, Eusebius transmitted the

---

37. The quoted material in this paragraph is adapted from Van Zoonen, "A Dance of Death," 208 (see above, note 6).

message that the established world network that created the boundaries of Christian society within its sociopolitical environment had to be strengthened and kept intact.

CHAPTER 6

Mission as Marketing Strategy

M ission to Gentiles was yet another aspect of the media revolution carried out by early Christianity. Communications with Gentiles (and Jews) in the first three centuries of the common era were performed through media channels of which Christian leaders made effective use. Their intensive activity can be understood against the background of the theological concept of the "marketing" potential outside the inner sphere of the Church. In this view the whole world was pervaded by the Logos, only waiting to be revealed.[1] The picture we get from the *Ecclesiastical History* is one of decisive action on the part of the Catholic organizational system within the worldly sphere in order to stimulate this potential constituency. The media channels discussed in the following pages were created, for example, by missionaries who set up outposts in pagan regions, sometimes remote and isolated, thus enlarging the organizational reach of the Church. These strategic bases became launching points for further expansion, that is, penetration into more of the outer public sphere. The common "charter" on which Catholic Christianity was based, the New Testament and related literature, was also employed as a media channel to reach new groups within the outer sphere. Other effective devices that played a

---

1. Eusebius's view has been well formulated by J. Rebecca Lyman, *Christology and Cosmology: Models of Divine Activity in Origen, Eusebius, and Athanasius* (Oxford: Clarendon, 1993), 88: "Theoretically, Eusebius organized his historical and literary defence around a fundamental conviction of God's power as active and discernible at all levels of reality. Human experience, whether historical or spiritual, was grounded in the saving will and providence of God."

significant role as media channels included apologies aimed at people in the higher echelons of society, the web of regional churches and catechetical schools, and the use of advertisement-like references to the Church and the faith. Media efforts were not only overt; we also find a great many hidden agents who became effective channels without being aware that they were promoting Christianity.

Christianity and Culture

Before dealing with the methods of mission, we should first investigate some of the basic terms which we will need in our discussion. Aylward Shorter, in *Toward a Theology of Inculturation*, deals with the history of inculturation in modern times; however, some of his observations can be applied to our case. He first distinguishes between two terms, *acculturation* and *inculturation*. He defines culture according to Clifford Geertz as "A system of inherited conceptions expressed in symbolic forms by means of which human beings communicate, perpetuate and develop their knowledge about, and their attitudes towards life," concluding that "culture is therefore essentially a transmitted pattern of meanings embodied in symbols, a pattern capable of development and change."[2] Shorter goes on to define *acculturation* as "the encounter between one culture and another, or the encounter between cultures," that is, "between two different sets of symbols and conceptions, two different interpretations of experience, two different social identities." Culture is made up of "intercommunicating ideas and forms of behaviour," and "the introduction of new behaviour entails an eventual change of ideas, and vice versa." Further, "behaviour and ideas cannot be separated from one another . . . acculturation is a historical process . . . in dealing with culture and the encounter between cultures, we are confronting a dynamic and diachronic phenomenon, and not a static, unchanging one."[3] This definition naturally leads to the notion of cultural domination: "Domination implies the unwelcome transference of foreign cultural traits: symbols, meanings, values and behaviour, from one culture to another."[4]

2. Aylward Shorter, *Toward a Theology of Inculturation* (Maryknoll, N.Y.: Orbis, 1988), 5.
3. Ibid., 7.
4. Ibid., 8.

Enculturation used in a sociological context refers to "the cultural learning process of the individual, the process by which a person is inserted into his or her culture."[5] *Inculturation,* says Shorter, is a theological concept, and he defines it as "the on-going dialogue between faith and culture or cultures. More fully, it is the creative and dynamic relationship between the Christian message and a culture or cultures.[6] Shorter adds three useful comments concerning inculturation that bear quoting at length:[7]

> We are not only talking about the first insertion of the Christian message into a hitherto non-Christian culture or cultures. . . . culture . . . is a developing process, and there must be, therefore, a continuous dialogue between faith and culture. . . . Indeed, there are times when the dialogue may be suspended, and culture gains, as it were, the upper hand, undermining or distorting the values of the Gospel. This is the situation dubbed by theologians as "culturalism." At such moments it is obviously vital to re-start the dialogue.
>
> Christian faith cannot exist except in a cultural form. When we speak of Christian faith or Christian life, we are necessarily speaking of a cultural phenomenon. It is a distinctive way of life that can only operate culturally. . . . When we describe inculturation as a dialogue between faith and culture, we are really speaking of a dialogue between a culture and the faith in cultural form, in the first instance a dialogue between the Christianized culture of the missionary and the hitherto un-Christianized culture to which he comes. . . .[8]
>
> When we speak of inculturation, we are referring to a phenomenon that transcends mere acculturation. It is the stage when a human culture is enlivened by the Gospel from within, a stage which presupposes a measure of reformulation or, more accurately, reinterpretation. . . . it is only when there is a truly critical symbiosis, and the Christian experience is really integrated, or — to use the term favoured by Pope Paul VI

5. Ibid., 5.

6. Ibid., 11.

7. Ibid., 11-12.

8. Shorter says further: "Before the 'new creation' . . . can take place there has to be an acculturation stage in which Christianity (in previous cultural form) seeks expression through elements proper to the new culture. It follows that Christian evangelization can only take place through the ordinary human process of acculturation, and that the message of the Gospel passes from culture to culture, and from history to history."

181

— "transposed," within the local culture, that we can speak of inculturation in the strict sense.

Moreover, "the reciprocal and critical interaction between the Christian faith and culture is a historical process. It is to be identified with the transfer of religious meaning between cultures, which, in Christian terms, is called 'mission' or 'evangelization.'"[9]

Since inculturation "seems to suggest that the process of mission or evangelization is a one-way process," Shorter introduces an additional concept, *interculturation,* according to which "Christianity is transformed by culture, not in a way that falsifies the message, but in a way in which the message is formulated and interpreted anew. When official Church statements declare, as they often do, that Christianity is enriched by the values of the culture that is being evangelized, it means that the Christian way of life is finding new scope and fuller understanding."[10]

Referring to the modern scene, Shorter comments that

it is God who speaks through strangers, and this "conditioning by strangers" is an important theme in the history of divine revelation. In the history of Christian mission, the message has always been brought by strangers in the first place, and the chain of tradition goes back ultimately to the original "stranger" who is Jesus Christ. One of the most valuable insights of the Second Vatican Council was that God's all-encompassing grace and activity is not limited by the visible institutions of the Church. With this truth in mind, it is easier to accept that missionary activity is a two-way process, and that inculturation is really an intercultural activity with intercultural benefits.[11]

Against this background we can ask whether mission as it appears in the *Ecclesiastical History* reveals a process of acculturation, inculturation, or interculturation. We shall see that Eusebius, without being aware of these particular terms, includes a great deal of what they encompass. Here it will suffice to say that, as we know from other sources as well, an enduring process of acculturation took place through the encounter of early Christianity with cultures in the outer public sphere; over the centuries both inculturation and interculturation became unavoidable. One of the

9. Ibid., 12-13.
10. Ibid., 14.
11. Ibid., 15-16.

main vehicles for acculturation and inculturation was the act of mission. This communicative action was not initiated only by the various visible agents of the Church; it was not necessarily an overt process. Eusebius presents mission as a hidden process as well, performed by agents outside the Church who were motivated by the Logos to act for the promotion of Christianity. Some of the agents described by Eusebius were aware of their vocation; others performed it without even knowing that they were actually helping to weave the new Christian network. It was Eusebius who granted them this historical role. The concept of mission performed by a stranger was not an innovation of Vatican II.

Historically, declares Eusebius, Christians were assigned the vocation of mission even prior to the appearance of Jesus Christ. In both his *Demonstratio Evangelica* and *Ecclesiastical History*, we learn that Christianity started with the beginning of the world. The patriarchs and early leaders of Israel were Christians who shared universal (good) traits. Moses saved the wayward Jews from slavery in Egypt and gave them the law in order to keep them in "civilized" shape. During the Mosaic period, the true Christian faith was hidden, and Moses' law could therefore be regarded as an icon and a symbol. Since the Jews did not fulfill the first covenant, they were punished; and since they did not acknowledge Jesus as their Messiah and slew both him and John the Baptist, they suffered destruction. Jews who put faith in Jesus as Messiah, on the other hand, were considered the "elect," and a select few among them became the apostles of Jesus. Thus after Judaism was eliminated (as an inferior kind of Christianity), Christianity began to reach out to all the Gentiles in the world. The Mosaic law, says Eusebius, was limited to Palestine and the Jews living there. It could not be applied in its entirety to the inhabitants of the *oikoumenē*.

Eusebius thus endows the Christian mission with a historical pedigree; his theology of mission views the Church's evangelism as a communicative action, both hidden and overt, that was embedded in Christianity from the start. This kind of communicative action turned Christianity into a world religion. Mission can be seen as the movement *(kinēsis)* that constituted the driving force of the grand strategy behind the media network of Christianity. Such a historical interpretation of mission also explains why Eusebius emphasizes the role of the canonical and extracanonical books adopted as the common "charter" by the Christian organization. Unlike the Mosaic law, which was valid only in Palestine, the New Testament was applicable to the whole world. There, in the outer public sphere, audiences of varied nature had to be addressed, and we will see in the following how different methods of mission were used to target different social segments. Mission to the masses was carried out differently than mission aimed at the higher strata of society.

Eusebius's emphasis on publicity and media performance had an impact on his own methods of presentation. Several channels or devices of media strategy can be discerned. We will begin with the formation of the canon.

The Formation of the Canon

The formation of the canon is dealt with in the *Ecclesiastical History* as an integral part of the history of the Church, an approach interesting in itself from an historiographic point of view.[12] In contrast to pagan literature, where the issue of canon does not exist, in the *Ecclesiastical History* it emerges as a significant theme within the historical dynamics of the early Church. One of the main reasons for this preoccupation with canon is the connection made by Eusebius, sometimes only implicitly, between mission and canon. The canonical and some extracanonical books became an important vehicle for spreading the religion. The early Church Fathers were aware that an effective organization must speak with one voice and that, to do this, it must have a common "charter" that can be referred to by all its participants.[13]

In Book 2 of the *Ecclesiastical History*, Eusebius writes,

> But a great light of religion shone on the minds of the hearers of Peter, so that they were not satisfied with a single hearing or with the unwritten teaching of the divine proclamation, but with every kind of exhortation besought Mark, whose Gospel is extant, seeing that he was Peter's follower, to leave them a written statement of teaching given them verbally, nor did they cease until they had persuaded him, and so became the cause of the Scripture called the Gospel according to Mark. (2.15.1)

12. Cf. in general Robert M. Grant, *Eusebius as Church Historian* (Oxford: Clarendon, 1980), Chap. 11.
13. For the necessity of a "frame of reference" (i.e., the Bible) in modern missionary work, see Alan R. Tippett, *Introduction to Missiology* (Pasadena, Calif.: William Carey Library, 1987), 13-16.

Eusebius adds that the apostle Peter "ratified the scripture for study in the churches" (2.15.2). This means that the first steps toward canonicity were performed in the inner public sphere. The "hearers" whom Eusebius mentions were probably people from Christian circles in Rome. The use of the canon in the inner public sphere is corroborated in 2.17.12, where we learn that the Therapeutai, whom Eusebius wrongly describes as Christians, probably read the Gospels and the writings of the Apostles as well as "some expositions of prophets after the manner of the ancients, such as are in the Epistle to the Hebrews and many other of the epistles of Paul." It is quite clear that the common text of this burgeoning world organization became the canon, which drew the boundaries among Christians, Gentiles, and Jews. The former had a common charter that made their communication with each other an easy task. Thus, although the second-century *Epistle to Diognetus* notes how similar Christians were to their neighbors in daily life,[14] their common text and organization nevertheless made them very different.

In Book 3 Eusebius writes,

> Now it would be clear from Paul's own words and from the narrative of Luke in the Acts that Paul, in his preaching to the Gentiles, laid the foundations of the churches from Jerusalem round about unto Illyricum. And from the Epistle which we have spoken of as indisputably Peter's, in which he writes to those of the Hebrews in the Dispersion of Pontus and Galatia, Cappadocia, Asia, and Bithynia, it would be clear from his own words in how many provinces he delivered the word of the New Testament by preaching the Gospel of Christ to those of the circumcision. But it is not easy to say how many of these and which of them were genuinely zealous and proved their ability to be the pastors of the churches founded by the Apostles, except by making a list of those mentioned by Paul. For there were many thousands of his fellow-workers and, as he called them himself, fellow-soldiers, of whom the most were granted by him memorial past forgetting, for he recounts his testimony to them unceasingly in his own letters, and, moreover, Luke also in the Acts gives a list of those known to him and mentions them by name. (3.4.1-4)

There follows a list of bishops appointed in different regions (3.4.5-11), including Timothy, Titus, Crescens, Linus, Clement, and Dionysius the Areopagite.

14. Shorter, *Toward a Theology of Inculturation*, 3.

From this evidence we can already highlight some important points from Eusebius's presentation. First, both hearers and speakers believed that oral communication alone was not effective; the common tradition adopted by Christians could remain accurate only if it were written down and passed on as Scripture. Second, in order for a text to become authoritative, Christians knew from the outset that it had to be granted a special status and sanction that was both religious and institutional. Third, the authoritative texts could be granted institutional sanction only if they had been authored by founders of the Church or close associates of the founders. Fourth, written letters to the communities were a prime media vehicle, and even some of the early extracanonical texts such as *1 Clement* were "publicly read in the common assembly in many churches both in the days of old and in our own time" (3.16.1).[15]

The formation of the canon was carried out within the inner public sphere.[16] An example of this process can be found in 3.24.1–3.25.7, where Eusebius has a long section on the problem of canonization. Here we cannot go into much detail, but Eusebius places books into three categories: "Recognized" (regarded as true and genuine and therefore "accepted without controversy by ancients and moderns alike"); "Disputed" (not universally accepted but known to most writers of the Church); and "Not Genuine" (rejected as forgeries of heretics).[17] These canonical distinctions constitute an integral part of the historical survey of the *Ecclesiastical History*.

Two aspects should be emphasized here. First, it is a well-known fact

15. Although no more than 10 to 15 percent of early Christians were able to read, the other 85 percent could be acquainted with Scripture, since "in Graeco-Roman society the illiterate had access to literacy in a variety of public settings . . . if most Christians were illiterate, it did not prevent them from participating in literacy or from becoming familiar with Christian texts. Those who had only a cursory contact with Christianity through missionary preaching or propaganda could hardly have failed to notice its reliance on texts and to hear them quoted" (Harry Y. Gamble, *Books and Readers in the Early Church: A History of Early Christian Texts* [New Haven and London: Yale University Press, 1995], 8).

16. On the formation of the canon, see Bruce M. Metzger, *The Canon of the New Testament: Its Origin, Development, and Significance* (Oxford: Clarendon, 1987).

17. Still useful is Friedrich Lücke, *Über den neutestamentlichen Kanon des Eusebius von Cäsarea* (Berlin: Reimer, 1816); and C. F. G. Heinrici, *Das Urchristentum in der Kirchengeschichte des Eusebius* (Leipzig: Edelmann, 1894). For Eusebius's classification of orthodox and unorthodox books, see Metzger, *Canon of the New Testament*, 201-7.

that already in antiquity religious organizations created and adopted a properly defined charter that contained their basic, common frames of reference. We find this, for instance, in Second Temple Judaism, in the Qumran *Rule of the Community*;[18] in rabbinic Judaism, with the Mishnah, Tosephta, and Talmud; and, of course, in the regulations of Christian monastic organizations. The orthodox church from its outset fought — in particular against heretics — for the establishment of one common and uniform corpus of authoritative literature for universal reference.[19] Since an organization of this nature can show its strength only if it is resolute in its dealings with the outer world, its effectiveness comes to the fore in a firm charter that constitutes the common bond of the communities within the inner public sphere. Secondly, the canonical books were employed by the orthodox Catholic organization as written texts for the promotion of its message to audiences in the outer sphere.[20] In antiquity, books were one of the most important media vehicles for spreading an idea.

But there is yet another reason why canonicity became such an important factor in the rise of the orthodox Church to world prominence, and here we may appeal again to the terms *inculturation* and *acculturation*. The appearance of heretics at an early stage of the Catholic Church's existence made it indispensable for orthodox Christians to have a well-defined written text, because some heretics undertook their own mission and competed with the orthodox Church through oral and written communication.[21] This they did by excluding some of the orthodox books, and in certain instances by adding ones of their own. Simon Magus and Menander are good examples. The latter declared that "he was the saviour who had been sent from above for the salvation of men from invisible aeons and taught that no one, not even of the angels who made the world, could survive unless they were first rescued through the magic art which

18. For a recent study of the *Rule of the Community*, see Sarianna Metso, *The Textual Development of the Qumran Community Rule* (Leiden: Brill, 1997).

19. See Metzger, *Canon of the New Testament*, 75-106. The soundness of the text itself became an important issue; see Bart D. Ehrman, *The Orthodox Corruption of Scripture: The Effect of Early Christological Controversies on the Text of the New Testament* (New York: Oxford University Press, 1993).

20. On the concern of the early Church Fathers with the distribution and availability of Christian books, cf. Gamble, *Books and Readers in the Early Church*, 82-143.

21. Cf. Metzger, *Canon of the New Testament*, 75-106. Orthodox Christians themselves tampered with the text of Scripture to suit their theological purposes; see Ehrman, *Orthodox Corruption of Scripture*.

was transmitted by him and through the baptism which he delivered" (3.26.1-2). As we have seen with the Montanists as well, interculturation can become a dangerous process in which the religion undergoes severe modifications by adopting aspects from the culture it wishes to transform. In fact, it is the religion rather than the local culture that ends up being transformed. Strict adherence to a canon and a set of dogmas was exactly what promised to limit such a process and to safeguard the encounter between Christianity and pagan culture as a process of inculturation, in which the religion "decides" what to accept and what to eliminate from the culture it wishes to transform.

Thus a canon — itself already interculturated — was considered a safe and clear frame of reference to fend off heretics like Simon, Menander, and the Montanists and to draw a clear and definite line separating acculturation, inculturation, and interculturation. The orthodox New Testament became a media framework that excluded competing orders of discourse in rival texts. But even those who attempted to discredit only parts of the canon (the Ebionites, for instance) were seen as groups who worked against the basic common charter of the organization, diminishing its effectiveness (3.27.4-5).

Eusebius was therefore extremely sensitive to canonization as a facet of the history of the early Church, and in 3.36.4 he adduces Ignatius's warning to Christians "to be on their guard against the heresies" by holding fast "to the tradition of the Apostles, to which he thought necessary, for safety's sake, to give the form of written testimony." In 4.23.12 he stresses that falsification of the Holy Scriptures constituted a menace to the Church (citing the complaint of Dionysius of Corinth concerning the falsification of both his own letters and "the Scriptures of the Lord"). In fact, Eusebius does not oppose the reading of disputed books in churches as long as there is a defined canon, authoritatively ratified (3.31.6; 4.23.11).[22]

The Old Testament was also considered a basic Church text, and Eusebius used it himself extensively in his *Demonstratio Evangelica*. In *Hist. Eccl.* 5.8.1 (cf. also 4.26.12-14) he says, "At the beginning of this work we made a promise to quote from time to time the sayings of the presbyters and writers of the church of the first period, in which they have delivered the traditions which came down to them about the canonical Scrip-

---

22. For public reading in the congregation, see Gamble, *Books and Readers in the Early Church*, 203-41 (Chapter 5, "The Uses of Early Christian Books").

tures." He then proceeds to cite Irenaeus's words about the New Testament and the Septuagint (5.8.2-15).

An important piece of information occurs also in 5.10.3. Here we have Bartholomew, "one of the Apostles, [who] had preached to them [the Indians] and had left them the writing of Matthew in Hebrew letters, which was preserved until the time mentioned." Whether this is true or not, it demonstrates the importance of the spread of the canonical books (even in Hebrew) for the act of mission.

The influence of the canon in daily life is emphasized in 6.3, where we learn that Origen decided at one stage to get rid of all his volumes of ancient pagan literature, even though they interested him very much, in order to devote his time to divine Scripture. Many Gentiles were impressed by his imitation of the way of life described in the Gospel. "Above all he [Origen] considered that those sayings of the Saviour in the Gospel ought to be kept which exhort us not [to provide] two coats nor to use shoes, nor, indeed, to be worn out with thoughts about the future" (6.3.10). This is an interesting piece of information; at a certain point in his life, Origen became aware of the dangers to the Christian religion inherent in the process of interculturation. It also shows that he was extremely confident in his own faith, which was based on a common charter.

In 6.14.1-7 Eusebius again tackles the issue of canon, this time in the context of his treatment of Clement of Alexandria. He mentions that Clement's *Hypotypōseis* "has given concise explanations of all the Canonical Scriptures, not passing over even the disputed writings." He goes on to cite Clement's defense of the Pauline authorship of the Epistle to the Hebrews, as well as Clement's information on "a tradition of the primitive elders with regard to the order of the Gospels" (of Mark and John).

In later books (7–10), Eusebius ceases to deal with the problem of canon; other, more burning issues occupy him. The problem of the canon was more or less settled in his own lifetime and therefore lacked any "news value." But the *Ecclesiastical History* still shows that the canon became the main source from which missionaries drew their message. Since the New Testament was itself the end product of a process of interculturation between Christianity and the dominant Greco-Roman culture,[23] it could easily be employed as a missionary text in a local pagan environment. Unlike the situation in Africa in the nineteenth century — where the Chris-

23. See F. Siegert, "La culture grecque, le message Chrétien," *Revue de Theologie et Philosophie* 125 (1993): 321-41.

tian canon, even in translation, remained an alien text to the inhabitants[24]
— the Greek canon, which had been formed in a milieu similar to the one
it was now addressing, became an easy repository of texts to use in spreading the religion among the Greek-speaking masses. When the canon was
closed, the risks of its being affected by interculturation were minimal.
The existence of the Old Testament in Greek also helped promote the new
religion, as did the Church's adoption of Hellenistic Jewish writers (Philo,
Aristobulus, Josephus, Demetrius, and Eupolemus) who argued that "Moses and the Jewish race went back further in their origins than the Greeks"
(6.13.7).

Why was the transforming of an oral tradition into a written, canonical one so important for the act of mission? A rather remote example may
suggest an answer. In a collection of papers dedicated to H. A. Innis, the
distinguished communications theorist G. G. Valaskakis illustrates and ex-
pands on Innis's observation concerning "the disturbances which have
characterized a shift from a culture dominated by one form of communication to another culture dominated by another form of communication
(for example, the movement from oral tradition to print communication
imposed by the West)."[25] She focuses on one specific subject, the expansion of Euro-Canadian control over the Inuit territories in southern Baffin
Island. While traders and whalers were the agents of social change, the
critical cultural role belonged to the missionaries, who introduced print-
ing and literacy. During the whaling period, local community leaders
could easily act as the incomers' agents without losing their traditional
roles. However, when whaling declined, the missionary impact became
very substantial, and local converts took a prominent part in missionary
activity. Literacy was central to the largely Protestant values being propa-
gated; it allowed personal consultation of the Bible and supplemented or
even supplanted the authority of the preacher. "The mode of communication [through literacy] had a particular function in the process of directed
change: the transfer of Christian authority from ministers to individual
converts."[26] At the same time that print was stabilizing missionary and

24. See Eugene Albert Nida, *Message and Mission: The Communication of the Christian Faith*, 2d ed. (South Pasadena, Calif.: William Carey Library, 1975).
25. G. G. Valaskakis, "The Other Side of Empire: Contact and Communication in Southern Baffin Island," in *Culture, Communication, and Dependency: The Tradition of H. A. Innis*, ed. William H. Melody, Liora Salter, and Paul Heyer (Norwood, N.J.: Ablex, 1981), 209-23.
26. Ibid., 214.

convert authority, the local shaman *(angakok)* leadership was threatened, for the shamans could no longer command group respect and cohesion through public performances that implied communication with supernatural powers. As they were relegated to the edges of the society, their activities were regarded with disfavor and people avoided contact with them even while continuing to fear them. Valaskakis goes into some detail about the language difficulty. Very few Inuit knew English, so translation had to precede literacy. A syllabic system was used that reinforced dialectal differences. These difficulties meant that missionaries concentrated on the basic Christian texts and made no attempt to widen their congregation's knowledge in other directions. The texts were energetically distributed and learned, even by rote if there was a scarcity of printed material.

This example can help us appreciate how early Christian missionaries considered the oral tradition preached to the Gentiles as less forceful than the written. Eusebius himself emphasizes this in his recounting of the story about Mark and his Gospel (and Ignatius and his warning). Eusebius was altogether certain that for the Church's mission to be effective, the common charter had to be well-distributed as a written document. If this view was implemented in reality by the Catholic Church, we may assume that more and more people gained easy access to written documents of great authority. The language of the canonical writings, Greek, was in most instances the same as the spoken language of pagans (this shows how eastern-minded Eusebius was, as if the western part of the Empire did not exist).[27] The example of the Inuit also helps us recognize that the inhabitants of the eastern Roman Empire, even if they were illiterate, could easily get the message from Christian agents who read the Bible aloud.[28] Also, as we learn from the *Ecclesiastical History,* this written document gave the missionaries great authority, even in remote places like India.[29] Christian media agents could always refer to their common charter, the canon, and not

---

27. Eusebius usually ignores the local languages other than Greek. For these languages, see William V. Harris, *Ancient Literacy* (Cambridge, Mass.: Harvard University Press, 1989), Chap. 7.

28. Harry Gamble has convincingly shown that even the majority of Christians who were illiterate became familiar with Christian texts because they were widely distributed and recited in public settings (*Books and Readers in the Early Church,* 1-15, 42-81, esp. 74).

29. According to Gamble, literacy "was undoubtedly a primary desideratum of Christian leaders and teachers from the earliest days" (*Books and Readers in the Early Church,* 9).

be dependent on magic. Unlike pagan secular books, the Christian canonical writings were endowed with authority, both religious and institutional. The canonical books spread quite rapidly in the eastern Empire and were therefore able to reach larger audiences and be influential as media vehicles.[30]

Books were one of the most important media vehicles in antiquity. Thus the spread of Christianity through a combination of oral mission and written text resulted in a wide publicity that highlighted the new religion and its leadership over against the leadership of the outer sphere (the local and Roman authorities).[31] This brought about a twofold process. First, influential Christian leadership was slowly integrated within the civil service of the outer sphere.[32] Second, in places where pagan leadership was more powerful than the rising Christian leadership, clashes ensued between the two. This latter process sometimes led to persecutions, which were in fact a manifestation of a conflict over leadership in the outer public sphere. The canonical books (and some of the extracanonical ones) created a menace to the local oral and written traditions in many places where mission was successful.[33] Sometimes they even disrupted the traditional

30. From its start, Christianity was not simply a proletarian movement, but one that attracted people from a variety of social levels. See Abraham J. Malherbe, *Social Aspects of Early Christianity,* 2d ed. (Philadelphia: Fortress, 1983); Wayne A. Meeks, *The First Urban Christians: The Social World of the Apostle Paul* (New Haven and London: Yale University Press, 1983). For the second and third centuries, see Dimitris J. Kyrtatas, *The Social Structure of the Early Christian Communities* (London: Verso, 1987). Gamble claims that Christianity used both original and translated texts in its missionary activity (*Books and Readers in the Early Church,* 130-32).

31. Gamble is right in concluding that "early Christian literature was disseminated more quickly and over a far wider area than were non-Christian writings and found a readership more numerous than the most ambitious pagan authors could have hoped for their works. The reasons are not difficult to discern" (*Books and Readers,* 140-41).

32. See in general Peter Brown, *Power and Persuasion in Late Antiquity: Towards a Christian Empire* (Madison: University of Wisconsin Press, 1992). For more detailed studies, see Werner Eck, "Das Eindringen des Christentums in den Senatorenstand bis zu Konstantin d. Gr.," *Chiron* 1 (1977): 381-406; Peter Lampe, *Die Stadtrömischen Christen in den ersten beiden Jahrhunderten: Untersuchungen zur Sozialgeschichte* (Tübingen: Mohr Siebeck, 1989); and T. M. Finn, "Social Morality, Imperial Service and the Spread of Christianity," *Studia Patristica* 17, no. 1 (1982): 31-37.

33. The Christian texts and their exegesis formed a self-contained culture separate from the surrounding pagan one; see Frances M. Young, *Biblical Exegesis and the Formation of Christian Culture* (Cambridge: Cambridge University Press, 1997).

linear understanding of history and time. We see this, for example, in the Church Fathers' emphasis that Christian thought was older than that of the Greeks.[34] The written canon was thus a well-defined historical frame of reference that Christian communities lived with daily as distinct from their pagan neighbors, who did not have such a binding text.[35] This in itself would create tensions between people of the inner and outer public spheres who suddenly found themselves living in different universes of tradition and history. In the case of the Inuit, new values were more easily accepted since they were introduced by missionaries with great authority and colonial backing. This was probably also the case with Christianity in antiquity, as we shall see later in this chapter.

The early transformation from oral tradition to written canon was seen by Eusebius as part of a mission strategy. He considered the canon and some related literature as the common charter of the Catholic organization that could be distributed everywhere and was binding on everyone of its members. Like the Inuit, who gained the ability to read the Scriptures in their syllabic script, speakers of Greek in the eastern Roman Empire could easily participate in the process of reading the charter (sometimes with the help of missionaries) in their own language and decide for themselves if they really wished to be converted. In certain instances, this procedure helped pagans to undergo the process of enculturation. Without knowing the number of biblical texts that were distributed, we can suppose that this phenomenon of a world organization disseminating one accepted uniform text was unique in antiquity.[36] No single pagan work, however eminent, could compete with such an aggressive distribution effort, as the historical outcome shows.

34. "There was no need to read Homer and Plato because they had in any case got all their best ideas from Moses" (Young, *Biblical Exegesis*, 292).

35. Harris, *Ancient Literacy*, 221: "What was most strikingly new was the organized community and the gradual accumulation of a group of virtually unchangeable texts. . . . The written word then came to exercise religious power in a somewhat novel way."

36. The great importance of the canonical and other religious writings for the Christian organization and its mission was apparently acknowledged by Diocletian when he burned books during persecution (Gamble, *Books and Readers*, 144-61); and by Constantine, who ordered fifty "Bibles" from Eusebius in 332 (*Vita Constantini* 4.36). See Metzger, *Canon of the New Testament*, 206; and Harris, *Ancient Literacy*, 285.

Missionaries and Their Methods

Adolf von Harnack's magisterial study of mission and missionaries in early Christianity remains the best discussion of this subject. He uses Eusebius extensively but more as a "factual" history of mission.[37] Our purpose is somewhat different, namely, to discuss mission as media in the *Ecclesiastical History.*

The Abgar-Jesus Correspondence

Already in the first book, Eusebius cites a correspondence between Abgar, king (or Toparch) of Edessa, and Jesus (1.13.6-10.). The story about Abgar and Jesus comes in the context of a report about a missionary, Thaddaeus, who was considered one of the "Seventy" (1.12.3-4).[38] Eusebius actually says that there were many more disciples of Jesus than seventy; he cites Paul's mention, in 1 Cor. 15:5-7, of the resurrected Lord's appearance to "above five hundred brethren" and takes Paul to imply that there were "numberless apostles." This means that he believed that all these people were potential missionaries, like Thaddaeus. At all events, Eusebius holds the opinion that Christian mission was undertaken in remote places such as Edessa even during Jesus' lifetime. He tells us that

> The divinity of our Lord and Saviour Jesus Christ became famous among all men because of his wonder-working power, and led to him myriads even of those who in foreign lands were far remote from Judaea, in the hope of healing from diseases and from all kinds of sufferings. In this way king Abgar, the celebrated monarch of the nations beyond the Euphrates, perishing from terrible suffering in his body, beyond human

37. Adolf von Harnack, *The Mission and Expansion of Christianity in the First Three Centuries,* 2 vols., trans. and ed. James Moffett, 2d ed. (London: Williams and Norgate; New York: G. P. Putnam's Sons, 1908). See also J. Foster, *After the Apostles: Missionary Preaching of the First Three Centuries* (London: SCM Press, 1951); and F. R. Wilson, "The Missionary Strategy of the Early Church" (Dissertation, Princeton Theological Seminary, 1956).

38. According to Sebastian Brock, "There seems to be no choice for the historian but to reject Eusebius's account of Thaddaeus' mission to Edessa as a legend without historical basis" ("Eusebius and Syriac Christianity," in *Eusebius, Christianity and Judaism,* ed. Harold W. Attridge and Gohei Hata [Detroit: Wayne State University Press, 1992], 227).

power to heal, when he heard much of the name of Jesus and of the miracles attested unanimously by all men, became his suppliant and sent to him by the bearer of a letter, asking to find relief from his disease. (1.13.1-2)

Interestingly enough, the missionary effort is not presented as initiated by Jesus; instead, he and his disciples react to Abgar's request. Jesus writes him a letter, but only after the resurrection does Thomas send Thaddaeus to Edessa. Eusebius claims that he is presenting the original correspondence, translated from the Syriac (1.13.6-22). In Abgar's letter to Jesus, the Toparch writes that he has heard about Jesus' healing ability and also about his wonders, and has decided that Jesus is either "God, and came down from heaven to do these things" or "a son of God for doing these things" (1.13.7). The letter does not add anything to the information we have in the New Testament concerning Jesus himself and thus may be fictitious. But Eusebius uses it to present the very beginnings of mission, which according to him started already in Jesus' lifetime.[39] That Abgar approached Jesus (rather than Jesus approaching him) is in accordance with Jesus' initial demand in the Synoptic Gospels to refrain from mission to the Gentiles (Matt. 10:5-6). In other words, according to the Gospels, no active mission to the Gentiles took place in Jesus' time, unless we accept Matt. 28:19 as genuine. But even then, it reflects wishful thinking rather than reality.

Jesus replies to Abgar, saying that he will send him one of his disciples who will be able to heal him. Then we are informed about Thaddaeus's mission to Abgar. He heals Abgar only after the latter has assured him that he believes in Jesus. Abgar is even carried away, saying that he had wished "to take force and destroy the Jews who crucified him [Jesus]" but had been prevented from doing so by the Roman Empire (1.13.15-16). When Abgar is healed and with him many others of the Edessenes, thus proving the power of Jesus, Thaddaeus asks Abgar to convene an assembly of all the citizens because he has been sent "to preach the word" (kēryxai ton logon, 1.13.20). When an assembly is convened, Thaddaeus makes a speech about Jesus' mission (apostolē) as it figures in the Gospels. According to the Ecclesiastical History the Abgar episode took place in the year 30 C.E.

---

39. As we have already noted, according to Eusebius the concept of mission was embedded in salvation history long before Jesus.

Eusebius's presentation is what matters here: the first steps of mission are performed in the outer public sphere during Jesus' lifetime (although at that time Christians had only started to establish their inner sphere). Mission is initiated by Abgar (a stranger), who brings about the spread of the Christian message. Thaddaeus enters the outer sphere (speaking to an assembly of the citizens of Edessa), using as a basis for mission the story about Jesus as it appears in the canon of the New Testament. The words he uses "out there" are simple and lack any complexity. Eusebius returns to this story in 2.1.6-8, saying that "Thaddaeus healed Abgar by the word of Christ, and amazed all the inhabitants by his strange miracles. By the mighty influence of his deeds he brought them to reverence the power of Christ, and made them disciples of the saving teaching." He adds that from that day on all the Edessenes were converted. In both passages Eusebius presents the first steps of mission as a combination of the word of God declared in public and performances of miracles and healing. Elsewhere he emphasizes that the Christian mission was based upon the concept that the tradition of knowledge *(gnōsis)* had been transmitted from Jesus to his disciples (2.1.4).

Conquering Geography

The martyrdom of Stephen was another important juncture for the beginnings of mission in the world. Near the beginning of Book 2, Eusebius writes,

> On the martyrdom of Stephen there arose the first and greatest persecution of the Church in Jerusalem by the Jews. All the disciples, with the single exception of the Twelve, were scattered throughout Judaea and Samaria; some, as the divine Scripture says, traversed as far as Phoenice, Cyprus and Antioch, but they were not yet in a position to venture to transmit the word of faith to the Gentiles, and announced it only to Jews. (2.1.8)

But Philip went to the Samaritans, and later we hear of Philip's mission to Ethiopia, "Tradition says that he [the officer of the queen of Ethiopia], who was the first of the Gentiles to receive from Philip by revelation the mysteries of the divine word and was the first fruits of the faithful throughout the world, was also the first to return to his native land" (2.1.13). When Eusebius tells us about Simon Magus, he says, "Seeing

196

that the faith in our Saviour and Lord Jesus Christ was already being given to all men, the enemy of men's salvation planned to capture the capital in advance, and sent there Simon . . . and by aiding the fellow's tricky sorcery won over to error many of the inhabitants of Rome" (2.13.1). Near the middle of the story, we hear that "no conspiracy, either of Simon, or of any other of those who arose at the time, succeeded in those Apostolic days; for the light of the truth and the divine Logos himself, which had shone from God upon men by growing up on the earth and dwelling among his own Apostles, was overcoming all things in the might of victory" (2.14.3). And at the end of the story about Simon, we hear again that Simon had no chance since Peter, "like a noble captain of God, clad in divine armour, he brought the costly merchandise of the spiritual light from the east to the dwellers of the west, preaching the Gospel of the light itself and the word which saves souls, the proclamation of the Kingdom of Heaven" (2.14.6).

Elsewhere Eusebius says,

> They say that this Mark was the first to be sent to preach in Egypt the Gospel which he had also put into writing, and was the first to establish churches in Alexandria itself. The number of men and women who were there converted at the first attempt was so great, and their asceticism was so extraordinarily philosophic, that Philo thought it right to describe their conduct and assemblies and meals and all the rest of their manner of life. (2.16.1-2)

Eusebius himself is not sure of this, ("they say"), and he offers the Jewish sect of Therapeutai as evidence, which is historically absurd. We will deal with this later. Be that as it may, in Eusebius's view Mark's mission was successful since new churches were established in Alexandria as a result of the distribution of his Gospel.

In 2.22.1 we learn about the apostle Paul that before his martyrdom he "spent two whole years in Rome in freedom, and preached the word of God without hindrance." Here Eusebius relies on the Book of Acts for his information.

The information we have just reviewed concerning the spread of Christianity in Egypt and Rome does not appear in the New Testament (except for the note that Paul preached for two years in Rome). It should therefore be seen as an effort on Eusebius's part to present mission as an important media asset of early Christianity that brought about its extensive diffusion. Even if these traditions circulated before his own time, he chose to include them in his *Ecclesiastical History*. He also stresses the geographical aspect of mission, telling us about the regions where Christian mission was already spreading at an early stage. The places mentioned in Books 1–2 include Edessa, Palestine, Syria, Ethiopia, Rome, Cyprus, and Egypt. Is it a coincidence that Edessa, Ethiopia, and Egypt are added to the regions mentioned in the New Testament as places where Paul carried out his missionary activity? Eusebius, so it seems, wished to cover more geographical ground than included in the Acts of the Apostles and in Paul's letters. Although he names only some regions, he repeats several times that Christianity was already a world religion from the outset.

Book 3 starts with an interesting passage:[40] in contrast to the miserable condition of the Jews that Eusebius describes in the previous books,

> the holy Apostles and disciples of our Saviour were scattered throughout the whole world. Thomas, as tradition relates, obtained by lot Parthia, Andrew Scythia, John Asia (and he stayed there and died in Ephesus), but Peter seems to have preached to the Jews in the Dispersion in Pontus and Galatia and Bithynia, Cappadocia, and Asia, and at the end he came to Rome and was crucified head downwards, for so he had demanded to suffer. (3.1.1-2)

Eusebius again wishes to fill in some of the regions that Paul did not visit (such as Parthia and Scythia), and this is highlighted by his statement that Paul fulfilled "the gospel of Christ from Jerusalem to Illyria and afterward was martyred in Rome under Nero. . . . This is stated exactly by Origen in the third volume of his commentary on Genesis" (3.1.3). Moreover, in 3.5.2 he relates the persecution of the apostles by the Jews and says that "other Apostles were driven from the land of Judaea by thousands of deadly plots. They went on their way to all the heathen, teaching their message in the power of Christ, for he said to them, 'Go and make disciples of all the heathen in my name'" (a gloss on Matt. 28:19, but lacking mention of baptism).

Thus, although Eusebius was extremely anxious to define the canon, he nevertheless based his *Ecclesiastical History* on extracanonical material that he probably considered hard evidence for the period covered by the

---

40. For a careful analysis of this passage, see E. Junod, "Origène, Eusèbe et la tradition sur la répartition des champs de mission des Apôtres (Eusèbe, Histoire ecclésiastique, III,1.1-3)," in *Les Actes des apocryphes des apôtres: christianisme et monde païen,* ed. François Bovon et al. (Geneva: Labor et Fides, 1981), 233-48.

New Testament.[41] In the case of mission, we have already seen that he uses this material in order to make the partial information he found in the canon more complete. As a result he gives his audience the impression that mission was more widespread in many regions than indicated in the New Testament. In this respect he works like a reporter who fills in information in order to complete a picture that seems to him lacking. This brings us to an important extracanonical missionary story.

Making Conversion Stick

In *Hist. Eccl.* 3.23.5-19, Eusebius tells a story about the evangelist John derived from Clement of Alexandria's *Who Is The Rich Man That Is Saved*. This account, which according to Clement was "a true tradition of John the Apostle preserved in memory," is probably apocryphal (like the story about John and Cerinthus in the public bath). It has a clear message: mission is a complex matter; the competing heathen are always "out there," and even if a person is at last converted to Christianity, the Gentiles can easily attract him to come back into the outer public sphere. In other words, the borders between the inner and outer public spheres were permeable because the marketplace was full of competition. According to the story, John was visiting the neighboring districts around Ephesus and entrusted the care of a young convert to the local bishop, "who took to his house the young man entrusted to him, brought him up, looked after him, and finally baptized him. After this he relaxed his great care and watchfulness, because he had set upon him the seal of the Lord as the perfect safeguard. But some idle and dissolute youths, familiar with evil, corrupted him in his premature freedom" (3.23.8-9). The young man became the chief of a group of brigands. When John discovered this, he went into the mountains to track down the young man. John was captured by brigands himself and asked to be brought to their leader, who happened to be the boy he had once converted. When the leader recognized John, his first reaction was to flee in shame.

> But John pursued with all his might, forgetting his age and calling out, 'Why do you run away from me, child, your own father, unarmed and

---

41. Eusebius did the same in his other compositions; see D. S. Wallace-Hadrill, *Eusebius of Caesarea* (London: Mowbray 1960), 59-71.

old? Pity me, child, do not fear me! You have still the hope of life. I will account to Christ for you. If it must be, I will willingly suffer your death, as the Lord suffered for us; for your life, I will give my own. Stay, believe; Christ sent me.' When he heard this he first stood looking down, then he tore off his weapons, then he began to tremble and to weep bitterly. He embraced the old man when he came up, pleading for himself with lamentations as best as he could, baptized a second time in his tears, but his right hand he kept back. But John assured him by pledges and pro-testations that he had found forgiveness for him with the Saviour, led him back, prayed and kneeled and kissed that right hand as though cleansed by his repentance. He brought him to the church, he prayed with many supplications, he joined with him in the struggle of continu-ous fasting, he worked on his mind by varied addresses and did not leave him, so they say, until he had restored him to the church, and thus gave a great example of true repentance and a great testimony of regen-eration, the trophy of a visible resurrection. (3.23.16-19)

This story demonstrates a strategy of mission other than the ones we will discuss later in this chapter, such as wonders and healings, distribution of written canonical material, preaching in public, and so on. Here we read about a more personal method. The constituency that is approached is also different: brigands in rough country. So far we have encountered a city assembly (Edessa), audiences in the large cities of Rome and Alexandria, a high official, and others. From this particular story we can learn a great deal about the techniques of mission and the difficulties involved in the act of conversion.[42] First we have the boy in the house of the elder (or bishop), and the required close control over his behavior (which the elder appar-ently failed to exert sufficiently); only then comes the act of baptism. These actions should have sufficed to produce a convert par excellence. But Eusebius wished to impress upon his readers that, since the boy did not in-ternalize the conversion, it went wrong, and he became a brigand. Then comes John's act of persuasion to bring the youth back into the inner sphere of the church. The youth laments bitterly, and John assures him that the Savior guarantees his forgiveness. The boy seems to have repented sincerely, and John kneels and prays while kissing the truant's right hand (which he had held back) as an act of purification. Only then does John

42. For literature on conversion, see Doron Mendels, *Identity, Religion and His-toriography: Studies in Hellenistic History* (Sheffield: Sheffield Academic Press, 1998), Chap. 24.

bring him back to the church, praying for him with many supplications, and fasting with him. He does not leave him for a moment (which shows what devotion one needs to make just one convert), until he finally returns him to the church. The story emphasizes that a formal conversion is not enough, and that much more has to be done before the convert truly internalizes Christianity. (The problem of the internalization of Christianity in the individual is echoed in Canon 2 of Nicaea.)[43] This incident, says Eusebius, happened at the end of the first century.

Miracles and Heretics

Another piece of information that Eusebius supplies concerning the early Christian missions comes in the context of a discussion of the apostolic succession. After distributing their property to the needy,

> These pious disciples of great men . . . took up the work of evangelists and were zealous to preach to all who had not yet heard the word of the faith, and to transmit the writings of the divine Gospels [to the Gentiles]. As soon as they had no more than laid the foundations of the faith in some strange place, they appointed others as shepherds and committed to them the task of tending those who had been just brought in, but they themselves passed on again to other lands and peoples, helped by the grace and co-operation of God, seeing that many strange miracles of the divine spirit were at that time still being wrought by them, so that whole crowds of men at the first hearing eagerly received in their souls the religion of the Creator of the universe. (3.37.1-3)

Interestingly enough, although Eusebius emphasizes the oral and written message, he says that miracles were then still a prominent part of the mission. He continues:

> It is impossible for us to give the number and the names of all who first succeeded the Apostles, and were shepherds or evangelists in the

43. In discussing qualifications for the clergy, Canon 2 declares that "time is necessary for the state of a catechumen, and a fuller probation after baptism." In some instances, it seems that Eusebius wished to demonstrate principles that would later be formulated in the Canons of Nicaea, and this, of course, is not accidental. For instance, Origen's castration and the opposition to it may be reflected in Canon 1, and Canon 3 deals with the *subintroductae* of Paul of Samosata.

churches throughout the world. It was, therefore, natural for us to record by name the memory only of those of whom the tradition still survives to our time by their treatises on the Apostolic teaching. (3.37.4)

This statement is followed by a survey of figures such as Clement of Rome, Ignatius, Polycarp, and Papias (3.38.1–3.39.17).

For his account of Polycarp here, Eusebius quotes Book 3 of Irenaeus's *Against Heresies:*

> And Polycarp also was not only instructed by apostles and conversed with many who had seen the Lord, but was also appointed bishop in Smyrna. . . . He constantly taught those things which he had learnt from the apostles, which also are the tradition of the church, which alone are true. To these facts all the churches in Asia bear witness, and the present successors of Polycarp, and he is a far more trustworthy and reliable witness of the truth than Valentinus and Marcion and the others who hold wrong opinions. In the time of Anicetus he visited Rome and converted many of the above mentioned heretics to the church of God, preaching that the one and only truth which he had received from the apostles was that which is the tradition of the church. (4.14.3-5)

Here we come across yet another aspect of mission within the Church, mission to heretics. This constituted an important front in the battle for the inner public sphere. To this context belong the letters sent by Dionysius of Corinth to many churches (4.23).[44] Eusebius describes Dionysius's letter to the Lacedaemonians as "an instruction in orthodoxy on the subject of peace and unity, and the letter to the Athenians is a call to faith and to life according to the gospel" (4.23.2). In his letter to the Nicomedians, Dionysius "combats the heresy of Marcion and compares it with the rule of the truth" (4.23.4). The missionary war within the inner public sphere is described very clearly in one of those general passages that Eusebius inserts from time to time. In 4.24.1 he says,

> Heretics were even then no less defiling the pure seed of apostolic teaching like tares, and the shepherds of the churches in every place, as though driving off wild beasts from Christ's sheep, excluded them at one time by rebukes and exhortations to the brethren, at another by their more complete exposure, by unwritten and personal inquiry and con-

44. On Dionysius of Corinth, see Johannes Quasten, *Patrology,* 4 vols. (Westminster, Md.: Christian Classics, 1986-92), 1:280-82.

versation, and ultimately correcting their opinions by accurate arguments in written treatises.

Catechetical Schools

To return to the outer public sphere: early Christian missionaries had excellent strategic bases for launching their activities when the catechetical schools were created.[45] Concerning the catechetical school in Alexandria, Eusebius says,

> At that time a man very famous for his learning named Pantaenus had charge of the life of the faithful in Alexandria, for from ancient custom a school of sacred learning existed among them. This school has lasted on to our time, and we have heard that it is managed by men powerful in their learning and zeal for divine things, but tradition says that at that time Pantaenus was especially eminent, and that he had been influenced by the philosophic system of those called Stoics. They say that he showed such zeal in his warm disposition for the divine word that he was appointed as a herald for the gospel of Christ to the heathen in the East, and was sent as far as India. For indeed there were until then many evangelists of the word who had forethought to use inspired zeal on the apostolic model for the increase and building up of the divine word. One of these was Pantaenus, and it is said that he went to the Indians, and the tradition is that he found there that, among some of those there who had known Christ, the Gospel according to Matthew had preceded his coming; for Bartholomew, one of the apostles, had preached to them and had left them the writing of Matthew in Hebrew letters, which was preserved until the time mentioned. Pantaenus, after many achievements, was at the head of the school in Alexandria until his death, and orally and in writing expounded the treasures of the divine doctrine. (5.10.1-4)

Whether this story is true or not, Eusebius wishes to show that mission was so widespread that it reached even India, which at that time was considered the far end of the earth, and that the text for mediating the mis-

45. See further A. Tuilier, "Les évangélistes et les docteurs de la primitive église et les origines de L'École (διδασκαλεῖον) d'Alexandrie," *Studia Patristica* 17 (1982): 738-49; and A. Van den Hoek, "The 'Catechetical' School of Early Christian Alexandria and Its Philonic Heritage," *Harvard Theological Review* 90, no. 1 (1997): 59-87.

sionary message was the Gospel of Matthew in Hebrew (this provides evidence for Eusebius's claim that Matthew was originally written in Hebrew; cf. *Hist. Eccl.* 6.25.4). He also wants to show that the catechetical school in Alexandria was the institution responsible for regional mission to the heathen.[46] And, here as elsewhere, he emphasizes that preaching became an important method in the act of mission.[47] This last observation was probably based on reality.

More information concerning the catechetical school as a missionary institution is to be found in 6.3.1-2, where we learn that, "since there was no one at Alexandria set apart for catechetical instruction (for all had been driven away by the threat of the persecution), some of the heathen approached him [Origen] to hear the word of God. Of these Plutarch is pointed out as being the first, who after a noble life was adorned also with a divine martyrdom; and the second Heraclas, Plutarch's brother. . . ." Later we have a more general statement: "At that time, however, Origen was engaged at Alexandria in the work of divine instruction for all, without reserve, who came to him by night and in the course of the day, devoting his whole time untiringly to the divine studies and his pupils" (6.8.6).[48] Eusebius gives the impression that the Christian mission assumed a strong intellectual character that abandoned the more mantic, healing, and prophetic methods. One of the finest means of intellectual mission was the teaching of Christianity through Greek philosophical concepts (cf. 6.18-19). This, of course, is a well-known device employed by the Church Fathers.[49] Here it will suffice to say

46. The large Christian libraries in the main Christian centers were no doubt a focus of attraction for many pagans. For these libraries, see Gamble, *Books and Readers in the Early Church*, 144-61.

47. For preaching on the basis of Scripture, see in general M. C. Murray, "Preaching, Scripture and Visual Imagery in Antiquity," *Christianesimo nella storia* 14, no. 3 (1993): 481-503.

48. In general for Origen and his school, see Henri Crouzel, *Origen*, trans. A. S. Worrall (Edinburgh: T & T Clark, 1989).

49. See, for instance, Edouard Des Places, *Eusèbe de Césarée Commentateur: Platonisme et écriture sainte* (Paris: Beauchesne, 1982); Henry Chadwick, *Early Christian Thought and the Classical Tradition: Studies in Justin, Clement, and Origen* (Oxford: Clarendon, 1966); Francis Dvornik, *Early Christian and Byzantine Political Philosophy: Origins and Background* (Washington, D.C.: Dumbarton Oaks Center for Byzantine Studies, 1966); Heinrich Doergens, *Eusebius von Casarea als Darsteller der griechischen Religion: Eine Studie zur Geschichte der altchristlichen Apologetik* (Paderborn: F. Schöningh, 1922); A. J. van der Aalst, *Aantekeningen bij de hellenisering van het christendom* (Nijmegen: Dekker & Van de Vegt; The Hague: Boekencentrum,

that inculturation (the transformation of the culture for religion's sake) served as an extremely attractive channel of mediatizing the Christian message to the more elevated parts of pagan society.

Penetrating the Outer Public Sphere

Eusebius tells us that Origen's fame reached so far that the "ruler of Arabia" wished to see him. Origen "duly arrived in Arabia, but soon accomplished the object of his journey thither, and returned again to Alexandria," and then "no small warfare broke out again in the city, and leaving Alexandria secretly he went to Palestine and abode in Caesarea. And although he had not yet received ordination to the presbyterate, the bishops there requested him to discourse and expound the divine Scriptures publicly in the church" (6.19.15-16). Thus we see Origen exercising a dual function, going into the outer public sphere, and teaching Scripture in the inner one (pagans from the outer sphere may have joined as well). Later we hear about a mission of Origen to the emperor's court:

> Origen's fame was now universal, so as to reach the ears of the emperor's mother, Mamaea by name, a religious woman if ever there was one. She set great store on securing a sight of the man, and on testing that understanding of divine things which was the wonder of all. She was then staying at Antioch, and summoned him to her presence with a military escort. And when he had stayed with her for some time, and shown her very many things that were for the glory of the Lord and the excellence of the divine teaching, he hastened back to his accustomed duties. (6.21.3-4)

This story demonstrates how the Christian mission penetrated more and more into the higher ranks of the outer public sphere.

That mission was inextricable from Christian thought we can also learn from the story told by and about Dionysius of Alexandria.[50] He was

---

1974); and Christian Gnilka, *Chresis: Die Methode der Kirchenväter im Umgang mit der antiken Kultur,* vols. 1 and 2 (Basel: Schwabe, 1986-93). See also Averil Cameron, *Christianity and the Rhetoric of Empire: The Development of Christian Discourse* (Berkeley: University of California Press, 1991).

50. On the concept of mission in the early Church, see E. Molland, "Besass die Alte Kirche ein Missionsprogramm und bewusste Missionsmethoden?" in *Die Alte Kirche,* ed. Heinzgünter Frohnes and Uwe W. Knorr (Munich: Kaiser, 1974), 51-67; and

banished from Alexandria to a remote place called Cephro, and there with some fellow Christians who joined him from both Cephro and Egypt

> God opened unto us a door for the word. And at first we were pursued, we were stoned, but afterwards not a few of the heathen left their idols and turned to God. Then for the first time was the word sown through our agency among those who had not formerly received it. It was, as it were, for this that God took us away to them, and, when we had fulfilled this ministration, took us away again. (7.11.13-14)

We may assume that the deputy prefect Aemilianus did not like this missionary enterprise, for later he wanted to remove them "to rougher, as he thought, and more Libyan-like places . . . assigning separate villages in the district for each party; but us he posted more on the road, so that we should be the first to be arrested" (7.11.14). In other words, it seems that in this particular case the Roman authorities did not like the missionary activity of Christians in the outer public sphere, which they wished to dominate completely and leave unchanged, socially and culturally.

Now that we have a picture of missionaries as depicted in the *Ecclesiastical History*, we should ask in what sense they contributed to the media revolution of early Christianity. To answer this question, we need to consult modern missiology.[51]

Early Christian missionaries worked with a clear frame of reference, the canon and some extrabiblical literature. They were motivated by the calls to and descriptions of mission in the New Testament. In Catholic Christianity the message to the Gentiles was defined and indisputable.[52] The missionary could find in the canon messages that were familiar to Gentiles, because the rhetoric, social codes, and universal values within the New Testament were taken from their own world. That the Hebrew Bible

C. and L. Pietri, eds., *Naissance d'une Chrétienté (250-430)*, vol. 2 of *Histoire du christianisme: Des origines à nos jours,* ed. Jean-Marie Mayeur et al. (Paris: Desclee, 1995), esp. Chaps. 2 (Saxer) and 3 (Pietri). There are also useful observations in David J. Bosch, *Transforming Mission: Paradigm Shifts in Theology of Mission* (Maryknoll, N.Y.: Orbis, 1991); and Per Beskow, "Crossing the Frontiers in the Second Century," *Studia Missionalia Upsaliensia* 11 (1969): 27-35.

51. For modern mission, see David J. Hesselgrave, *Communicating Christ Cross-Culturally: An Introduction to Missionary Communication,* 2d ed. (Grand Rapids: Zondervan, 1991).

52. See Tippett, *Introduction to Missiology,* 13-16.

and the New Testament existed in Greek in the first centuries of the common era eased the process of approaching pagans. Terms known from the pagan vocabulary of political, moral and social discourse were used by Christian missionaries and accepted by hearers within their own framework of symbols and ideas. Hence the message was a mixture of "identificational" and "extractionist" approaches to mission.[53]

The strategies of Christian mission have not changed dramatically throughout the ages. Although neither early Christian missionaries nor the Church Fathers studied the discipline of missiology, they were nevertheless aware of many devices of mediatizing to Gentiles, both Greeks and others. This does not mean that they were always successful in their efforts, but from the outset they were aware of the methods necessary for communication with people in the outer public sphere. In fact, they mastered the basics of mission (sometimes even better than missionaries in Africa in the nineteenth century). For effective mission, one needs a communicator (C), a message (M), and a receptor (R).[54] Early Christian missionaries evidently knew what kind of methods to employ according to the type of audience they hoped to reach — an assembly in a city, an accidental gathering, the Roman or local aristocracy, the emperor's court, or students in catechetical schools. In other words, they were "receptor-oriented." "The communicator, to communicate the message effectively, must be 'receptor-oriented'. . . . Accuracy and correctness, then, will have to be evaluated at R's end of the communication process even more than at C's."[55] Missionaries in the first centuries used formal rites of passage (baptism) and probably even tolerated heathen interpretations of their holy message. Another principle of modern missiology already known to missionaries in antiquity was awareness of the so-called "personal mission," the sharing of life with the receptor: "Communication is most effective when M is understood by R to relate specifically to life as R lives it."[56]

According to Eusebius there were missionaries (including some of the Church Fathers, such as Clement of Alexandria and Origen) who went out to the Gentiles with a message that had syncretistic aspects; for example, it was common to present Christian ideas within a pagan literary and philosophical framework. Was this merely a missionary strategy or an in-

---

53. See Charles H. Kraft, *Christianity in Culture: A Study in Dynamic Biblical Theologizing in Cross-cultural Perspective* (Maryknoll, N.Y.: Orbis, 1979), 147-53.
54. Ibid.
55. Ibid., 148.
56. Ibid., 150.

tentional inculturation process? Probably both. But this aspect has been exhaustively researched and so will not be discussed here since it relates to the content of the message rather than its medium.[57] Here it will suffice to say that the early Christian message as formulated within pagan cultural frameworks reflects what Charles H. Kraft calls the "identificational" approach: "In this approach communicators become familiar with the conceptual framework of the receptor and attempt to fit their communication to the categories and felt needs of that frame of reference."[58] But this identificational message was mostly meant for educated people who were familiar with Greek literature and philosophy. This again shows that the Catholic Church as an organization geared its media efforts to the nature of the audiences it approached.

Social Aid and Moral Example

In 3.19-20 we hear (through Hegesippus) that the emperor Domitian arrested the grandsons of Judas, the brother of Jesus "according to the flesh," and accused them of being of the house of David. They said in their defense that Christ and his kingdom were "neither of the world nor earthly, but heavenly and angelic, and it would be at the end of the world, when he would come in glory to judge the living and the dead and to reward every man according to his deeds." Domitian released them, and then, Eusebius says, "when they were released they were the leaders of the churches, both for their testimony and for their relation to the Lord" (3.20.4-6). In 3.32.6 he adds, "They came therefore and presided over every church as witnesses belonging to the Lord's family." This qualifies as a missionary story since these figures publicly revealed the Christian message to the emperor.

From Eusebius we get the impression that an important asset for active mission was the moral position of Christians within their pagan society. They became an example of good, moral, and sometimes even "normal" behavior. Eusebius wishes to show throughout his history how the Catholic Church represents the right order in society. This right order is

---

57. For instance, the exegesis of Scripture with methods taken from the pagan philosophical schools resulted in a canon that replaced the traditional schools of Hellenistic culture; see Young, *Biblical Exegesis*.

58. Kraft, *Christianity in Culture*, 153.

demonstrated in many ways, such as helping the sick and setting a moral example by maintaining purity within family life (no adultery or celibacy) and in embodying such virtues as honesty, peace, simplicity, love of neighbor, and love of God. Thus Eusebius, unlike Thucydides for instance, makes the presentation of the right order of society a high priority in his historiography. He selects the social issues at stake from the universal and general arsenal of Greco-Roman values in addition to the ones that were strictly Christian.

For Gentiles in the outer public sphere who could not read, or who were not interested in reading or listening to the Christian "charter," the personal moral stance radiated by the Christian organization became an important media asset. But not only on the illiterate did Christians make an impression. Their example of good behavior was mentioned by the emperor Trajan himself (3.33).[59] Eusebius relies upon Tertullian for a summary of Pliny's famous letter to Trajan, which stated that "beyond their unwillingness to offer sacrifice to idols, he had found nothing wicked in them [the Christians]. He also mentioned this, that the Christians arose at dawn and sang a hymn to Christ as a God, and in order to preserve their teaching forbade murder, adultery, covetousness, robbery, and suchlike" (3.33.3). Pliny himself here becomes a media agent of the Christians by showing how Christians keep the social order better than their Gentile neighbors.

Eusebius introduces into his missionary stories various incidents that demonstrate the good order of Christian individuals and communities. One of these incidents can be found in 4.17, where Eusebius picks up a story from Justin. It tells about a converted woman who tried to persuade her husband to convert, "relating the doctrine to him." He refused and continued with his wayward behavior. Then she decided to divorce him since she "thought it was wicked to continue consorting with a husband who tried every kind of pleasure contrary to the law of nature and to righteousness" (4.17.3). Her family persuaded her to stay with her husband, but then he went to Alexandria and behaved even worse. Thus in order "not to be a partner of wickedness and impiety," she divorced him at last. Her husband, who disliked her conversion (since she had previously be-

59. For Trajan and the Christians, see Günther Gottlieb and Pedro Barcelo, eds., *Christen und Heiden in Staat und Gesellschaft des zweiten bis vierten Jahrhunderts: Gedanken und Thesen zu einem schwierigen Verhältnis* (Munich: E. Vogel, 1992), 6-21; and Robert L. Wilken, *The Christians as the Romans Saw Them* (New Haven and London: Yale University Press, 1984), 1-30.

haved immorally, like himself), "brought an accusation alleging that she was a Christian." She filed a petition with the emperor. Then her husband turned against her teacher in Christian doctrine, Ptolemy, who was ordered to be executed by Urbicius. Lucius, who came forward in Ptolemy's defense, argued before Urbicius, "What is the reason for punishing this man who has not been convicted of adultery or fornication or murder or theft or robbery or, in a word, of having done anything wrong, but merely confesses that he bears the Christian name? Your judgement, Urbicius, is unworthy of the emperor called Pius, or of Caesar's son, the philosopher, or of the sacred Senate." Urbicius ordered him to be executed as well. As with "unfinished" stories in our mass media, Eusebius does not care to tell us the end of the woman. But the story demonstrates what the Christian message was about. It was essentially moral and universal, and thus could easily be perceived by pagans. Universal moral values constituted a facet of Christianity that could be presented in clear and simple terms to everyone in the outer sphere. This type of approach did not entail a complicated theological message, if one thinks in terms of media performance. Eusebius emphasizes that the Christian Lucius even got the opportunity to state this message in public (before the hostile Roman authorities and others). Regardless of its media value, its content was what made it accessible to a large audience of pagans (but not to Jews, who themselves adhered to the same moral values, and did not need the Christian missionary message in this respect).

In a letter to the Roman community[60] addressed to its bishop, Soter, Dionysius of Corinth writes,

> This has been your custom from the beginning, to do good in manifold ways to all Christians, and to send contributions to the many churches in every city, in some places relieving the poverty of the needy, and ministering to the Christians in the mines, by the contribution which you have sent from the beginning, preserving the ancestral custom of the Romans, true Romans as you are. (4.23.10)

No doubt this kind of Christian behavior became well known in the outer public sphere. The Christian mission knew how to "scratch where it itches," as Kraft describes it in his ninth principle of mission:[61] "historical,

---

60. For letters as a significant communicative device, see Gamble, *Books and Readers in the Early Church*, 95-101.
61. Kraft, *Christianity in Culture*, 150.

technical, theoretical, and academic presentations may contribute to R[eceptor]'s store of information but they rarely affect the person's behavior unless, via application and illustration, lessons are extracted from them and related to R[eceptor]'s day-to-day life." Also, in terms of the medium employed, namely, the presentation of these cases in the *Ecclesiastical History*, Eusebius's missionary cases can be evaluated in line with Kraft's principle "that personal experiences of C[ommunicator] and case studies from the lives of others are often effective techniques for making messages specific to R[eceptor]'s life."[62]

In 5.5 Eusebius relates the story of how the prayers of Christians serving in the army of Marcus Aurelius resulted in a miraculous rain shower that kept his troops from dying of thirst. The story dramatizes what an impression Christians made on their immediate neighbors in the outer and institutional public spheres (here the army).[63] The great missionary asset of the account comes through in Eusebius's commentary on it:

> This story is both told among writers who are foreign to our faith who have undertaken to write of the times of the above mentioned emperors, and has also been recorded by Christians. By the heathen writers, inasmuch as they were strangers to the faith, the miracle is related, but it was not confessed that it happened through the prayers of Christians; but in our own writers, inasmuch as they are friends of the truth, what happened has been described in a simple and harmless fashion. Among these would also be Apolinarius, who states that after that time the legion which had wrought the miracle through prayer had received a name from the emperor appropriate to what had happened, and was called in Latin the "Thundering Legion." Tertullian is also a worthy witness of these things, who in addressing in Latin an apology for our faith to the Senate, which we have quoted already, confirmed the story with more and clearer proof. (5.5.3-5)

Eusebius thus emphasizes that in many fields of life Christians not only provided an outstanding moral example, but also contributed by their pure behavior to the welfare of society.[64]

---

62. Ibid., 150.

63. See Jaroslav Pelikan, *The Finality of Jesus Christ in an Age of Universal History: A Dilemma of the Third Century* (London: Lutterworth, 1965), 55-56.

64. This is emphasized by Rodney Stark, *The Rise of Christianity: A Sociologist Reconsiders History* (Princeton: Princeton University Press, 1996).

The Example of Origen

This brings us to Origen and the example he gave in his private life. (The story of his castration is perhaps not the best model one can think of, since it was rejected by the Church Fathers themselves and elicited a strong reaction later in Canon 1 in Nicaea.) In a summary statement of Origen's virtue, Eusebius says,

> And by displaying proofs such as these of a philosophic life to those who saw him, he naturally stimulated a large number of his pupils to a like zeal, so that, even among the unbelieving Gentiles and those from the ranks of learning and philosophy, some persons of no small account were won by his instruction. By his agency these very persons received the faith of the divine Word truly in the depth of the soul . . . insomuch that even some of them were arrested and perfected by martyrdom. (6.3.13)[65]

What, then, was the nature of this marvelous example that Origen gave? We learn, for instance, that he disposed of all his volumes of ancient pagan literature and devoted himself to divine Scripture; he lived like an ascetic, walking barefoot and abstaining from wine and "all except necessary food"; and he took many of Jesus' sayings at face value in daily life. By "persevering in cold and nakedness and going to the extremest limit of poverty, he greatly astounded his followers" (6.3.10-11). Unlike the Cynics and the Stoics, Origen combined his ascetic life with the religious sanctions given through Holy Scripture, and he lived even more strictly than these philosophers did. Thus Eusebius emphasizes that Origen's way of living made such an impression that even pagan intellectuals converted, and their conversion was not skin-deep, but spiritually internalized. Origen also became so extreme that he rejected in a symbolic manner an imminent process of interculturation by studying only Scripture and renouncing pagan literature.[66] In his

---

65. The first half of Book 6 is an example of a biography, which Christians liked to write about eminent individuals within the Church. See Patricia Cox Miller, *Biography in Late Antiquity: A Quest for the Holy Man* (Berkeley: University of California Press, 1983), esp. 134; and Cameron, *Christianity and the Rhetoric of Empire*, 57, and Chap. 3. See also Cameron in *Portraits: Biographical Representation in the Greek and Latin Literature of the Roman Empire*, ed. M. J. Edwards and Simon Swain (Oxford: Clarendon, 1997), 145-75.

66. For this process see Young, *Biblical Exegesis*, 292.

Demonstratio Evangelica, Eusebius says that asceticism is the best way of life (1.8.[29]).

Reaching the Higher-Ups

From the many cases we have already seen, we can deduce that Eusebius was aware of what missionaries were confronted with in daily life, namely, that the act of conversion could not be completed if the Christian values were not fully internalized. The case of John and the brigand demonstrated this problem concerning the lower strata of the population. But even in the higher echelons of society, the difficulty remained a serious one. Eusebius demonstrates this through a striking story about the Roman emperor Philip (244-249 C.E.).

> It is recorded that he, being a Christian, wished on the day of the last paschal vigil to share along with the multitude the prayers at the church, but was not permitted to enter by him who was then presiding, until he confessed and numbered himself among those who were reckoned to be in sins and were occupying the place of penitence; for that otherwise, had he not done so, he would never have been received by [the president] on account of the many charges made concerning him. And it is said that he obeyed readily, displaying by his actions how genuine and pious was his disposition towards the fear of God. (6.34.1)

This may be seen as another example of a missionary story designed to show how successful Christianity was in all parts of society, reaching the emperor himself, who in reality was probably not even aware that he had turned Christian. (We are reminded of a similar story about the Seleucid ruler Antiochus IV in 2 Maccabees 9.)[67] But even the emperor could not enter the inner public sphere if he did not wholeheartedly undergo conversion and manifest an internalized Christianity.

Whereas in Books 1–5 of the *Ecclesiastical History* (covering the first and second centuries) Eusebius emphasizes the mission to the lower segments of the population within the outer public sphere, in Books 6–10 he lingers on the mission directed at the more aristocratic part of society, culminating in emperors who became Christians even before Constantine the

---

67. Cf. my *Identity, Religion and Historiography,* Chap. 20.

Great.[68] Such stories were also more salable in terms of media performance, an important consideration for Eusebius. For instance, the martyrdom of Marinus from Caesarea in Palestine represents the conversion
of people of higher social strata who had adopted Christianity. Marinus
was "honoured by high rank in the army and distinguished besides by
birth and wealth" (7.15.1). So, too, Astyrius, who took away the body of
Marinus after he was martyred; he was a "member of the Roman Senate, a
favourite of emperors, and well known to all for birth and wealth"
(7.16.1).

Helping the Brother and the Neighbor

The Christian purchase on moral and social values is prominent also in the
information we get from Dionysius of Alexandria concerning the terrible
plague in Alexandria in the middle of the third century. He relates that to
the Christians it was "no less than the other misfortunes, a source of discipline and testing. For indeed it did not leave us untouched, although it attacked the heathen with great strength" (7.22.6). Now he tells at great
length how the Christians cared for each other in such a way that they did
not fear death. He even compares their activity to the act of martyrdom.
This was a lesson for the heathen since their

> conduct . . . was the exact opposite . . . even those who were in the first
> stages of the disease they thrust away, and fled from their dearest. They
> would even cast them in the roads half dead, and treat the unburied
> corpses as vile refuse, in their attempts to avoid the spreading and conta-
> gion of the death-plague; a thing which, for all their devices, it was not
> easy for them to escape. (7.22.10)

Although the plague did not recognize frontiers between the outer and inner public spheres, it is remarkable how in the mid-third century such a
dichotomy existed between Christians and their Gentile neighbors in daily
life. At that time, the Christians did not come to the assistance of the pa-

---

68. Hence it is not surprising that fourth-century Christianity was "far from being a 'popular' movement" but "reflected the sharp divisions in Roman society: its upper echelons were occupied by highly cultivated persons, drawn from the class of urban
notables" (Brown, *Power and Persuasion in Late Antiquity,* 76; cf. Robin Lane Fox, *Pagans and Christians* [New York: Knopf, 1986], 265-93).

gans for two reasons: they evidently feared the diminution of their numbers, knowing that their communities would suffer even more if they helped the sick Gentiles around them; and they were very careful to discern who was a true Christian, as we have seen in the case of the emperor Philip and as the whole baptismal dispute shows. Nevertheless, the behavior of Christians within their inner public sphere in times of severe plague no doubt impressed their pagan neighbors.

But there was a development. More than fifty years later, during the terrible circumstances of the plague in Maximin Diaia's reign, Christians did help their heathen neighbors:

> Such were the wages received for the proud boasting of Maximin and for the petitions presented by the cities against us; while the proofs of the Christians' zeal and piety in every respect were manifest to all the heathen. For example, they alone in such an evil state of affairs gave practical evidence of their sympathy and humanity: all day long some of them would diligently persevere in performing the last offices for the dying and burying them (for there were countless numbers, and no one to look after them); while others would gather together in a single assemblage the multitude of those who all throughout the city were wasted with the famine, and distributed bread to them all, so that their action was on all men's lips, and they glorified the God of the Christians, and, convinced by the deeds themselves, acknowledged that they alone were truly pious and God-fearing. (9.8.13-14)

Thus within fifty to sixty years a dramatic change had occurred. How can we explain this change? From the *Ecclesiastical History* we get the impression that the Christians had obtained more and more strategic positions in the outer and institutional public spheres. The integration of Christians following the mid-third-century persecution was also recognized by pagan society in general. Christians were apparently more acceptable as a force to be reckoned with, hence the broad public was willing to receive their assistance, especially when the (pagan) authorities were helpless. And the Christians had greater self-assurance in acting within the outer public sphere since their numbers had considerably increased since the mid-third century.

Public Performances

Eusebius introduces Justin Martyr as one who "in the garb of philosopher ... served as ambassador of the word of God and contended in his writings for the faith" (4.11.8). Although this may be just a metaphorical turn of phrase, in certain circumstances early Christian missionaries did appear in the guise of Greek philosophers in order to reach an educated Gentile audience. But Eusebius also mentions mission performed through writings.

The Genre Apology

The *apology* was a special literary genre adapted by Christians from the second century onward in their efforts to present a reasoned defense of their faith in the face of pagan prejudice. Apologies were sent to Roman emperors and were also addressed to educated Gentiles in general.[69] How many people were really converted or even convinced by these writings remains an unanswerable question.[70] But the frequent use of this kind of literature may perhaps indicate its effectiveness. We have already seen that fierce verbal attacks against heretics in early Christianity's inner public sphere had great media value. Apologies, by contrast, were directed outwards. What Eusebius says about Justin is therefore important for our argument: "The same Justin laboured powerfully against the Gentiles, and addressed other arguments, affording a defense *(apologia)* for our faith, to the emperor Antoninus, called Pius, and to the Senate of the Romans, for he was living in Rome" (4.11.11). We may question at what point in the process of mission Christians began to address their audiences aggressively, and in what circumstances they just stepped forward with their *kerygma*. The answer is complex, since it depends upon the kind of audi-

---

69. Cf. the excellent survey of Paul Corby Finney, *The Invisible God: The Earliest Christians on Art* (New York: Oxford University Press, 1994), 15-38, esp. 29-30.

70. See Gamble, *Books and Readers in the Early Church*, 112-13. On the intended readership of the apologies, Gamble says, "Perhaps the most plausible assumption is that they were open letters to the emperor, that is, sent to the emperor and at the same time circulated among Christians and, so far as possible, among the general public — or at least its educated elements" (p. 112). Regarding their impact on pagans, he says, "If pagans could be induced to read such works, they could hardly be expected to go to the trouble or expense of obtaining the copies they read. It has to be supposed that Christians produced the copies and insinuated them among non-Christian readers" (p. 113).

ence they were addressing. Eusebius shows again how alert he was to the publicity asset of mission, by selecting information that indicated the exposure of Christianity to the emperor and the Roman senate. As with our modern mass media, it did not matter whether the press was good or bad, true or false; what counted was the publicity itself.

Of Justin we read again in 4.16.1 that

> In their time too Justin, whom we mentioned a little earlier, after delivering to the rulers mentioned a second book in behalf of our opinions, was adorned with divine martyrdom when the philosopher Crescens, who strove in life and behaviour to justify the name cynic which he bore, instigated the plot against him, for Justin had often defeated him in debate in the presence of hearers, and finally bound on himself the trophies of victory by his martyrdom for the truth of which he was an ambassador.

Now comes an extract from Justin's *Apology*, emphasizing the public scene of the debates:

> "I [Justin] too expect to be plotted against by one of those who have been mentioned, and to be stretched on the rack, or even by Crescens, that lover not of wisdom but of boasting, for the man is not worthy to be called 'philosopher' seeing that he publicly testifies about what he does not know, to the effect that the Christians are atheists and impious, and he does this to gain the grace and pleasure of the many who have been deceived." (4.16.3)

Later Justin insists that Crescens "knows nothing of our position, or, if he does know, does not dare say so because of the listeners, and, as I said before, is proved to be a man who loves not wisdom but reputation and does not even honour the saying of Socrates, worthy of affection as it is" (4.16.6). Hence public debates were meant to increase the exposure of the Christian presence. We hear more about Justin in 4.18.1-3: he sent treatises to Antoninus Pius and his children and to the Roman Senate, and also to Antoninus Verus, and a second treatise against the Greeks entitled *A Confutation*.

Needless to say, Eusebius adduces these pieces of information in order to impress his readers with the variety of media channels employed by the early Church, which in this particular case penetrated the highest levels of the Roman administration. Along the same lines, we learn about

Tertullian's evidence concerning the "Thundering Legion," mentioned above:

> Tertullian is also a worthy witness of these things, who in addressing in Latin an apology for our faith to the Senate, which we have quoted already, confirmed the story with more and clearer proof. In his writing he says that letters of Marcus, the most prudent emperor, were still extant, in which he testifies himself that when his army was on the point of destruction in Germany from lack of water it had been saved by the prayers of the Christians, and Tertullian says that the emperor also threatened death to those who attempted to accuse us. (5.5.5-6)

In 6.36.3 Eusebius mentions a letter from Origen to the emperor Philip and another one "to his wife Severa, and various other letters to various persons." We can assume that even a limited distribution of apologies had a cumulative effect and contributed to the publicity Christianity was striving for. Whatever the reactions of pagans and Jews to the disputes, they brought Christianity more and more into the marketplace, and its flow of ideas circulated in the outer public sphere. (The Jews did not use such methods in a systematic manner, which suggests that they had no interest in mission.) We may assume that the market segment most hospitable to this kind of mission was the more elevated one including aristocratic and intellectual people.

Oral Presentations

As we have already seen, oral presentations were no less important in Eusebius's view. In 5.21.3-5 he tells us about the martyr Apollonius, who "when the judge begged and prayed him to defend himself before the senate, made before everyone a most learned defence of the faith for which he was a martyr." Eusebius adds, "The words of Apollonius before the judge and the answers which he made to the interrogation of Perennius, and all the defence which he made to the senate, can be read by anyone who wishes in the compilation which we have made of the ancient martyrs" (5.21.5). Here again it becomes quite obvious how Christians acted. Whatever circumstances they faced, they took the opportunity to promote their ideas in the midst of the outer public sphere — in local senates, the Roman senate, various institutions such as the army, judicial courts, the agora, and so forth. Eusebius presents Apollonius as a man who attained great success by the mere fact that he got a hearing in the Roman senate. Regardless of whether Apollonius convinced many senators, Eusebius considers the man's witness an important contribution to mission and the promotion of Christianity. Moreover, Eusebius deemed it necessary to present the publicity campaigns of Christianity elaborately. When all these factors are taken together, we once again get the strong impression that he thought of the rise of Christianity in terms of a media revolution.

Christian Art

Another channel of communication that emerges in the *Ecclesiastical History* is the presence of Christian art in the outer public sphere. In Book 7 Eusebius describes statues in the town of Caesarea Philippi (called Paneas by the Greeks), in northern Palestine:

> For they say that she who had an issue of blood, and who, as we learn from the sacred Gospels, found at the hands of our Saviour relief from her affliction, came from this place and that her house was pointed out in the city, and that marvellous memorials of the good deed, which the Saviour wrought upon her, still remained. For [they said] that there stood on a lofty stone at the gates of her house a brazen figure in relief of a woman, bending on her knee and stretching forth her hands like a suppliant, while opposite to this there was another of the same material, an upright figure of a man, clothed in comely fashion in a double cloak and stretching out his hand to the woman; at his feet on the monument itself a strange species of herb was growing. . . . This statue, they said, bore the likeness of Jesus. And it was in existence even to our day, so that we saw it with our own eyes when we stayed in the city. And there is nothing wonderful in the fact that those heathen, who long ago had good deeds done to them by our Saviour, should have made these objects, since we saw the likenesses of His apostles also, of Paul and Peter, and indeed of Christ Himself, preserved in pictures painted in colours. And this is what we should expect, for the ancients were wont, according to their pagan habit, to honour them as saviours, without reservation, in this fashion. (7.18.1-4)

Interestingly enough, Eusebius does not oppose these statues.[71] They were

71. Here Eusebius was in line with the majority of Christians. On Eusebius and icons in general, see Moshe Barasch, *Icon: Studies in the History of an Idea* (New York:

a common phenomenon by the third century and during Eusebius's own lifetime. Christianity was thus promoted by the visual arts, and in this respect the medium of mission was created ingeniously by the local Christians themselves. By this syncretistic act they represented Christianity with a static media device in the midst of the public sphere. But the act also demonstrates the sensitivity of the Catholic Church organization concerning various local audiences (doing something the Jews at that time could never permit). This example shows again that missionary media devices varied according to the audience targeted. From early on Christians were sophisticated in what we call marketing.[72] They knew what suited one segment of society and what fitted another, and when pagans erected statues representing figures of the New Testament, they accepted this, albeit reluctantly. Interculturation took its toll, and many years later icons would be more than welcome in the Catholic Church.

Hidden Agents of Mission

In the introduction to the *Ecclesiastical History* Eusebius declares that Jesus' "acts and sufferings were such as were consistent with the prophecies which foretell that man and God shall live together to do marvellous deeds, and to teach to all Gentiles the worship of the father" (1.2.23). This statement expresses the conviction that God and man will act together for the purpose of missionizing the Gentiles. Let us look at some examples.

Near the beginning of Book 2, Eusebius relates an apocryphal story about the emperor Tiberius and the Roman Senate. The story appears in two versions. In both, Tiberius becomes a promoter of Christianity. In Tertullian's version (translated by Eusebius from Latin), we learn that no one in the empire could be declared god without the approval of the Roman Senate.

New York University Press, 1992), 141-57. Finney, *Invisible God,* Chaps. 5-6, shows how from 200 C.E. onwards most Christians became receptive to art and used it freely. He says that in the Antonine-Severan period "the new religionists could again begin to acquire the kind of material visibility that hitherto they lacked" (p. 289). See also J. Gutmann, "Early Christian and Jewish Art," in *Eusebius, Christianity and Judaism,* ed. Attridge and Hata, 270-87.

72. For marketing, see William M. Pride and O. C. Ferrell, *Marketing: Concepts and Strategies,* 6th ed. (Boston: Houghton Mifflin, 1989).

Tiberius therefore, in whose time the name of Christian came into the world, when this doctrine was reported to him from Palestine, where it first began, communicated it to the Senate, and made it plain to them that he favoured the doctrine, but the Senate, because it had not itself tested it, rejected it; but he continued in his own opinion and threatened death to the accusers of the Christians. (2.2.6)

To this citation Eusebius adds, "For heavenly providence had designed putting this in his mind in order that the word of the Gospel (*euangeliou logos*) might have an unimpeded beginning, and traverse the earth in all directions. Thus by the power and assistance of Heaven the saving word began to flood the whole world with light like the rays of the sun" (2.2.6–2.3.1). Here Eusebius presents the supreme secular authority itself as an unwitting means of spreading mission. Mission is thus presented by Eusebius as not only an overt strategy of the Church but a manifestation of God working through external agents who do not even know that they are contributing to the gradual spread of Christianity. Strangers, therefore, could also become media vehicles of mission in the outer public sphere.

In another case, while describing the Therapeutai mentioned by Philo Judaeus (2.16-17), Eusebius says that from Philo's very "accurate description of the life of our ascetics it will be plain that he not only knew but welcomed, reverenced, and recognized the divine mission of the apostolic men of his day, who were, it appears, of Hebrew origin, and thus still preserved most of the ancient customs in a strictly Jewish manner" (2.17.2). It should be emphasized that Eusebius reads into the practices of the Therapeutai many elements that he found in the monastic organizations of his own time.[73] These, as we know, themselves became an important means for spreading the Christian mission. Eusebius may have had this fact in mind when he described the Therapeutai, saying that their "race is found in many places in the world" (2.17.7). His efforts to argue that the Therapeutai lived according to the Gospel are designed to support his view that in the first century Christianity was already widespread in the world ("the writer [Philo] referred to has given in his own writing a description of this, which exactly agrees with the manner which is still observed by us and by us alone" [2.17.22]). At the end of his

73. See G. P. Richardson, "Philo and Eusebius on Monasteries and Monasticism: The Therapeutae and Kellia," in *Origins and Method: Towards a New Understanding of Judaism and Christianity: Essays in Honour of John C. Hurd*, ed. Bradley H. McLean (Sheffield: JSOT Press, 1993), 334-59.

description, Eusebius writes, "Anyone who has a love of accurate knowledge of these things can learn from the narrative of the author quoted already, and it is plain to everyone that Philo perceived and described the
first heralds *(tous prōtous kērykas)* of teaching according to the Gospel
and the customs handed down from the beginning by the apostles"
(2.17.23-24). Eusebius actually views the Therapeutai, who in reality
were Jews, as active agents of mission since they constituted a perfect example of "Christian" purity and handed down teachings from the apostles themselves. Unlike Tiberius, the Therapeutai were not a hidden
Gentile agent of mission but rather a "Christianized" Jewish entity. This
agent too was not aware in reality that it was Christian, but Eusebius
views it as playing an active role within the organizational web that was
responsible for mission in the world.

Eusebius also treats the emperor Trajan as a stranger who promoted
the Christian faith and who supported the notion that Christians constituted a wonderful model of good order in society.[74] A letter attributed by
Eusebius to Marcus Aurelius can also be interpreted as wishful thinking on
the part of Christians. This letter has a Roman emperor put Christianity
on the public agenda (since it was "published at Ephesus in the Council of
Asia," 4.13.7).[75] And then in a quotation from Melito's *To Antoninus* (i.e.,
Marcus Aurelius), Eusebius repeats an idea he has already expressed elsewhere, that the Roman Empire itself was a prime contributor to the rise of
Christianity:

> Our philosophy first grew up among the barbarians, but its full flower
> came among your nation in the great reign of your ancestor Augustus,
> and became an omen of good to your empire, for from that time the
> power of the Romans became great and splendid. You [Marcus Aurelius]
> are now his happy successor, and shall be so along with your son
> [Commodus], if you protect the philosophy which grew up with the em-
> pire and began with Augustus. Your ancestors nourished it together with
> the other cults, and the greatest proof that our doctrine flourished for
> good along with the empire in its noble beginning is the fact that it met
> no evil in the reign of Augustus, but on the contrary everything splendid
> and glorious according to the wishes of all men. (4.26.7-8)

74. Cf. *Hist. Eccl.* 3.33.3; see Wilken, *The Christians as the Romans Saw Them,* 28.
75. For problems concerning the authenticity of this letter, see H. J. Lawlor and
J. E. L. Oulton, *Eusebius, Bishop of Caesarea: The Ecclesiastical History and the Martyrs
of Palestine,* 2 vols. (London: SPCK, 1927-28), 2:128-29.

These lines are followed immediately by an epitome containing a survey of the relations of the Roman authorities with the Christians. In other words, Eusebius emphasizes, from the outset there existed a symbiotic relation between the Roman Empire and Christianity. There were of course some evil emperors, but the general course of history shows that the Roman Empire existed in order to bring about the spread and success of Christianity in the world. This view is supported by the story about the so-called "Thundering Legion" mentioned above. According to 5.5.6-7,

> Tertullian says that the emperor [Marcus Aurelius] also threatened death to those who attempted to accuse us. The author goes on as follows: "What kind of laws are these which wicked, unrighteous, and cruel men use against us alone? Vespasian did not observe them although he conquered the Jews. Trajan partially allowed them, but forbade Christians to be sought out. Neither Hadrian, though busy in all curious matters, nor Pius, as he is called, ratified them."

The emperors Philip and Valerian were also regarded as practicing Christians. This is in line with Eusebius's notion that whenever an emperor was kind to Christians this was a sign of the manifestation of the Logos through an important stranger. This approach can be found as well in a letter of Dionysius of Alexandria cited by Eusebius:

> "For not a single one of the emperors before him [Valerian] was so kindly and favourably disposed towards them, not even those who were said to have been openly Christians, as he manifestly was, when he received them at the beginning in the most intimate and friendly manner; indeed all his house had been filled with godly persons, and was a church of God. But the master and ruler of the synagogue of the Egyptian magicians persuaded him to get rid of them." (7.10.3)

We get a clearer picture of officials and emperors as hidden agents of Christianity from Eusebius's remark about Macrian, who urged Valerian away from Christianity. In Eusebius's view, Macrian was a bad guy. According to another quoted excerpt from Dionysius, Macrian

> "did not understand the universal Providence, nor did he suspect the judgement of Him who is before all and through all and over all. Therefore he has come to be at enmity with His Catholic Church, and so alienated and estranged himself from God's mercy and banished himself as far as possible from his own salvation, in this proving true his name. . . .

223

For Valerian, being induced by him to this course of action, was given over to insults and reproaches, according to that which was said to Isaiah." (7.10.6-7)

Later in Book 7, Eusebius describes Aurelian's attitude toward Christianity:

Such indeed was the disposition of Aurelian towards us at that time. But as his reign advanced, he changed his mind with regard to us, and was now being moved by certain counsels to stir up persecution against us; and there was great talk about this on all sides. But as he was just on the point of so doing and was putting, one might almost say, his signature to the decrees against us, the divine Justice visited him, and pinioned his arms, so to speak, to prevent his undertaking. Thus it was clearly shown for all to see that the rulers of this world would never find it easy to proceed against the churches of Christ, unless the hand which champions us were to permit this to be done, as a divine and heavenly judgement to chasten and turn us, at whatsoever times it should approve. (7.30.20-21)

Thus, the further we get into the third century, the more overt and outspoken the hidden agents become. According to Eusebius, some of the emperors who ruled before Constantine the Great already anticipated his conversion to Christianity. During the reigns of Philip and Valerian, circumstances were not yet ripe for a complete revolution, but Eusebius makes it clear that Christianity was on the agenda of the Roman emperors long before Constantine, indeed, even as far back as Augustus. Eusebius believes that the Logos worked within many agents in the outer public sphere who from time to time were hindered by evil powers of various kinds. These powers were an obstacle to actions performed under free will. Eusebius regards the victory of Christianity in 312 C.E. not only as a triumph of one religion over others, but as the complete triumph of the public over the unknown. Constantine the Great became an overt Christian who publicly promoted Christianity and communicated its message openly and freely throughout the outer public sphere. Catholic Christianity was victorious in the battle over the public sphere not just because it was a better religion, but because it knew how to promote itself through mission and other media channels. Christianity's media revolution in the marketplace of ancient religion was perhaps one of its greatest achievements.

Advertisements

The *Ecclesiastical History* contains many general statements concerning the spread of Christianity and the flourishing of the Church. These assertions can be seen as having the status that advertisements have in our own modern media systems.

In 2.3.1 Eusebius says that by "the power and assistance of Heaven the saving word *(ho sōtērios logos)* began to flood the whole world with light like the rays of the sun."[76] This expression recurs in the *Ecclesiastical History*, in particular in the first books. Eusebius continues:

> At once, in accordance with the divine Scriptures, the voice of its inspired evangelists and Apostles "went forth to the whole earth and their words to the end of the world." In every city and village arose churches crowded with thousands of men, like a teeming threshing floor. Those who by hereditary succession and original error had their souls bound by the ancient disease of the superstition of idols were set free . . . by the power of Christ through the teaching of his followers and their wonderful deeds. They rejected all the polytheism of the demons and confessed that there is only one God, the Creator of the universe. Him they honoured with the rites of true piety by the divine and rational worship which was implanted by our Saviour in the life of men. But indeed it was when the grace *(charis)* of God was already being poured out even on the other nations — when faith in Christ had been received, first by Cornelius with all his house in Palestinian Caesarea through divine manifestations and the ministration of Peter, and also by many other Greeks in Antioch, to whom those preached who had been scattered in the persecution about Stephen, and the Church in Antioch was already flourishing and multiplying — it was at that moment and in that place, when so many of the prophets from Jerusalem were also present, and with them Barnabas and Paul and a number of the other brethren besides them, that the name of Christians was first given, as from a fresh and life-giving fountain. (2.3.1-3)

Eusebius wishes his readers to believe that the Christian faith enjoyed worldwide acceptance and celebrity from the outset, even though in reality it was then an almost unknown religion. Generalizations of this nature can

---

76. On the Logos in Eusebius, see H. Berkhof, *Die Theologie des Eusebius von Caesarea* (Amsterdam, 1939), 67-162.

be found in political discourse in modern times, and in Eusebius's case they show that the number of Christians in the world was one of his great concerns. Let us look at some more examples of generalizations of this kind concerning mission.

When Eusebius deals with Flavia Domitilla, he says in 3.18.4 that "the teaching of our faith shone so brilliantly in the days described that even writ- ers foreign to our belief did not hesitate to commit to their narratives the persecutions and the martyrdoms in it, and they even indicated the time ac- curately."[77] Here it is made very clear that persecutions and martyrdoms were witnesses to the shining of the faith, and that pagans had a great admi- ration for this process of martyrdom. According to 3.37.1, a passage cited above, "These pious disciples of great men built in every place on the foun- dations of the churches laid by the Apostles. They spread the preaching and scattered the saving seeds of the kingdom of Heaven, sowing them broadcast through the whole world." In 4.2.1, right before his brief description of the revolt of Diaspora Jews under Trajan (the so-called Polemos Quietus), Eusebius issues another advertisement for the success of Christianity: "While the teaching of our Saviour and the church were flourishing daily and moving on to further progress the tragedy of the Jews was reaching the climax of successive woes." After mentioning Aelia Capitolina, built on the ruins of Jerusalem after the Bar Kochba revolt, Eusebius writes:

> Like brilliant lamps the churches were now shining throughout the world, and faith in our Saviour and Lord Jesus Christ was flourishing among all mankind, when the devil who hates what is good, as the en- emy of truth, ever most hostile to man's salvation, turned all his devices against the church. (4.6.4–7.1)

In our discussion of heresies (Chapter 4 above), we have seen some aspects of counter-mission performed by heretics. Here we may note that the advertisements for the orthodox Catholic Church were probably used as counter propaganda to the mission initiated by heretics. Eusebius at one point even admits this:

> By using these ministers the demon who rejoices in evil accomplished the piteous enslavement to perdition of those who were thus deceived

---

77. See H. B. Green, "Matthew 28:19, Eusebius and the *lux orandi,*" in *The Making of Orthodoxy: Essays in Honour of Henry Chadwick,* ed. Rowan Williams (Cam- bridge: Cambridge University Press, 1989), 124-41.

by them, and brought much weight of discredit upon the divine word among the unbelieving Gentiles, because the report which started from them was scattered calumniously on the whole race of Christians. It was especially in this way that it came to pass that a blasphemous and wicked suspicion concerning us was spread among the heathen of those days, to the effect that we practised unspeakable incest with mothers and sisters and took part in wicked food. Yet this did not long succeed, for the truth vindicated itself and as time went on shone ever more brightly. For by its power the machinations of its enemies were refuted; though new heresies were invented one after another, the earlier ones flowed into strange multiple and multifarious forms and perished in different ways at different times. But the brightness of the universal and only true church proceeded to increase in greatness, for it ever held to the same points in the same way, and radiated forth to all the race of Greeks and barbarians the reverent, sincere, and free nature, and the sobriety and purity of the divine teaching as to conduct and thought. Thus with the lapse of time the calumnies against the whole teaching were extinguished, and our doctrine remained as the only one which had power among all and was admitted to excel in its godliness and sobriety, and its divine and wise doctrines. So that no one has dared to continue the base implications of calumny against our faith, such as those who were opposed to us were formerly accustomed to use. (4.7.10-14)

This paragraph sheds light on previous passages as well. In fact, Eusebius is a great believer in slogans with a powerful order of discourse. He thinks powerful slogans can fend off heretics and also be of great media value where the Gentile audience is concerned.

In Book 5 we meet with yet another advertisement:

And at the same time in the reign of Commodus our treatment was changed to a milder one, and by the grace of God peace came on the churches throughout the whole world. The word of salvation began to lead every soul of every race of men to the pious worship of the God of the universe, so that now many of those who at Rome were famous for wealth and family turned to their own salvation with all their house and with all their kin. This was unendurable to the demon who hates good, envious as he is by nature, and he again stripped for conflict, and prepared various devices against us. (5.21.1-2)

Here the advertisement changes somewhat; instead of making a general

and exaggerated statement, Eusebius informs us that people from different races looked for salvation (i.e., became Christians) and that in Rome
the process occurred among the elite of the outer public sphere, who were
more susceptible to the intellectual, written mission of Christianity.

We have already noted that as we proceed to later books we encounter fewer advertisements of such a general nature. In Book 6, Eusebius asserts that "the faith was increasing and our doctrine was boldly
proclaimed in the ears of all" (6.36.1). And, speaking of the "freedom"
before the persecution of Diocletian, Eusebius notes in Book 8, "With
what favour one might note that the rulers in every church were honoured by all procurators and governors! And how could one fully describe those assemblies thronged with countless men, and the multitude
that gathered together in every city, and the famed concourses in the
places of prayer" (8.1.5). Although the following sentence is not a "missionary" one, it is worth quoting; it relates to the declaration in 313 C.E.
concerning the end of persecution in the Empire: "For when the divine
and heavenly grace showed that it watched over us with kindly and pro-
pitious regard, then indeed our rulers also, those very persons who had
long time committed acts of war against us, changed their mind"
(8.16.1). The same note is sounded about the termination of the troubles
during Maximin Daia's reign:

> After these things were thus accomplished, God, the great and heavenly
> Champion of the Christians, when He had displayed His threatening
> and wrath against all men by the aforesaid means, in return for their ex-
> ceeding great attacks against us, once again restored to us the bright and
> kindly radiance of His providential care for us. Most marvellously, as in
> a thick darkness, he caused the light of peace to shine upon us from
> Himself, and made it manifest to all that God Himself had been watch-
> ing over our affairs continually. (9.8.15)

Like the statement at 8.16.1, this one differs from the ones concerning the
spread of Christianity that appear in the first books of the *Ecclesiastical
History*. The general advertisements are completely missing from the last
four books, replaced by the statements quoted above. The reason may be
that advertisements were no longer a necessity at a time when Christianity
was in reality widespread, that is, in the late third and the beginning of the
fourth century.

Let us now examine the nature of these advertisements by considering and applying some findings of modern research. Kim B. Rotzoll, in an article entitled "Advertisements,"[78] argues,

> Advertisements are overwhelmingly used with persuasive intent. That is, the advertisers are striving to alter behavior and/or our levels of awareness, knowledge, attitude and so on . . . their intents can range from altering behavior to affecting the way people think about a particular social or economic position. The results of their efforts can range from enormously influential to a waste of the advertiser's money.[79]

In Eusebius's general statements, we can easily detect this intent to change people's behavior (to convert them to Christianity) by overwhelming them with the enormous success of the spread of the faith. But this is not the whole picture. Rotzoll speaks of "advertising by producers of consumer goods to reach individuals," and explains that "this is often called 'general' or 'national' advertising, because it involves advertising from a single company (the 'producer' of the good or service) to an audience over a large geographic area — a region, or perhaps an entire country. . . . The purpose is generally to attempt to encourage preference for a particular brand."[80] (An example would be a typical advertisement for Coca-Cola.) The nature of Eusebius's statements is obvious; he approaches the individual but strives to encompass all the individuals of the whole Roman Empire by declaring that the whole world had already become Christian (like the advertisement implying that everybody in the world drinks Coca-Cola, a claim that statistically is surely not true but that increases pressure on any individual to drink it).

Rotzoll also distinguishes between non-controllable (external) and controllable (internal) factors in the potential use of advertising:[81]

> *The non-controllable (external) factors* — the most obvious external factor is the socio-economic system in which the advertiser finds himself. . . . One is advised, then, to approach advertisements with some un-

78. Kim B. Rotzoll, "Advertisements," in *Discourse and Communication: New Approaches to the Analysis of Mass Media Discourse and Communication,* ed. Teun A. van Dijk (Berlin and New York: de Gruyter, 1985), 94-105. See also C. C. Rohde and C. R. C. Pellicaan, "Advertising and the Legitimacy Crisis of Eastern Europe," in *Communication in Eastern Europe: The Role of History, Culture, and Media in Contemporary Conflicts,* ed. Fred L. Casmir (Mahwah, N.J.: Lawrence Erlbaum, 1995), 133-62.

79. Rotzoll, "Advertisements," 94.

80. Ibid., 95-96.

81. Ibid., 96.

derstanding of the expectations of advertising in that particular *culture.* These expectations are, of course, closely aligned with the more general 'world view' of the country regarding such fundamental assumptions as the 'rationality' of man, the relationship of the individual and the state, etc. . . . Advertisers are often quite powerless to affect many other factors that may strongly influence the opportunities for their successful use of advertising. The most obvious within a culture is the complexity of the individual. . . . Advertisers must . . . make certain assumptions about the particular combination of these factors when they prepare their advertisements. Given the host of potential influences on individual behavior in the absence of, or in addition to, advertising, then, this factor explains one of the most important characteristics of contemporary advertising — the uncertainty of its outcome. . . . Other non-controllable factors could include changes in the age of the population. . . . occupational shifts . . . and general social norms . . . etc. *Controllable (internal) factors* are linked to the problems of "what will be produced? At what price? Where will it be distributed? How will it be promoted?"[82]

Eusebius's advertisement-like claims are influenced by both sets of factors. Although he could not foresee many factors working within the society in which he launched his propaganda slogans, he could and did control the "end product"; he believed that the kingdom of God would be there in the future, as he clearly says in one of his advertisements.

Rotzoll also deals with the "symbol package," which reflects

assumptions about the likely motivational elements on the part of the potential 'market.' . . . Human communication is on a conceptual level. We are able to transmit 'pictures in the heads' through the use of verbal (predominantly words) and non-verbal (music, art, photography, graphics, gestures, etc.) symbols. Unlike our normal person-to-person symbolic communication forms, advertisements:

— Are overwhelmingly persuasive in intent. For example, the use of information by an advertiser can still be considered a means to the end of persuasion.

— Lack immediate feedback. The feedback from most advertisements is inferred, usually in the form of some action taken on the part of the 'target' audience. For example, if sales go up, the advertising campaign is seen to be 'working.' As we have seen, however, the abundance of potential influences on behavior other than (or in addition to) adver-

82. Ibid., 96-98.

tising, makes such an assumption more an act of faith than a statement of fact.

— Are . . . characterized by repetition. Much manufacturer advertising tends to involve the repetition of the same message (often *ad nauseam* in the broadcast media).

— Commonly involve hyperbole, 'puffing,' exaggeration, fancy. Part of this can be explained by the *caveat emptor* character of the market system. Perhaps of greater interest is the idea . . . that advertising serves as a form of 'alleviating imagery' of many of us, offering a world far more interesting, glamorous, sinful, alluring, clean, better ordered, and exciting than that we find around us. Thus, we may be seen to welcome the blandishments of advertisements at the same time that we may be annoyed by their repetition, lack of 'taste' and the like.[83]

The similarities with "advertisements" in the *Ecclesiastical History* speak for themselves. Let us just point out here the element of repetition as well as the element of hyperbole, namely, the presentation of a more vivid, powerful and glamorous world as a product (namely that Christianity has already become a powerful world-wide religion that does only good to society). We of course cannot know what the direct feedback was. We may assume, however, that Eusebius expresses the kind of verbal slogans employed by the Catholic Church from an early date. But this is not the whole story.

Rotzoll goes on to say,

Given these characteristics for virtually all advertising messages, the particular qualities of any one can be further analyzed by considering the advertiser's presumed *strategy* and *technique*. *Strategy* basically involves *what* is to be said. This is a decision that can be seen as an end product of many of the non-controllable and controllable factors discussed earlier. For example — A manufacturer of a video disc player attempts to 'position' it as an alternative to video tape recorder/players as well as other brands.[84]

We shall see in a moment that Eusebius is extremely cautious about the terminology that he chooses for his repetitious advertisements, which pose an alternative to the bad quality and weakness of pagan society in the outer public sphere.

83. Ibid., 99.
84. Ibid., 100.

Concerning the technique of advertising, Rotzoll says,

> *Technique*, then, involves *how* to say it. . . . The advertiser faces an almost infinite number of choices among the verbal and non-verbal symbols to implement the advertising strategy. To use the examples above: The video manufacturer could choose to be extremely informative, with heavy reliance on words and, perhaps, diagrams. He could also elect to emphasize the end product — i.e. the program *on* the video disc — with emphasis on arresting scenes from familiar movies.[85]

Eusebius reflects awareness of the *how*, the technique, of successful promotion; he usually knows where to position the advertisements (usually at junctures where the historical situation offers good prospects for the advance of Christianity, or when reality looks grim). One of his methods is to repeat the advertisements, which shows that he believed in their powerful impact on his readers. We may, once again, assume that Eusebius here expresses the order of discourse that was circulating in the Catholic Church before his time.[86]

In a paper entitled "Advertising as a Cultural Text,"[87] James Hay (drawing on the thought of Roland Barthes) maintains,

> Advertising is not as much a *social language* (in the sense of an already given and coherent system of discourse) as it is a *textual* operation practiced through and amidst a variety of discourses and forms used — not only, but in a significant way — for the regeneration of the cultural life of a social formation . . . An ad is an institutionalized textual practice (advertising) that operates through a variety of signifying practices and media. . . . While advertising, as a textual practice, may encourage or enable groups . . . to construct relationships among signs, these signs must first be (are) understood as already processed objects in a popular culture. Meaning is thus constructed around texts through a variety of 'discourses,' and in this sense an ad can be said to have a variety of 'power centers'. . . . A given expression can be interpreted as many times, and in as many ways, as it has actually been interpreted in a given cultural

---

85. Ibid.

86. For the distinction between "structured" and "unstructured" advertisements, see Rotzoll, "Advertisements," 101-3.

87. James Hay, "Advertising as a Cultural Text (Rethinking Message Analysis in a Recombinant Culture)," in *Rethinking Communication*, vol. 2, ed. Brenda Dervin et al. (Newbury Park, Calif.: Sage Publications, 1989), 129-52.

MISSION AS MARKETING STRATEGY

framework. . . . style is in some respects a key to understanding how ads, in their endless attempts to underscore or enable readings of difference, territorialize and deterritorialize the meanings of culture for their audiences.[88]

Against this theoretical background we can analyze some of the terms appearing in Eusebius's advertisements. Some of the terms he uses were extremely meaningful and powerful within the society where he lived. For the Gentiles words and phrases such as "power," "whole world," "divine manifestation," "famous for wealth and family," "churches crowded with thousands of men," "faith increasing," "shone brilliantly," "flourishing daily," "fresh and life-giving fountain," and "flourishing among all mankind" had a special socioeconomic and political meaning. These terms, combined with distinctively Christian discourse, created new connotations but left no room for doubt about who was responsible for all the good things mentioned.

Eusebius's advertisements mirror the aspirations of the audience he wished to target, pagans among whom Christian missionaries were operating. His intended audience aspired to achieve the values and goals that his advertisements lauded. The terminology characteristic of his repetitive advertisements was taken from power language used in the outer and institutional public spheres and was combined with symbols from the inner, Christian sphere. His advertisements thus function as verbal and conceptual bridges between these two worlds. This explains why Eusebius uses advertisements when he is dealing with the first two centuries of the common era. Later, when the outer and institutional public spheres saw a gradual increase in the number and influence of Christians, there was no more need for such overwhelming advertisements. The expectations voiced in them had been fulfilled by the end of the third century, at least in the eyes of Eusebius.

88. Ibid., 137-41.

EPILOGUE

The Triumph of Christian Publicity

A gainst the background of what we have seen in the preceding chapters, we may assume that Diocletian and his successors, Galerius,
Maxentius, Maximin, and Licinius, persecuted the Christians because they
posed an increasing threat to the society and the state. The Roman authorities feared the unknown, an organizational web that seemed to be ani-
mated by a mysterious power that attracted more and more public attention. Its wide-ranging penetration into the institutional public sphere in
the last quarter of the third century was evidently effective,[1] and disputes
within circles of Christians who served in the administration only highlighted their presence and the exposure they enjoyed (*Hist. Eccl.* 8.1). The
rulers started the persecution after 299, since by then it was clear that the
Christians had increased considerably in numbers and public power.[2]
Christians who served in the imperial administration and army became a
high priority target before the official persecution and during the persecution itself.

This state of affairs can be compared to conditions under the politics
of fear launched by Senator Joseph R. McCarthy when he was hunting

1. For instance 8.1.3: "Why need one speak of those in the imperial palaces and
of the supreme rulers, who allowed the members of their households — wives, children
and servants — to practice openly *(parrēsiazomenois)* to their face the divine word and
conduct, and — one might say — permitted them even to boast of the freedom accorded to the faith?"
2. P. S. Davies, "The Origin and Purpose of the Persecution of AD 303," *Journal
of Theological Studies* 40 (1989): 92-94.

Communists in the United States government.[3] With hindsight we know that Communism was not a real and massive threat in the United States in the early Fifties, but McCarthy was successful in his war against "honorable men" since he understood the technique of intimidation and the media's ability to give it exposure.[4] The latter, most of which opposed him, gave his demagoguery constant publicity, fostering fear of him and making him more celebrated than he merited.[5] But the hysterical fear of the American authorities who were impressed by McCarthy's propaganda concerning a Communist conspiracy proliferated against the background of the Cold War and the problematic American involvement in Asia.[6]

A similar fear concerning a mysterious network creeping into the public sphere may have triggered the persecution under Diocletian and his successors.[7] From the *Ecclesiastical History* we get the impression that Christians were increasingly penetrating the institutional public sphere, and their vague identity and numbers inspired alarm in the authorities. Thus came the moment when political logic was displaced by fear, and persecution began. It is hard to believe that Diocletian, Galerius, and the others were suddenly so carried away by pagan pressure that they decided overnight to eliminate the Christians. One pagan prophecy associated with Diocletian cannot be the whole reason for persecution, and one therefore has to consider seriously the fear of the undefined but increasing power of Christians within the administration and the army (*Hist. Eccl.* 8.1; Appendix 1.1).

However, Constantius and later his son Constantine understood at an early stage of their rise to power what the others had failed to grasp (*Hist. Eccl.* 8; Appendix 1.4-5). They realized that the Christian organization, by then woven into the public sphere, could be harnessed to their own political interests and constitute another power base that could strengthen their own hold on society.[8] In fact, one of the most notorious

3. See Robert Griffith, *The Politics of Fear: Joseph R. McCarthy and the Senate* (Lexington: University Press of Kentucky, 1970), esp. Chap. 4.

4. Ibid.

5. See Edwin R. Bayley, *Joe McCarthy and the Press* (Madison: University of Wisconsin Press, 1981).

6. Griffith, *Politics of Fear.*

7. For the persecution under Diocletian, see Fergus Millar, *The Emperor in the Roman World: 31 BC–AD 337* (London: Duckworth, 1977), 572ff.; and G. E. M. De Ste. Croix, "Aspects of the 'Great Persecution,'" *Harvard Theological Review* 47 (1954): 75-109.

8. Constantine himself, in discussing his conversion, mentions bishops in his court in 312 (*Vita Constantini* 1.28ff. and 1.39ff.).

persecutors at the time, Maximin, understood this advantage of the Christian organization extremely well. But instead of using it to advance his interests (as did Constantius and even more so Constantine), he tried to imitate the Christian organization by creating a competing pagan one (at some point between 311-313): "Maximin himself appointed as priests of the images in each city and, moreover, as high priests, those who were especially distinguished in the public services and had made their mark in the entire course thereof. These persons brought great zeal to bear on the worship of the gods whom they served" (9.4.2).[9]

Eusebius was aware of this development. In Books 9–10 of the *Ecclesiastical History* (as well as in the first books of the *Vita Constantini*), he reproduces verbatim the edicts of toleration of Christians published by the successors of Diocletian (but not all those that promulgated persecution).[10] That toleration of Christians and Christianity was important news to be transmitted is obvious. But in line with what we have argued throughout this book, we should emphasize another reason that induced Eusebius to quote the favorable edicts verbatim: they so clearly demonstrate the publicity victory of Christianity over all the other religions in the marketplace. No religion but Christianity received such publicity and exposure from the imperial edicts, which were put up everywhere in the public sphere (and not just in one local temple or another). Even when toleration is mentioned (as, for example, in the Edict of Milan), not one of the pagan religions is referred to by name. In other words, by quoting these edicts Eusebius wished to show that Christianity was the real winner because it received enormous publicity. Christianity was thus promoted by the emperors themselves. We have already seen that Eusebius quoted official documents only when he deemed it necessary for media performance (in the case of synods, for instance); the prominence he gives to public edicts is therefore quite natural.

While we cannot enter here into the question of the imperial edicts,

---

9. For an analysis of this passage against the background of Lactantius's account (*De Mortibus Persecutorum* 36.4-5), see O. Nicholson, "The 'Pagan Churches' of Maximinus Daia and Julian the Apostate," *Journal of Ecclesiastical History* 45, no. 1 (1994): 1-10. The *Scriptores Historiae Augustae* (Severus Alexander 43.6-7) probably attributes to Hadrian and Severus a similar motivation.

10. For these edicts, see S. Mitchell, "Maximinus and the Christians in A.D. 312: A New Latin Inscription," *Journal of Roman Studies* 78 (1988): 111-112. On Books 9–10, see the still useful discussion of Richard Laqueur, *Eusebius als Historiker seiner Zeit* (Berlin and Leipzig: de Gruyter, 1929), Chaps. 3-4.

we shall cite a few instances illustrating the above.[11] First, the Edict of Toleration issued by Galerius, Constantine, and Licinius, published just before Galerius's death in 311. In 8.17.2 Eusebius says concerning this edict that "imperial ordinances were promulgated in each city." In 9.1.1 he says again, "The recantation of the imperial will set forth above was promulgated broadcast throughout Asia and in the neighbouring provinces." Even if Eusebius exaggerates the extent of the distribution, the fact remains that he wants his readers to believe that the edict reached everybody in the Empire. He in fact offers a Greek translation to show how the emperor publicly announced the return of Christians to the public sphere, and earlier he comments that Galerius "openly confessed to the God of the universe; then he called those around him, and commanded them without delay to cause the persecution against Christians to cease, and by an imperial law and decree to urge them to build their churches and to perform their accustomed rites, offering prayers on the Emperor's behalf" (8.17.1). Then comes the ordinance itself, concluding with the emperor(s)' declaration "that Christians may exist again and build the houses in which they used to assemble, always provided that they do nothing contrary to the order. . . . they may be enabled to live free from care in their own homes" (8.17.9-10).

Eusebius again insists on the importance of publicity when he informs us that Maximin, who was reluctant to distribute the news of the edict (and is also absent from the list of emperors appearing in it),

> was by no means pleased with what was written, and instead of making known the letter set forth above gave verbal commands to the rulers under him to relax the war against us. For since he might not otherwise gainsay the judgement of his superiors, he put in a corner the law set forth above; and taking measures how it might never see the light of day in the districts under him, by an oral direction he commanded the rulers under him to relax the persecution against us. (9.1.1)

He adds that the provincial rulers communicated the news to each other, and he then cites a letter by one of them, Sabinus (9.1.2-6). The

---

11. For a good survey of the edicts, see Timothy D. Barnes, "The Constantinian Settlement," in *Eusebius, Christianity and Judaism,* ed. Harold W. Attridge and Gohei Hata (Detroit: Wayne State University Press, 1992), 635-57; and Mitchell, "Maximinus and the Christians," 111-14. On Eusebius's attitude towards Diocletian and his successors, see Robert M. Grant, "Eusebius and Imperial Propaganda," in *Eusebius, Christianity and Judaism,* ed. Attridge and Hata, 664-83.

tone of this letter expresses Maximin's reluctance to tolerate Christianity.[12] When Christians were released from prisons and mines as a result of the imperial edict, one could witness "churches thronged in every city, and crowded assemblies, and the rites performed thereat in the customary manner. And every single one of the unbelieving heathen was in no small degree amazed at these happenings, marvelling at the miracle of so great a change, and extolling the Christians' God as alone great and true" (9.1.8). The verb *thaumazein* ("to be amazed") used to denote the reaction of the heathen is used here exactly in the same manner as it was in the case of martyrdom and thus is not necessarily a negative term.[13]

In 9.9.13 we hear about the letter of Maximin to the governors "under him" written after the victory of the Milvian bridge (October 312). The letter is quoted verbatim in 9.9a.1-9; apparently, it was written only after "the advocates of peace and piety, [Constantine and Licinius], had written to him to allow this, and had conceded it to all their subjects by means of edicts and laws" (9.9a.12). The edict itself employs rhetoric that propagates Christianity, as for instance the declaration that the banishment of Christians had actually harmed the public good: "But when under happy auspices I came for the first time to the East, and learnt that in certain places very many persons who were able to serve the public good were being banished . . . I gave orders . . ." (9.9a.2). Later, in the spring of 313, when Maximin was hard-pressed in his conflict with Licinius, he published another edict,[14] this time with more specified instructions for the freedom of Christians. At that time he was forced by difficult circumstances to publish it himself from the imperial center (and not just to write letters to his governors, who secretly transmitted the message among themselves) in order for it to be plain "to all" (9.10.10). At this dangerous juncture even Maximin could no longer resist the open act of publication and distribution of the imperial act. Edicts against Christians kept them constantly on the agenda, but the ones declaring that they should be tolerated — and that even offered apologies from anti-Christian emperors — granted them enormous publicity, launched by the highest imperial authority. At the same time, the edicts constituted a splendid opportunity for Eusebius to

12. Cf. *Hist. Eccl.* 9.2.1; and Mitchell, "Maximinus and the Christians," 113-14.

13. This shows again that Christians received a great deal of attention because of their unfamiliar and different position within pagan society.

14. For the date of publication, see Mitchell, "Maximinus and the Christians," 115.

present the Christians as victorious in the battle for exposure and publicity within the marketplace.

In 10.5.2-14 the so-called Edict of Milan, published by Licinius in the summer of 313, is given verbatim in Greek translation (a Latin version was transcribed by Lactantius in *De Mortibus Persecutorum* 48).[15] The letter shows clearly how Christians were being returned by imperial edict to the inner public sphere (thus opening up the public and institutional ones as well). For instance:

> "And this, moreover, with special regard to the Christians, we resolve: That their places, at which it was their former wont to assemble, concerning which also in the former letter dispatched to thy Devotedness a definite ordinance had been formerly laid down . . . that these they should restore to these same Christians without payment or any demand for compensation, setting aside all negligence and doubtfulness; and if any chance to have received them by gift, that they should restore them with all speed to these same Christians." (10.5.9)

The edict itself again stresses that in order that "the form which our enactment and generosity takes may be brought to the knowledge of all, it is fitting that this which we have written be set forth by the order and published everywhere, and brought to the knowledge of all, to the intent that the enactment which embodies this our generosity may escape the notice of no one" (10.5.14). In other words, the reestablishment of the shattered inner public sphere is formally and publicly declared. When Constantine

---

15. In *Vita Constantini* 1.28-31, Eusebius highlights the episode of the so-called *Labarum* (the standard bearing the Chi-Rho) and presents it as a publicity victory for Christianity: "The emperor constantly made use of this sign of salvation as a safeguard against every adverse and hostile power, and commanded that others similar to it should be carved at the head of all his armies" (1.31). It is surprising that Eusebius ignores this episode altogether in the *Ecclesiastical History,* where, as we have seen, he was so alert to the publicity of Christianity. Was the *Labarum* really a later invention? See further Rudolf Egger, "*Das Labarum,* die Kaiserstandarte der Spätantike," in *Römische Antike und frühes Christentum: Ausgewählte Schriften von Rudolf Egger zur Vollendung seines 80. Lebensjahres,* ed. Artur Betz und Gotbert Moro (Klagenfurt: Verlag des Geschichtsvereines für Karnten, 1963), 2:325-44. See also Averil Cameron, "Eusebius' *Vita Constantini* and the Construction of Constantine," in *Portraits: Biographical Representation in the Greek and Latin Literature of the Roman Empire,* ed. M. J. Edwards and Simon Swain (Oxford: Clarendon, 1997), 161-63. For the problem of the authenticity of the *Vita Constantini,* see Timothy D. Barnes, *Constantine and Eusebius* (Cambridge, Mass.: Harvard University Press, 1981). Barnes himself affirms Eusebius's authorship.

became sole emperor in 324, Christianity was elevated to an official religion; a publicity campaign carried out by the imperial court itself helped make this possible, as the first two books of Eusebius's *Vita Constantini* show.[16] As our short survey has indicated, the promotion of Christians and Christianity by the fourth-century emperors was a gradual process that culminated in a publicity victory for Christianity thanks to Constantine in 324.

Throughout this study we have seen that Eusebius paid a great deal of attention to the publicity that Christianity both sought and enjoyed during the three centuries covered in the *Ecclesiastical History*. Publicity, both good and bad, was to him an important aspect of Christianity's rise to the status of an official world religion. The combined energies of several media channels and devices — the public displays of martyrdom, the vociferous and colorful competition among heresies within Christianity, the aggressive mission of the Church, and the flow of communication in its worldwide organizational web, as well as the imperial edicts for and against Christians — all these contributed to the victory Christianity gained over its pagan competitors in the marketplace of religion. This is the picture that emerges in the *Ecclesiastical History*. To recognize these factors is, again, by no means to deny that the message itself — the attractive theology of Christianity to many within the public sphere — was also a crucial factor in the religion's success; but without effective media to propagate that message, it is doubtful whether the new faith would have been able to have the impact or to attain the status that it did.

We have also seen that Eusebius's methods of presentation in the *Ecclesiastical History* reflect his recognition of historiography as an important media channel in its own right. He deliberately designed this work to be accessible to the masses, not just to an intellectual elite, and he clearly intended it to help promote Christianity within the marketplace. In writing this history, Eusebius adopted many compositional devices from his predecessors, but he developed them into a *system*. This act, combined with his missionary agenda, makes the genre of the *Ecclesiastical History* unique in the annals of Greek and Hellenistic historiography.

---

16. We also have evidence of an increase in the number of Christian inscriptions at this time; see Ramsay MacMullen, *Christianizing the Roman Empire (A.D. 100-400)* (New Haven and London: Yale University Press, 1984), 102-3.

Bibliography

Aalst, A. J. van der. *Aantekeningen bij de hellenisering van het christendom.* Nijmegen: Dekker & Van de Vegt; The Hague: Boekencentrum, 1974.

Adler, William. "Eusebius' *Chronicle* and Its Legacy." In *Eusebius, Christianity and Judaism,* edited by Harold W. Attridge and Gohei Hata, 467-91. Detroit: Wayne State University Press, 1992.

Aland, Barbara. "Marcion: Versuch einer neuen Interpretation." *Zeitschrift für Theologie und Kirche* 70 (1973): 420-47.

Argyle, M. "Non-verbal Communication in Human Social Interaction." In *Non-Verbal Communication,* edited by Robert A. Hinde. Cambridge: Cambridge University Press, 1972.

Asp, K. "Mass Media as Molders of Opinion and Suppliers of Information." In *Mass Communication Review Year Book,* edited by C. Wilhoit and C. Whitney, vol. 2, 332-54. Beverly Hills: Sage Publications, 1981.

Attridge, Harold W., and Gohei Hata, eds. *Eusebius, Christianity and Judaism.* Detroit: Wayne State University Press, 1992.

Aune, David E. *Prophecy in Early Christianity and the Ancient Mediterranean World.* Grand Rapids: Eerdmans, 1983.

Barasch, Moshe. *Icon: Studies in the History of an Idea.* New York: New York University Press, 1992.

Bardy, Gustave. *Paul de Samosate: Étude historique.* Louvain: "Spicilegium sacrum lovaniense" bureaux; Paris: E. Champion, 1923.

Barnes, Timothy D. "The Constantinian Settlement." In *Eusebius, Christianity and Judaism,* edited by Harold W. Attridge and Gohei Hata, 635-57. Detroit: Wayne State University Press, 1992.

―――. *Constantine and Eusebius.* Cambridge, Mass.: Harvard University Press, 1981.

243

————. *The New Empire of Diocletian and Constantine.* Cambridge, Mass.: Harvard University Press, 1982.

Bauer, Walter. *Orthodxy and Heresy in Earliest Christianity.* Edited by Robert Kraft and Gerhard Krodel. Philadelphia: Fortress, 1971.

Baumeister, Theofried. *Genese und Entfaltung der altkirchlichen Theologie des Martyriums.* Bern: Peter Lang, 1991.

Bayley, Edwin R. *Joe McCarthy and the Press.* Madison: University of Wisconsin Press, 1981.

Beard, Mary, John North, and Simon Price. *Religions of Rome.* Vol. 1. New York: Cambridge University Press, 1998.

Bell, A. "Telling Stories." In *Media Texts, Authors and Readers: A Reader,* edited by David Graddol and Oliver Boyd-Barrett, 100-18. Clevedon, England and Philadelphia: Multilingual Matters and The Open University, 1994.

Bennett, W. Lance. *News, The Politics of Illusion.* 2d ed. New York: Longman, 1988.

Berger, Peter L. *The Social Reality of Religion.* London: Faber, 1969.

Berkhof, H. *Die Theologie des Eusebius von Caesarea.* Amsterdam, 1939.

Beskow, Per. "Crossing the Frontiers in the Second Century." *Studia Missionalia Upsaliensia* 11 (1969): 27-35.

Bienert, Wolfgang A. *Dionysius von Alexandrien: Zur Frage des Origenismus im 3. Jahrhundert.* Berlin: de Gruyter, 1978.

Blanchetière, F. "Le Montanisme originel." *Revue des sciences religieuses* 52 (1978): 118-34 and 53 (1979): 1-22.

Blankenberg, W. "News Accuracy: Some Findings on the Meaning of the Term." *Journalism Quarterly* 47 (1970): 375-86.

Blumler, J. G. "Producers' Attitudes towards the TV Coverage of an Election." In *The Sociology of Mass Media Communicators,* edited by Paul Halmos, 85-115. Keele: University of Keele, 1969.

Bommes, Karin. *Weizen Gottes: Untersuchungen zur Theologie des Martyriums bei Ignatius von Antiochien.* Cologne: Hanstein, 1976.

Bosch, David J. *Transforming Mission: Paradigm Shifts in Theology of Mission.* Maryknoll, N.Y.: Orbis, 1991.

Bowersock, G. W. *Martyrdom and Rome.* Cambridge: Cambridge University Press, 1995.

Boyer, J. H. "How Editors View Objectivity." *Journalism Quarterly* 58 (1981): 24-28.

Brennecke, H. C. "Zum Prozess gegen Paul von Samosata: Die Frage nach der Verurteilung des Homoousios." *Zeitschrift für die neutestamentliche Wissenschaft* 75 (1984): 270-90.

Brent, Allen. *Cultural Episcopacy and Ecumenism: Representative Ministry in*

Church History from the Age of Ignatius of Antioch to the Reformation, with Special Reference to Contemporary Ecumenism. Leiden: Brill, 1992.

Brock, Sebastian. "Eusebius and Syriac Christianity." In *Eusebius, Christianity and Judaism,* edited by Harold W. Attridge and Gohei Hata, 212-34. Detroit: Wayne State University Press, 1992.

Brown, Peter. *The Body and Society: Men, Women, and Sexual Renunciation in Early Christianity.* New York: Columbia University Press, 1988.

———. *Power and Persuasion in Late Antiquity: Towards a Christian Empire.* Madison: University of Wisconsin Press, 1992.

Brox, Norbert. *Zeuge und Märtyrer: Untersuchungen zur frühchristlichen Zeugnis-Terminologie.* Munich: Kösel, 1961.

Burke, J. "Eusebius on Paul of Samosata: A New Image." *Kleronomia* 7 (1975): 8-20.

Burnett, Ron. *Cultures of Vision: Images, Media, and the Imaginary.* Bloomington: Indiana University Press, 1995.

Burrus, V. "Rhetorical Stereotypes in the Portrait of Paul of Samosata." *Vigiliae Christianae* 43 (1989): 215-25.

Buschmann, Gerd. *Martyrium Polycarpi: Eine formkritische Studie: Ein Beitrag zur Frage nach der Entstehung der Gattung Märtyrerakte.* Berlin: de Gruyter, 1994.

Calhoun, Craig, ed. *Habermas and the Public Sphere.* Cambridge, Mass.: MIT Press, 1992.

Cameron, Averil. *Christianity and the Rhetoric of Empire: The Development of Christian Discourse.* Berkeley: University of California Press, 1991.

———. "Eusebius' *Vita Constantini* and the Construction of Constantine." In *Portraits: Biographical Representation in the Greek and Latin Literature of the Roman Empire,* edited by M. J. Edwards and Simon Swain, 145-75. Oxford: Clarendon, 1997.

Campenhausen, Hans von. "Das Martyrium in der Mission." In *Die Alte Kirche,* edited by Heinzgünter Frohnes and Uwe W. Knorr, 71-85. Munich: Kaiser, 1974.

Cancik, H., and J. Rupke, eds. *Reichsreligion und Provinzialreligion.* Tübingen: Mohr Siebeck, 1997.

Canetti, Elias. *Masse und Macht.* Frankfurt: Fischer Taschenbuch, 1980.

Cary, M., and H. H. Scullard. *A History of Rome down to the Reign of Constantine.* 3d ed. London: Macmillan, 1975.

Caspar, Erich. *Die älteste römische Bischofsliste: Kritische Studien zum Formproblem des eusebianischen Kanons sowie zur Geschichte der ältesten Bischofslisten und ihrer Entstehung aus apostolischen Sukzessionenreihen.* Hildesheim: Gerstenberg, 1975.

Cerulo, Karen A. "Putting It Together: Measuring the Syntax of Aural and Visual Symbols." In *Vocabularies of Public Life: Empirical Essays in Symbolic Structure*, edited by Robert Wuthnow, 111-129. London and New York: Routledge, 1992.

Cezard, Leonce. *Histoire Juridique des Persécutions contre les Chrétiens de Neron a Septime-Severe (64 à 202)*. Rome: "L'Erma" di Bretschneider, 1967.

Chadwick, Henry. "Enkrateia." In *Reallexikon für Antike und Christentum*, vol. 5, 343-65. Stuttgart: Hiersemann, 1950-78.

————. *Early Christian Thought and the Classical Tradition: Studies in Justin, Clement, and Origen*. Oxford: Clarendon, 1966.

Chesnut, Glenn F. *The First Christian Histories: Eusebius, Socrates, Sozomen, Theodoret, and Evagrius*. 2d ed. Macon, Ga.: Mercer University Press, 1986.

Clark, Elizabeth A. "Eusebius on Women in Early Church History." In *Eusebius, Christianity and Judaism*, edited by Harold W. Attridge and Gohei Hata, 256-69. Detroit: Wayne State University Press, 1992.

Clarke, G. W., "Double Trials in the Persecution of Decius." *Historia* 22 (1973): 650-63.

Coleman, K. M. "Fatal Charades: Roman Executions Staged as Mythological Enactments." *Journal of Roman Studies* 80 (1990): 44-73.

Crouzel, Henri. "Le Christianisme de l'emperéur Philippe l'Arabe." *Gregorianum* 56 (1975): 545-50.

————. *Origen*. Translated by A. S. Worrall. Edinburgh: T & T Clark, 1989.

Cureton, William, ed. *History of the Martyrs in Palestine by Eusebius*. London, 1861.

Curran, James. "Communications, Power and Social Order." In *Culture, Society and the Media*, edited by Michael Gurevitch et al., 202-35. London and New York: Methuen, 1982.

Curran, James, and Michael Gurevitch, eds. *Mass Media and Society*. London: E. Arnold, 1991.

Daniélou, Jean. *Gospel Message and Hellenistic Culture*. Translated, edited, and with a postscript by John Austin Baker. London: Darton, Longman & Todd, 1973.

Davies, P. S. "The Origin and Purpose of the Persecution of AD 303." *Journal of Theological Studies* 40 (1989): 66-94.

Declerck, J. H. "Deux nouveaux fragments attribués à Paul de Samosate." *Byzantium* 54 (1984): 116-40.

Dehandschutter, B. "The Martyrium Polycarpi: A Century of Research." In *Aufstieg und Niedergang der Römischen Welt*, vol. II.27.1, edited by Hildegard Temporini, 485-522. Berlin: de Gruyter, 1993.

Den Boer, W. "Some Remarks on the Beginning of Christian Historiography." *Studia Patristica* 4 (1959): 348-62.

DeSimone, Russell J. *The Treatise of Novatian the Roman Presbyter on the Trinity: A Study of the Text and the Doctrine.* Rome: Institutum Patristicum Augustinianum, 1970.

Des Places, Edouard. *Eusèbe de Césarée Commentateur: Platonisme et écriture sainte.* Paris: Beauchesne, 1982.

De Ste. Croix, G. E. M. "Aspects of the 'Great Persecution.'" *Harvard Theological Review* 47 (1954): 75-109.

Dijk, Teun A. van. *News Analysis: Case Studies of International and National News in the Press.* Hillsdale, N.J. and London: Erlbaum, 1988.

Doergens, Heinrich. *Eusebius von Casarea als Darsteller der griechischen Religion: Eine Studie zur Geschichte der altchristlichen Apologetik.* Paderborn: F. Schöningh, 1922.

Douglas, Mary. *Natural Symbols: Explorations in Cosmology.* London: Barrie & Rockliff: Cresset, 1970.

Downey, Glanville. *A History of Antioch in Syria from Seleucus to the Arab Conquest.* Princeton: Princeton University Press, 1961.

Drijvers, Han J. W. "Marcionism in Syria: Principles, Problems, and Polemics." *The Second Century* 6, no. 3 (1987-88): 153-72.

Droge, Arthur J. "The Apologetic Dimensions of the Ecclesiastical History." In *Eusebius, Christianity and Judaism,* edited by Harold W. Attridge and Gohei Hata, 492-509. Detroit: Wayne State University Press, 1992.

Droge, Arthur J., and James D. Tabor. *A Noble Death: Suicide and Martyrdom among Christians and Jews in Antiquity.* San Francisco: HarperSanFrancisco, 1992.

Dvornik, Francis. *Early Christian and Byzantine Political Philosophy: Origins and Background.* Washington, D.C.: Dumbarton Oaks Center for Byzantine Studies, 1966.

Eck, Werner. "Das Eindringen des Christentums in den Senatorstand bis zu Konstantin d. Gr." *Chiron* 1 (1977): 381-406.

Eckstein, Arthur M. *Moral Vision in the Histories of Polybius.* Berkeley: University of California Press, 1995.

Edwards, M. J., and Simon Swain, eds. *Portraits: Biographical Representation in the Greek and Latin Literature of the Roman Empire.* Oxford: Clarendon, 1997.

Egger, Rudolf. "*Das Labarum,* die Kaiserstandarte der Spätantike." In *Römische Antike und frühes Christentum: Ausgewählte Schriften von Rudolf Egger zur Vollendung seines 80. Lebensjahres,* edited by Artur Betz und Gotbert Moro, vol. 2, 325-44. Klagenfurt: Verlag des Geschichtsvereines für Karnten, 1963.

Ehrman, Bart D. *The Orthodox Corruption of Scripture: The Effect of Early Christological Controversies on the Text of the New Testament.* New York: Oxford University Press, 1993.

Errington, R. M. "Constantine and the Pagans." *Greek, Roman, and Byzantine Studies* 29 (1988): 309-18.

Fairclough, Norman. *Media Discourse.* London: Arnold, 1995.

Farina, Raffaele. *L'impero e l'imperatore Cristiano in Eusebio di Cesarea: La Prima teologia politica del Cristianesimo.* Zurich: Pas Verlag, 1966.

Feige, Gerhard. *Die Lehre Markells von Ankyra in der Darstellung seiner Gegner.* Leipzig: Benno, 1991.

Finley, M. I., and H. W. Pleket. *The Olympic Games: The First Thousand Years.* New York: Viking, 1976.

Finn, T. M. "Social Morality, Imperial Service and the Spread of Christianity." *Studia Patristica* 17, no. 1 (1982): 31-37.

Finney, Paul Corby. *The Invisible God: The Earliest Christians on Art.* New York: Oxford University Press, 1994.

Fischer, J. A. "Angebliche Synoden des 2. Jahrhunderts." *Annuarium Historiae Concilium* 9 (1977): 241-52.

———. "Die antimontanistischen Synoden des 2.-3. Jahrhunderts." *Annuarium Historiae Concilium* 6 (1974): 241-73.

Fiske, John. *Introduction to Communication Studies.* 2d ed. London: Routledge, 1990.

Foakes-Jackson, F. J. *Eusebius Pamphili, Bishop of Caesarea in Palestine and First Christian Historian: A Study of the Man and His Writings.* Cambridge: W. Heffer & Sons, 1933.

Fornara, Charles W. *The Nature of History in Ancient Greece and Rome.* Berkeley: University of California Press, 1983.

Foster, J. *After the Apostles: Missionary Preaching of the First Three Centuries.* London: SCM Press, 1951.

Fowden, Garth. *Empire to Commonwealth: Consequences of Monotheism in Late Antiquity.* Princeton: Princeton University Press, 1993.

Fowler, Roger. "Hysterical Style in the Press." In *Media Texts, Authors and Readers: A Reader,* edited by David Graddol and Oliver Boyd-Barrett, 90-99. Clevedon and Philadelphia: Multilingual Matters and the Open University, 1994.

Frend, W. H. C. *Martyrdom and Persecution in the Early Church: A Study of a Conflict from the Maccabees to Donatus.* Oxford: Blackwell, 1965.

Friedländer, Saul. *Nazi Germany and the Jews: The Years of Persecution, 1933-1939.* New York: HarperCollins, 1997.

Frohnes, Heinzgünter, and Uwe W. Knorr, eds. *Die Alte Kirche.* Munich: Kaiser, 1974.

Furman, Frida Kerner. *Beyond Yiddishkeit: The Struggle for Jewish Identity in a Reform Synagogue.* Albany: State University of New York Press, 1987.

Gamble, Harry Y. *Books and Readers in the Early Church: A History of Early Christian Texts.* New Haven and London: Yale University Press, 1995.

Gans, Herbert J. *Deciding What's News: A Study of CBS Evening News, NBC Nightly News, Newsweek, and Time.* New York: Pantheon Books, 1979.

Ghiberti, Giuseppe, ed. *La missione nel mondo antico e nella Biblia: XXX Settimana Biblica Nazionale (Roma 12-16 settembre 1988).* Bologna: EDB, 1990.

Glasser, T. L. "Competition and Diversity among Radio Formats: Legal and Structural Issues." *Journal of Broadcasting* 28, no. 2 (1984): 127-42.

Gnilka, Christian. *Chresis: Die Methode der Kirchenväter im Umgang mit der antiken Kultur.* Vols. 1 and 2. Basel: Schwabe, 1984-93.

Gödecke, Monika. *Geschichte als Mythos: Eusebs "Kirchengeschichte."* Frankfurt am Main: P. Lang, 1987.

Golding, P. "The Missing Dimension — News Media and the Management of Social Change." In *Mass Media and Social Change*, edited by Elihu Katz and Tamas Szecsko, 63-81. London: Sage Publications, 1981.

Goodman, Martin. *Mission and Conversion: Proselytizing in the Religious History of the Roman Empire.* Oxford: Clarendon, 1994.

Gottlieb, Günther, and Pedro Barcelo, eds. *Christen und Heiden in Staat und Gesellschaft des zweiten bis vierten Jahrhunderts: Gedanken und Thesen zu einem schwierigen Verhältnis.* Munich: E. Vogel, 1992.

Graddol, David, and Oliver Boyd-Barrett, eds. *Media Texts, Authors and Readers: A Reader.* Clevedon and Philadelphia: Multilingual Matters and the Open University, 1994.

Grant, Robert M. *Eusebius as Church Historian.* Oxford: Clarendon, 1980.

————. "Eusebius and Imperial Propaganda." In *Eusebius, Christianity and Judaism*, edited by Harold W. Attridge and Gohei Hata, 664-83. Detroit: Wayne State University Press, 1992.

————. "Eusebius and the Martyrs of Gaul." In *Les Martyrs de Lyon (177): Colloque international du Centre national de la recherche scientifique, Lyon, 20-23 septembre 1977*, edited by Jean Rougé and Robert Turcan, 129-36. Paris: Editions du C.N.R.S., 1978.

————. *Gnosticism and Early Christianity.* New York: Columbia University Press, 1959.

Green, H. B. "Matthew 28:19, Eusebius and the *lux orandi.*" In *The Making of Orthodoxy: Essays in Honour of Henry Chadwick*, edited by Rowan Williams, 124-41. Cambridge: Cambridge University Press, 1989.

Greenberg, Gerald S. *Tabloid Journalism: An Annotated Bibliography of English-Language Sources.* Westport, Conn.: Greenwood Press, 1996.

Gregoire, Henri. *Les persécutions dans l'empire Romain*. Brussels: Palais des Academies, 1950.

Griffith, Robert. *The Politics of Fear: Joseph R. McCarthy and the Senate*. Lexington: University Press of Kentucky, 1970.

Grillmeier, Alois. *Christ in Christian Tradition from the Apostolic Age to Chalcedon (451)*. Translated by J. S. Bowden. New York: Sheed and Ward, 1965.

———. "Neue Fragmente zu Paul von Samosata?" *Theologie und Philosophie* 65 (1990): 392-94.

Gülzow, Hennecke. *Cyprian und Novatian: Der Briefwechsel zwischen den Gemeinden in Rom und Karthago zur Zeit der Verfolgung des Kaisers Decius*. Tübingen: Mohr Siebeck, 1975.

Gustafsson, B. "Eusebius' Principles in Handling His Sources, as Found in His 'Church History,' Books I-VII." *Studia Patristica* 4 (1961): 429-41.

Gutmann, J. "Early Christian and Jewish Art." In *Eusebius, Christianity and Judaism*, edited by Harold W. Attridge and Gohei Hata, 270-87. Detroit: Wayne State University Press, 1992.

Habermas, Jürgen. *The Structural Transformation of the Public Sphere: An Inquiry into a Category of Bourgeois Society*. Translated by Thomas Burger. Cambridge, Mass.: MIT Press, 1989.

Hall, S. G. "Women among the Early Martyrs." In *Martyrs and Martyrologies: Papers Read at the 1992 Summer Meeting and the 1993 Winter Meeting of the Ecclesiastical History Society*, edited by Diana Wood, 1-21. Oxford: Blackwell, 1993.

Halton, T. "Hegesippus in Eusebius." *Studia Patristica* 17 (1982): 688-93.

Hamman, A.-G. *Das Gebet in der Alten Kirche*. Berlin: Lang, 1989.

Hardwick, Michael E. *Josephus as an Historical Source in Patristic Literature Through Eusebius*. Atlanta: Scholars Press, 1989.

Harnack, Adolf von. *History of Dogma*. 3 vols. Translated from the 3d German edition by Neil Buchanan. Boston: Little, Brown, 1897-1910.

———. *Marcion: The Gospel of the Alien God*. Translated by John E. Steely and Lyle D. Bierma. Durham, N.C.: Labyrinth, 1990.

———. *The Mission and Expansion of Christianity in the First Three Centuries*. 2 vols. Translated and edited by James Moffett. 2d ed. London: Williams and Norgate; New York: G. P. Putnam's Sons, 1908.

———. "Die Reden Pauls von Samosata . . ." *Theologische Literaturzeitung* 50 (1925): 227-32.

———. "Die Reden Pauls von Samosata an Sabinus [Zenobia?] und seine Christologie." *Sitzungsberichte der preussischen Akademie der Wissenschaften* 22 (1924): 130-51.

Harris, William V. *Ancient Literacy.* Cambridge, Mass.: Harvard University Press, 1989.

Hay, James. "Advertising as a Cultural Text (Rethinking Message Analysis in a Recombinant Culture)." In *Rethinking Communication,* vol. 2, edited by Brenda Dervin et al., 129-52. Newbury Park, Calif.: Sage Publications, 1989.

Hefele, Charles Joseph. *A History of the Christian Councils from the Original Documents to the Close of the Council of Nicaea, A.D. 325.* 2 vols. 2d ed. Translated and edited by William R. Clark. Edinburgh: Clark, 1883-96.

Heine, Ronald E., ed. *The Montanist Oracles and Testimonies.* Macon, Ga.: Mercer University Press, 1989.

Heinrici, D. C. F. G. *Das Urchristentum in der Kirchengeschichte des Eusebius.* Leipzig: Edelmann, 1894.

Held, Virginia. *The Public Interest and Individual Interests.* New York: Basic Books, 1970.

Helgeland, J. "Christians and the Roman Army from Marcus Aurelius to Constantine." In *Aufstieg und Niedergang der Römischen Welt,* vol. II.2.23, edited by Hildegard Temporini, 724-834. Berlin: de Gruyter, 1979.

Henten, J. W. Van. "The Martyrs as Heroes of the Christian People: Some Remarks on the Continuity between Jewish and Christian Martyrology, with Pagan Analogies." In *Martyrium in Multidisciplinary Perspective,* edited by M. Lamberigts and P. van Deun, 303-22. Leuven: Leuven University Press, 1995.

Hesselgrave, David J. *Communicating Christ Cross-Culturally: An Introduction to Missionary Communication.* 2d ed. Grand Rapids: Zondervan, 1991.

Hoffmann, R. Joseph. *Marcion: On the Restitution of Christianity: An Essay on the Development of Radical Paulinist Theology in the Second Century.* Chico, Calif.: Scholars Press, 1984.

Instinsky, H. U. *Bischofsstuhl und Kaiserthron.* Munich: Kösel, 1955.

———. "Offene Fragen um Bischofsstuhl und Kaiserthron." *Römische Quartalschrift für christliche Altertumskunde und Kirchengeschichte* 66 (1971): 68-73.

Jacklin, P. "Representative Diversity." *Journal of Communication* 28, no. 2 (1978): 85-88.

Jones, A. H. M. *The Cities of the Eastern Roman Provinces.* 2d ed. Oxford: Clarendon, 1971.

Junod, E. "Origène, Eusèbe et la tradition sur la répartition des champs de mission des Apôtres (Eusèbe, Histoire ecclésiastique, III,1.1-3)." In *Les Actes des apocryphes des apôtres: christianisme et monde païen,* edited by Francois Bovon et al., 233-48. Geneva: Labor et Fides, 1981.

Kinzig, Wolfram. *Novitas Christiana: Die Idee des Fortschritts in der Alten Kirche bis Eusebius.* Göttingen: Vandenhoeck & Ruprecht, 1994.

Klijn, A. F. J., and G. J. Reinink. *Patristic Evidence for Jewish-Christian Sects.* Leiden: Brill, 1973.

Kofski, A. "Apologetics and Polemics against the Pagans in the Writings of Eusebius of Caesarea." Dissertation, Hebrew University of Jerusalem, 1990.

Kraft, Charles H. *Christianity in Culture: A Study in Dynamic Biblical Theologizing in Cross-cultural Perspective.* Maryknoll, N.Y.: Orbis, 1979.

Kurtz, L. R. "The Politics of Heresy." *American Journal of Sociology* 88 (1983): 1085-1115.

Kyrtatas, Dimitris J. *The Social Structure of the Early Christian Communities.* London: Verso, 1987.

Lampe, Peter. *Die Stadtrömischen Christen in den ersten beiden Jahrhunderten: Untersuchungen zur Sozialgeschichte.* Tübingen: Mohr Siebeck, 1989.

Lane Fox, Robin. *Pagans and Christians.* New York: Knopf, 1986.

Laqueur, Richard. *Eusebius als Historiker seiner Zeit.* Berlin and Leipzig: de Gruyter, 1929.

Larsen, J. A. O. *Greek Federal States: Their Institutions and History.* Oxford: Clarendon, 1968.

Lawlor, H. J. "The *Hypomnemata* of Hegesippus." In *Eusebiana: Essays on the Ecclesiastical History of Eusebius, Bishop of Caesarea,* 1-107. Oxford: Clarendon, 1912.

Lawlor, H. J., and J. E. L. Oulton. *Eusebius, Bishop of Caesarea: The Ecclesiastical History and the Martyrs of Palestine.* 2 vols. London: SPCK, 1927-28.

Le Boulluec, Alain. *La notion d'hérésie dans la littérature grecque IIe-IIIe Siècle.* 2 vols. Paris: Études augustiniennes, 1985.

Liebes T., and E. Katz, "Patterns of Involvement in TV Fiction." *European Journal of Communication* 1, no. 2 (1986): 151-72.

Lieu, Judith, John North, and Tessa Rajak, eds. *The Jews among Pagans and Christians in the Roman Empire.* London and New York: Routledge, 1992.

Lo sport nel mondo antico: ludi, munera, certamina a Roma. Rome: Museo della Civilta Romana, 1987.

Löhr, Winrich Alfried. *Basilides und seine Schule: Eine Studie zur Theologie- und Kirchengeschichte des Zweiten Jahrhunderts.* Tübingen: Mohr Siebeck, 1996.

Loofs, Friedrich. *Paulus von Samosata: Eine Untersuchung zur altkirchlichen Literatur und Dogmengeschichte.* Leipzig: Hinrichs, 1924.

Lücke, Friedrich. *Über den neutestamentlichen Kanon des Eusebius von Cäsarea.* Berlin: Reimer, 1816.

Lüdemann, Gerd. *Heretics: The Other Side of Early Christianity.* Translated by John Bowden. Louisville: Westminster John Knox, 1996.

Lyman, J. Rebecca. *Christology and Cosmology: Models of Divine Activity in Origen, Eusebius, and Athanasius.* Oxford: Clarendon, 1993.

MacDonald, Dennis Ronald. *The Acts of Andrew and the Acts of Andrew and Matthias in the City of the Cannibals.* Atlanta: Scholars Press, 1990.

MacMullen, Ramsay. *Christianizing the Roman Empire (A.D. 100-400).* New Haven and London: Yale University Press, 1984.

————. *Paganism in the Roman Empire.* New Haven and London: Yale University Press, 1981.

Malherbe, Abraham J. *Social Aspects of Early Christianity.* 2d ed. Philadelphia: Fortress, 1983.

Mann, Michael. *The Sources of Social Power: A History of Power from the Beginning to A.D. 1760.* 2 vols. Cambridge: Cambridge University Press, 1986-93.

Markschies, Christoph. *Valentinus Gnosticus? Untersuchungen zur Valentinischen Gnosis mit einem Kommentar zu den Fragmenten Valentins.* Tübingen: Mohr Siebeck, 1992.

McClelland, J. S. *The Crowd and the Mob: From Plato to Canetti.* London and Boston: Unwin Hyman, 1989.

McLeod, J. M., et al. "On Understanding and Misunderstanding Media Effects." In *Mass Media and Society,* edited by James Curran and Michael Gurevitch, 235-66. London: Arnold, 1991.

McPhee, Robert D. "Organizational Communication: A Structurational Exemplar." In *Rethinking Communication,* vol. 2, edited by Brenda Dervin et al., 199-212. Newbury Park, Calif.: Sage Publications, 1989.

McQuail, Denis. *Analysis of Newspaper Content.* London: H.M. Stationery Office, 1977.

————. *Mass Communication Theory: An Introduction.* London: Sage Publications, 1994.

————. *Media Performance: Mass Communication and the Public Interest.* London: Sage Publications, 1992.

Meeks, Wayne A. *The First Urban Christians: The Social World of the Apostle Paul.* New Haven and London: Yale University Press, 1983.

Melucci, Alberto. *Nomads of the Present: Social Movements and Individual Needs in Contemporary Society.* London: Hutchinson Radius, 1989.

Mendels, Doron. *Identity, Religion and Historiography: Studies in Hellenistic History.* Sheffield: Sheffield Academic Press, 1998.

————. *The Rise and Fall of Jewish Nationalism.* 2d ed. Grand Rapids: Eerdmans, 1997.

Metzger, Bruce M. *The Canon of the New Testament: Its Origin, Development, and Significance.* Oxford: Clarendon, 1987.

Millar, Fergus. *The Emperor in the Roman World: 31 BC–AD 337.* London: Duckworth, 1977.

————. "Paul of Samosata, Zenobia and Aurelian: The Church, Local Culture and Political Allegiance in Third-Century Syria." *Journal of Roman Studies* 61 (1971): 1-17.

Miller, Patricia Cox. *Biography in Late Antiquity: A Quest for the Holy Man.* Berkeley: University of California Press, 1983.

————. *Dreams in Late Antiquity: Studies in the Imagination of a Culture.* Princeton: Princeton University Press, 1994.

Mitchell, Stephen. *Anatolia: Land, Men, and Gods in Asia Minor.* Vol. 2, *The Rise of the Church.* Oxford: Clarendon, 1993.

————. "Maximinus and the Christians in A.D. 312: A New Latin Inscription." *Journal of Roman Studies* 78 (1988): 105-24.

Mitnick, Barry M. *The Political Economy of Regulation: Creating, Designing, and Removing Regulatory Forms.* New York: Columbia University Press, 1980.

Molland, E. "Besass die Alte Kirche ein Missionsprogramm und bewusste Missionsmethoden?" In *Die Alte Kirche,* edited by Heinzgünter Frohnes and Uwe W. Knorr, 51-67. Munich: Kaiser, 1974.

Momigliano, Arnaldo. "Pagan and Christian Historiography in the Fourth Century A.D." In *Essays in Ancient and Modern Historiography,* 107-26. Oxford: Blackwell, 1977.

Mosshammer, Alden A. *The "Chronicle" of Eusebius and Greek Chronographic Tradition.* Lewisburg, Penn.: Bucknell University Press, 1979.

Mowlana, Hamid. *Global Communication in Transition.* London: Sage Publications, 1996.

Murray, M. C. "Preaching, Scripture and Visual Imagery in Antiquity." *Christianesimo nella storia* 14, no. 3 (1993): 481-503.

Musurillo, Herbert. *The Acts of the Christian Martyrs.* Oxford: Clarendon, 1972.

Nautin, Pierre. *Lettres et écrivains chrétiens des IIe et IIIe siècle.* Paris: Cerf, 1961.

Nicholson, O. "The 'Pagan Churches' of Maximinus Daia and Julian the Apostate." *Journal of Ecclesiastical History* 45, no. 1 (1994): 1-10.

Nida, Eugene Albert. *Message and Mission: The Communication of the Christian Faith.* 2d ed. South Pasadena, Calif.: William Carey Library, 1975.

Nixon, C. E. V. "Constantinus oriens imperator: Propaganda and Panegyric: On Reading Panegyric 7 (307)." *Historia* 42, no. 2 (1993): 229-46.

Norris, F. W. "Paul of Samosata: Procurator Ducenarius." *Journal of Theological Studies*, n.s., 35 (1984): 50-70.

North, J. "The Development of Religious Pluralism." In *The Jews among Pagans and Christians in the Roman Empire*, edited by Judith Lieu, John North, and Tessa Rajak, 174-93. London: Routledge, 1992.

Pagels, Elaine. *The Origin of Satan*. New York: Random House, 1995.

Park, Robert E. "News as a Form of Knowledge." In *On Social Control and Collective Behavior: Selected Papers*, 32-52. Edited by Ralph H. Turner. Chicago: University of Chicago Press, 1967.

Pearson, Birger A. "Eusebius and Gnosticism." In *Eusebius, Christianity and Judaism*, edited by Harold W. Attridge and Gohei Hata, 291-310. Detroit: Wayne State University Press, 1992.

Pelikan, Jaroslav. *The Finality of Jesus Christ in an Age of Universal History: A Dilemma of the Third Century*. London: Lutterworth, 1965.

Perkins, Judith. *The Suffering Self: Pain and Narrative Representation in the Early Christian Era*. London and New York: Routledge, 1995.

Perrone, Lorenzo. "L'enigma di Paolo di Samosata: Dogma, chiesa e società nella Siria del III Secolo: prospettive di un ventennio di studi." *Cristianesimo nella storia* 13, no. 2 (1992): 253-327.

Pietri, C. and L., eds. *Naissance d'une Chrétienté (250-430)*. Vol. 2 of *Histoire du christianisme: Des origines à nos jours*. Edited by Jean-Marie Mayeur et al. Paris: Desclee, 1995.

Portmann, W. "Zu den Motiven der diokletianischen Christenverfolgung." *Historia* 39 (1990): 212-48.

Potter, D. "Martyrdom as Spectacle." In *Theater and Society in the Classical World*, edited by Ruth Scodel, 53-88. Ann Arbor: University of Michigan Press, 1993.

Pourkier, Aline. *L'hérésiologie chez Épiphane de Salamine*. Paris: Beauchesne, 1992.

Price, S. R. F. *Rituals and Power: The Roman Imperial Cult in Asia Minor*. Cambridge: Cambridge University Press, 1984.

Pride, William M., and O. C. Ferrell. *Marketing: Concepts and Strategies*. 6th ed. Boston: Houghton Mifflin, 1989.

Quasten, Johannes. *Patrology*. 4 vols. Westminster, Md.: Christian Classics, 1986-92.

Richardson, G. P. "Philo and Eusebius on Monasteries and Monasticism: The Therapeutae and Kellia." In *Origins and Method: Towards a New Understanding of Judaism and Christianity: Essays in Honour of John C. Hurd*, edited by Bradley H. McLean, 334-59. Sheffield: JSOT Press, 1993.

Riedmatten, Henri de. *Les actes du procès de Paul de Samosate: Étude sur la christologie du IIIe au IVe siècle*. Fribourg: Editions St-Paul, 1952.

Riepl, Wolfgang. *Das Nachrichtenwesen des Altertums, mit besonderer Rücksicht auf die Römer.* Leipzig: Teubner, 1913.

Ritter, A. M. "Dogma und Lehre in der Alten Kirche." In *Handbuch der Dogmengeschichte,* vol. 1, 129ff. Freiburg: Herder, 1982.

Robert, Louis, with G. W. Bowersock and C. P. Jones. *Le martyre de Pionios, prêtre de Smyrne.* Washington, D.C.: Dumbarton Oaks, 1994.

Robinson, John P., Mark R. Levy, et al. *The Main Source: Learning from Television News.* Beverly Hills: Sage Publications, 1986.

Rohde, C. C., and C. R. C. Pellicaan. "Advertising and the Legitimacy Crisis of Eastern Europe." In *Communication in Eastern Europe: The Role of History, Culture, and Media in Contemporary Conflicts,* edited by Fred L. Casmir, 133-62. Mahwah, N.J.: Lawrence Erlbaum, 1995.

Rotzoll, Kim B. "Advertisements." In *Discourse and Communication: New Approaches to the Analysis of Mass Media Discourse and Communication,* edited by Teun A. van Dijk, 94-105. Berlin and New York: de Gruyter, 1985.

Rougé, Jean, and Robert Turcan, eds., *Les Martyrs de Lyon (177): Colloque international du Centre national de la recherche scientifique, Lyon, 20-23 septembre 1977.* Paris: Editions du C.N.R.S., 1978.

Sacks, Kenneth S. *Diodorus Siculus and the First Century.* Princeton: Princeton University Press, 1990.

Sample, R. L. "The Christology of the Council of Antioch (268 c.e.) Reconsidered." *Church History* 48 (1979): 18-26.

Sato, Y. "Martyrdom and Apostasy." In *Eusebius, Christianity and Judaism,* edited by Harold W. Attridge and Gohei Hata, 619-634. Detroit: Wayne State University Press, 1992.

Saxer, Victor. *Bible et hagiographie: texte et thèmes bibliques dans les actes des martyrs authentiques des premiers siècles.* Bern: Lang, 1986.

Schaffert, Richard W. *Media Coverage and Political Terrorists: A Quantitative Analysis.* New York: Praeger, 1992.

Scheidweiler, E. "Paul von Samosata." *Zeitschrift für die neutestamentliche Wissenschaft* 46 (1955): 116-29.

Schepens, G. "Polemic and Methodology in Polybius' Book XII." In *Purposes of History: Studies in Greek Historiography from the 4th to the 2nd Centuries B.C.,* edited by H. Verdin, G. Schepens, and E. de Keyser, 39-61. Louvain: University of Leuven Press, 1990.

Schmid, Alex P. and Janny de Graaf. *Violence as Communication: Insurgent Terrorism and the Western News Media.* London and Beverly Hills: Sage Publications, 1982.

Schneemelcher, Wilhelm, ed. *New Testament Apocrypha.* Vol. 2, *Writings Re-*

lating to the Apostles, Apocalypses, and Related Subjects. English translaton edited by R. McL. Wilson. Louisville: Westminster John Knox, 1992.

Schoedel, William R. *Ignatius of Antioch: A Commentary on the Letters of Ignatius of Antioch.* Philadelphia: Fortress, 1985.

Schudson, M. "The Sociology of News Production Revisited." In *Mass Media and Society,* edited by James Curran and Michael Gurevitch, 141-159. London: Arnold, 1991.

Schürer, Emil. *The History of the Jewish People in the Age of Jesus Christ (175 B.C.–A.D. 135).* Vol. 1. Revised and Edited by Geza Vermes and Fergus Millar. Edinburgh: T & T Clark, 1973.

Schürer, Ernst, Manfred Keune, and Philip Jenkins, eds. *The Berlin Wall: Representations and Perspectives.* New York: Lang, 1996.

Schulz, W. "Mass Media and Reality." Paper presented at the Sommatie Conference, Veldhoven, Netherlands, 1988.

Schwartz, E. "Eusebios von Caesarea." *Real-encyklopädie der classischen Altertumswissenschaft,* vol. 6, part 1 (1907), cols. 1370-1439.

Shannon, Claude, and Warren Weaver. *The Mathematical Theory of Communication.* Urbana: University of Illinois Press, 1963.

Shaw, B. D. "Body/Power/Identity: Passions of the Martyrs." *Journal of Early Christian Studies* 4, no. 3 (1996): 269-312.

————. "The Passion of Perpetua." *Past & Present* 139 (1993): 3-45.

Shoemaker, Pamela J. *Gatekeeping.* Communication Concepts 3. Newbury Park, Calif.: Sage Publications, 1991.

Shorter, Aylward. *Toward a Theology of Inculturation.* Maryknoll, N.Y.: Orbis, 1988.

Sieben, Hermann Josef. *Die Konzilsidee der Alten Kirche.* Paderborn: Schöningh, 1979.

Siegert, F. "La culture grecque, le message Chrétien." *Revue de Theologie et Philosophie* 125 (1993): 321-41.

Signorielli, Nancy, and Michael Morgan, eds. *Cultivation Analysis: New Directions in Media Effects Research.* Newbury Park, Calif.: Sage Publications, 1990.

Silk, Mark. *Unsecular Media: Making News of Religion in America.* Urbana: University of Illinois Press, 1995.

Stark, Rodney. *The Rise of Christianity: A Sociologist Reconsiders History.* Princeton: Princeton University Press, 1996.

Stevenson, J. *Studies in Eusebius.* Cambridge: Cambridge University Press, 1929.

Stommel, E. "Bischofsstuhl und hoher Thron." *Jahrbuch für Antike und Christentum* 1 (1958): 52-78.

257

Stroumsa, Gedaliahu A. G. *Another Seed: Studies in Gnostic Mythology.* Leiden: Brill, 1984.

Sullivan, D. L. "Establishing Orthodoxy: The Letters of Ignatius of Antioch as Epideictic Rhetoric." *The Journal of Communication and Religion* 15, no. 2 (1992): 71-86.

Tardieu, Michel. *Trois Mythes Gnostiques: Adam, Éros et les animaux d'Égypte dans un écrit de Nag Hammadi (II,5).* Paris: Études augustiniennes, 1974.

Taylor, W. L. "Cloze Procedure: A New Tool for Measuring Readability." *Journalism Quarterly* 30 (1953): 415-33.

Thomas, G. "La condition sociale de L'Église de Lyon en 177." In *Les Martyrs de Lyon (177): Colloque international du Centre national de la recherche scientifique, Lyon, 20-23 septembre 1977,* edited by Jean Rougé and Robert Turcan, 93-106. Paris: Editions du C.N.R.S., 1978.

Thompson, J. B. "Social Theory and the Media." In *Communication Theory Today,* edited by David Crowley and David Mitchell, 27-49. Cambridge: Polity, 1994.

Tippet, Alan R. *Introduction to Missiology.* Pasadena, Calif.: William Carey Library, 1987.

Trebolle Barrera, Julio. *The Jewish Bible and the Christian Bible: An Introduction to the History of the Bible.* Leiden: Brill; Grand Rapids: Eerdmans, 1998.

Tuilier, A. "Les évangélistes et les docteurs de la primitive église et les origines de L'École (διδασκαλεῖον) d'Alexandrie." *Studia Patristica* 17 (1982): 738-49.

Turner, H. E. W. *The Pattern of Christian Truth: A Study in the Relations between Orthodoxy and Heresy in the Early Church.* London: Mowbray, 1954.

Twomey, Vincent. *Apostolikos Thronos: The Primacy of Rome as Reflected in the Church History of Eusebius and the Historico-apologetic Writings of Saint Athanasius the Great.* Münster: Aschendorff, 1982.

Valaskakis, G. G. "The Other Side of Empire: Contact and Communication in Southern Baffin Island." In *Culture, Communication, and Dependency: The Tradition of H. A. Innis,* edited by William H. Melody, Liora Salter, and Paul Heyer, 209-23. Norwood, N.J.: Ablex, 1981.

Vallée, Gérard. *A Study in Anti-Gnostic Polemics: Irenaeus, Hippolytus, and Epiphanius.* Waterloo, Ont.: Wilfrid Laurier University Press, 1981.

Van den Hoek, A. "The 'Catechetical' School of Early Christian Alexandria and Its Philonic Heritage." *Harvard Theological Review* 90, no. 1 (1997): 59-87.

Van Zoonen, Liesbet. "A Dance of Death: New Social Movements and Mass Media." In *Political Communication in Action: States, Institutions, Movements,*

Audiences, edited by David Paletz, 201-22. Cresskill, N.J.: Hampton, 1996.

Völker, Walther, ed. *Quellen zur Geschichte der Christlichen Gnosis.* Tübingen: Mohr, 1932.

———. "Von Welchen Tendenzen lies sich Eusebius bei Abfassung seiner 'Kirchengeschichte' leiten?" *Vigiliae Christianae* 4 (1950): 157-80.

Vogt, Hermann Josef. *Coetus Sanctorum: Der Kirchenbegriff des Novatian und die Geschichte seiner Sonderkirche.* Bonn: Hanstein, 1968.

Walbank, F. W. *Polybius.* Berkeley: University of California Press, 1972.

Wallace-Hadrill, D. S. *Eusebius of Caesarea.* London: Mowbray 1960.

Watson, Duane F. "Nicolaitans." In *The Anchor Bible Dictionary,* 6 vols., edited by David Noel Freedman, 4:1106-7. New York: Doubleday, 1992.

Weimann, Gabriel, and Conrad Winn. *The Theatre of Terror: Mass Media and International Terrorism.* New York: Longman, 1994.

Wiedemann, Thomas E. J. *Emperors and Gladiators.* London and New York: Routledge, 1992.

Wilken, Robert L. *The Christians as the Romans Saw Them.* New Haven and London: Yale University Press, 1984.

Williams, D. E. "Probing Cultural Implications of War-Related Victimization in Bosnia-Hercegovina, Croatia, and Serbia." In *Communication in Eastern Europe: The Role of History, Culture, and Media in Contemporary Conflicts,* edited by Fred L. Casmir, 277-311. Mahwah, N.J.: Lawrence Erlbaum, 1995.

Wilson, F. R. "The Missionary Strategy of the Early Church." Dissertation, Princeton Theological Seminary, 1956.

Winkelmann, Friedhelm. *Euseb von Kaisareia: Der Vater der Kirchengeschichte.* Berlin: Verlags-Anstalt Union, 1991.

Witten, Marsha. "The Restriction of Meaning in Religious Discourse: Centripetal Devices in a Fundamentalist Christian Sermon." In *Vocabularies of Public Life: Empirical Essays in Symbolic Structure,* edited by Robert Wuthnow, 19-38. London and New York: Routledge, 1992.

Wojtowytsch, Myron. *Papsttum und Konzile von den Anfängen bis zu Leo I (440-461): Studien zur Entstehung der Überordnung des Papstes über Konzile.* Stuttgart: Hiersemann, 1981.

Wyatt, Clarence R. *Paper Soldiers: The American Press and the Vietnam War.* New York: Norton, 1993.

Young, Frances M. *Biblical Exegesis and the Formation of Christian Culture.* Cambridge: Cambridge University Press, 1997.

Index of Ancient Literature

Index of Modern Authors

Index of Main Subjects

Abgar, correspondence with Jesus, 194-96

advertisements, 225-33

Antioch, life in the city, 31-50

art, Christian, 219-20

audience of Eusebius, 9-30, 38-45, 60, 67-68, 115, 120, 123, 132-36, 166-75, 225-33

bishopric, 31-50, 151-77

canon, formation of, 184-93

catechetical schools, 203-5

charter of the Church, 151-77, 179-80, 184, 209

Christianity and culture, 180-84

Constantine, 235-41

conversion, 199-201

Diocletian, persecution of, 96-105, 235-37

edicts, imperial, 235-41

Eusebius: editorial decisions of, 69-70, 81-90, 98-102, 107-9, 123, 173-75; rhetoric of hysteria, 145-47; use of genres, orders of discourse, voices, images, 162-77; use of space and time, 106-7, 196-99

heresy, 111-50; as media asset, 112-17, 184-93

heretics: Basilides, 128-29; Beryllus, 153-54; Carpocrates, 130-31; Cerinthus, 125-28; Ebionites, 123-24; Marcion, 131-36; Menander, 122-23; 187-88; Montanus, 137-42, 152, 188; Nicolaitans, 125-28; Novatian, 151-77; Papias, 125-28; Paul of Samosata, 31-50, 158; Saturninus, 128-29; Simon Magus, 118-21, 187-88

Historiography, Classical and Hellenistic, 1-11, 16-17, 21-23, 29-30, 35, 46-49, 69, 84, 102, 107, 119, 122-23, 125, 138-39, 175-76

literary *topoi*, 65-67

market competition, 132-36

martyrdom, 14-15, 51-109; of Alexander the Phrygian, 28-30, 78-79; of Ignatius, 56-58, 158-59; of James the Just, 14-15, 53-56; of Justin, 70-71; of Lyons and Vienne, 71-81; of Marinus, 95-96; of Paul the Apostle, 52-53; of Polycarp, 58-70; of Stephen, 52-53

media history, 2-30, 66-67

269